WRITING FOR WOMEN

GENDER IN WRITING

Series Editor: Kate Flint, Fellow and Tutor in English,
Mansfield College, Oxford

Difference in language, in subject matter, in form. This series seeks to
explore what is distinctive about women's and men's writing, and to
examine the theories of sexuality which attempt to explain these
differences. Writings of all periods and genres will be looked at from a
variety of radical perspectives: some explicitly feminist, others examining masculinity, homosexuality and gender politics as they are con-
structed through the writing and reading of texts. The series will draw on
recent developments in literary theory in order to examine all aspects of
gender in writing.

WRITING FOR WOMEN
The Example of Woman as Reader in Elizabethan Romance

———

CAROLINE LUCAS

OPEN UNIVERSITY PRESS
MILTON KEYNES · PHILADELPHIA

Open University Press
12 Cofferidge Close
Stony Stratford
Milton Keynes MK11 1BY

and
1900 Frost Road, Suite 101
Bristol, PA 19007, USA

First Published 1989

British Library Cataloguing in Publication Data

Lucas, Caroline
   Writing for women: the example of woman as reader in
   Elizabethan romance. — (Gender in writing)
   1. Literature. Feminist criticism
   I. Title
   801'.95

   ISBN 0–335–09018–4
       0–335–09017–6 (pbk)

Library of Congress Cataloging in Publication Number Available

Typeset by Quadra Graphics, Oxford
Printed in Great Britain by St. Edmundsbury Press Limited,
Bury St. Edmunds, Suffolk

For Sarah

Contents

Preface

Feminist scholarship has shown us that no theoretical approach or critical perspective is politically neutral; all are inevitably coloured by political, cultural, social and personal factors. I shall explain here, then, that my position is that of a white, middle-class English woman and feminist, with one foot precariously placed in the male-dominated academic world as a 'feminist academic' (this book started life as a Ph.D. thesis), and the other foot placed in more direct political activism within the Green Party, where I currently work. I approach the texts as a 'woman reader', a position both defined by experience and created as a construct.

Although in my analysis of particular romances I shall distinguish between the different classes of the women readers (Sidney's *Arcadia* and Lyly's *Euphues*, for example, were originally intended for an aristocratic readership, although by the early seventeenth century both had become the reading matter of the middle classes), I shall often refer to sixteenth-century women readers in general. Ruth Kelso, in her *Doctrine for the Lady of the Renaissance*, demonstrates that the theory which called for submission and obedience from women did not differentiate between different classes, and she suggests that although there were significant and growing class differences among women during the Renaissance, they none the less constituted a distinct group within the discourse of patriarchal theory.

Many of the prose romances have been marginalized on several counts; with a few exceptions (notably Sidney and Lyly), they have been dismissed as popular literature for the unlearned, or regarded simply as the sources for more well-known works (Greene's *Pandosto* was the principal source for Shakespeare's *The Winter's Tale*, for example, and Lodge's *Rosalynde* for *As You Like It*). They have been further marginalized as 'women's books'. Clara Reeve, writing a history of romance in 1785, observes that:

> The learned men of our own country, have in general affected a contempt for this kind of writing, and looked upon Romances, as proper furniture only for a Lady's library.
>
> (*The Progress of Romance*, p. xi)

This work is an attempt to reclaim these 'women's books', to suggest ways of reading them which both reveal the designs they have on us and allow us to reappropriate them for our own use, and to demonstrate that these texts are in fact far more complex and sophisticated than has previously been supposed.

Reliable modern editions of texts have been used when available. In quotations from early texts I have modernized the use of u and v, i and j, and the use of the long s; unusual printer's contractions have been expanded, and roman substituted for black-letter gothic type. Original spelling and punctuation have been retained except for the silent correction of some obvious errors.

I should like gratefully to acknowledge the following: Princeton University Press for quotation from Walter Davis, *Idea and Act in Elizabethan Fiction*, copyright © 1969 Princeton University Press, Princeton, N.J.; Yale University Press for quotation from Walter Davis and Richard Lanham, *Sidney's Arcadia*, copyright © 1965 Yale University Press, New Haven, Conn.; Harvard University Press for quotation from Stanley Fish, *Is There A Text In This Class?*, copyright © 1980 President and Fellows of Harvard College, Cambridge, Mass.; Johns Hopkins University Press for quotation from Elizabeth Flynn and Patrocinio Schweickart (eds), *Gender and Reading*, copyright © 1986 The Johns Hopkins University Press, Baltimore, Md.; Robin Hood for quotation from 'Studies in Some Collections of Romantic Novelle', Unpublished Dissertation, University of Oxford 1973; Annette Kolodny for quotation from 'Dancing Through the Minefield', *Feminist Studies* 6, copyright © 1980 Annette Kolodny; University of North Carolina Press for quotation from John Lievsay, *Stephano Guazzo and the English Renaissance 1575–1675*, copyright © 1961 University of North Carolina Press, Chapel Hill, N.C.; University of Wisconsin Press for quotation from Annabel Patterson, *Censorship and Interpretation*, copyright © 1984 Board of Regents of University of Wisconsin System; University of Michigan Press for quotation from K.T. Rowe, 'Romantic Love and Parental Authority in Sidney's *Arcadia*', *University of Michigan Contributions in Modern Philology* 4, copyright © 1947 University of Michigan Press, Mich.

I should like to thank Sarah Jones for her invaluable criticism, warm understanding, and much needed encouragement and support; Gareth Roberts for his shrewd insights and constructive comments; Katrina Biggart for her advice and unfailing enthusiasm; Penny Kemp for her generosity and interest; and Keith Garland for his care, patience and humour. I should also like to thank Kate Flint for her help in revising the final typescript. Most of all this book is indebted to the meticulous typing skills and kindness of Judy Maciejowska.

Introduction

When the armour, worn less often, began to grow rusty in the great halls, and the nobles, coming forth from their coats-of-mail like the butterfly from the chrysalis, showed themselves all glistening in silk, pearls in their ears, their heads full of Italian madrigals and mythological similes, a new society was formed, salons of a kind were organized, and the role of the women was enlarged. English medieval times had been by no means sparing of compliments to them. But there is a great difference between celebrating in verse fair, slim-necked ladies, and writing books expressly for them.

(J.J. Jusserand, *The English Novel in the Age of Shakespeare*, 1890; reprinted London 1901, pp. 88–9)

Jusserand's charming picture of the Renaissance might be altogether dismissed for its inaccuracy and exaggeration were it not for his last sentence; for Jusserand is one of the very few critics of this period to have both registered that in the last quarter of the sixteenth century men were writing for women, and to have recognized its significance. A large proportion of the books they were addressing to women were prose romances. In the following pages I will be exploring this phenomenon, examining the complex relation of women to romance, and locating the political implications of romances written for women by men.

Until now, these texts have been surveyed only in so far as they contribute to a preconceived chronological study of English fiction, or in their relation to the inception of the realist novel, or as storehouses of sources and influences. They have never been approached on their own terms. Because these works are primarily about women and for women, it seems not only reasonable but also necessary to approach them as a 'woman reader'. Using feminist critical theories of reading, I shall explore the dynamic process in which reader and narrator engage, studying the implications for women living 400 years ago, and increasing, I hope, the texts' accessibility for women reading today.

The first part of my study focuses on the growing literacy of women in the second half of the sixteenth century and the rise of a new female readership, and outlines the range of books which were being written for them. Romances appear to have been particularly popular, and I examine the double-edged nature of these works, which both reinforce patriarchal prescriptions for female behaviour, and simultaneously offer women a version of themselves as far more independent, powerful and significant than they would have experienced themselves in any other area of their lives. I outline the basis for a feminist reader-response methodology with which to approach these texts, before moving on to a brief examination of the history and nature of Elizabethan prose romances, and an indication of the limitations of previous critical approaches to them.

The second part explores in depth the romances of four authors in particular who wrote specifically for women: George Pettie, Robert Greene, Barnaby Rich and Sir Philip Sidney. The woman reader whom these writers envisage is a particularly active one. Her attention is constantly being called for by the narrator within the text; he appeals to her to agree with his observations, to heed closely what he is saying, to follow his advice, and to apply the story to her own life. She is offered a variety of often inconsistent, self-contradictory and self-destructive roles to play; crucially, she can refuse to adopt them, becoming, in Judith Fetterley's term, a 'resisting reader'.[1]* By recognizing the more oppressive designs these texts have on us, and by disengaging from them, women can instead revalue the romances as important domains of women's independence and power. And we can speculate that it was precisely these versions of women's independence and power which drew women readers of the sixteenth century to these works.

The second half of the sixteenth century has frequently been seen as a period of unprecedented freedom for women, and it has been assumed – as Jusserand assumes in the opening extract – that the Renaissance ushered in a 'rebirth' for women just as it did for (some) men. Burckhardt's famous work on the period, *The Civilization of the Renaissance in Italy* (1860), for example, contains the remarkable assertion that:

---

*Superscript numerals refer to numbered notes at the end of the book.

> To understand the higher forms of social intercourse at this period
> we must keep before our minds the fact that women stood on a
> footing of perfect equality with men,[2]

a statement belied by its location in a tiny chapter headed 'The position
of women'. More recently, feminist historians have questioned whether
this model of Renaissance history actually fits women's history. Joan
Kelly-Gadol argues that there was in fact no renaissance for women – at
least not during the Renaissance. On the contrary, she suggests, women
suffered a noticeable restriction of their scope and powers.[3]

One place where women might have experienced themselves as
powerful, however, is within the discourse of romantic fiction. Feminists
have recognized that the period of courtship, on which most romance
focuses, is one in which social consensus puts women's concerns at the
centre of attention, both in fiction and in life. Peter Laslett wisely
counsels us not to treat literature as if it were some kind of pre-
sociological sociology, and as if social reality were simply and unproblematically reflected in artistic forms,[4] but it will be helpful at least to
indicate that the notion of romantic love was not a foreign one in the
lives of ordinary people during the period. Historians Alan Macfarlane
and Ralph Houlbrooke refute the notion that there was little affection
between courting and married couples. Houlbrooke makes clear that
marriage based on love and free consent was a long-established ideal,
although the extent of this freedom depended in practice on political,
economic and social circumstances,[5] while Macfarlane, basing his
research on depositions and examinations taken in matrimonial cases
before ecclesiastical courts, concludes that the sixteenth-century evidence speaks plainly of romantic love.[6]

The nature of the power offered by fictional romances is always
ambivalent, as much recent feminist scholarship has indicated,[7] and this
is even more the case when those romances are written by men. Linda
Woodbridge, in her study of the literary debate over women which was
flourishing during this period, concludes that paradox most accurately
expresses the essence of the age.[8] Paradox is central to Renaissance
literature as it was habitual in Renaissance thought; and she finds one
manifestation of that paradox in the widespread insistence on describing
women in general as weak and vulnerable while portraying individual
women as strong and independent. This is precisely what happens in
much Elizabethan romance: it is generally peopled by assertive,
energetic, powerful women but attempts are consistently made to
neutralize that power. Barnaby Rich, for example, typically characterizes
his female characters as active, resourceful and intelligent, and his
women readers as passive and helpless; while George Pettie simultaneously expands and develops the roles of the female characters he found
in his sources and yet finally withdraws from the radical implications of

his own work and imposes a premature and repressive closure on the text.

The romances are primarily about women and for women – but they are written by men, so that women's relationship to language is often at best oblique, most apparent in gaps and silences; the silence of Agrippina, for example, a formidable woman of heroic stature who, after the death of her husband in Pettie's version of the story, pines away to death without him; according to tradition, she outlived her husband by many years and retained an active political life.

And as the female characters are often finally silenced, so there are attempts at silencing the woman reader. Each of the romance authors I study constructs a role for the woman reader which is prescriptive and repressive; the narrator constantly anticipates her reactions and arrogates her response. Gary Waller's observations about the struggle of women to be heard within male discourse can be applied to the encoding of women within the discourse of male-authored romance:

> To enter history an oppressed or under-privileged class can speak only through or against the dominant discourse and disrupt only by its negation or subdued silences – but we can say that such silence finally does speak (even if it is not acknowledged as having been said by being stated within the privileged monumentality of a text), and it is the critic's responsibility to make those silences speak.[9]

In Elizabethan romances, women readers are an 'absent presence'. The methodology which I outline in Chapter 1 proposes strategies for reading which make those silences 'speak', and which allow the woman reader to read against the grain and to resist the marginalization which she is offered, so that finally the romances can be reread and revalued as the strongly woman-centred texts which they can be. And we can speculate that while women in the sixteenth century would probably never have thought of themselves as 'reading against the grain', they might have individually and perhaps unconsciously valued the romances particularly for the powerful women who – despite authorial intentions – finally dominate these works.

★ ★ ★

The period which this study focuses on runs approximately from the publication of William Painter's *Palace of Pleasure* in 1566 to the end of the sixteenth century. Painter was one of the earliest Elizabethan fiction writers to recognize the market potential of a growing female readership, and the following 40 years witnessed a huge and sudden rise in the number of fiction titles which were published, many of which were romances. This period would seem to be the first time in English literary history that women were recognized as constituting a specific reader-ship, and it is a phenomenon which has been largely overlooked, both by literary historians and by critics of the romance. Ann Rosalind Jones, for example, in an essay on popular romance erroneously states, '. . . it is only recently that romance has been aimed so exclusively at women',[10] and indeed in the collection of essays in which hers appears, entitled *The Progress of Romance*, Elizabethan romance is left out altogether.[11]

My own use of the term 'romance' requires some explanation. In the early Middle Ages the word had referred to the languages of the vernacular rather than Latin, but this meaning gradually became more specialized, referring to a certain sort of story in the vernacular which was characterized by chivalric knights and ladies, and stories of love and adventure. Indeed, the romance as a literary genre has often been exclusively associated with medieval literature, but of course its antecedents went back far beyond twelfth-century Europe and its influence persisted long after the Middle Ages. Several scholarly works have traced the influence of medieval romance on Elizabethan fiction in general,[12] although in Chapter 2 I shall demonstrate that the romances of Sidney and Greene were in fact more indebted to the Greek romance tradition, while Pettie and Rich call heavily upon the Italian novelle. For the purpose of this study, however, the most important difference between medieval romance and the Elizabethan romances which I examine is one of focus. In medieval romance, it is the male who is the subject of the passion. What happens at the end of the sixteenth and beginning of the seventeenth centuries – and even more forcefully so in popular modern romances – is that the focus shifts from man as subject to woman as object of the romantic tale, and it is this object, not the male subject, with whom the reader is asked to identify. Juliet Mitchell, summarizing this process, observes: 'In other words, romance has moved from being about a male subject to becoming a commodity about women, for women'.[13] And it is on these romances, in which the interest is predominantly on love and courtship rather than on chivalric adventure, and in which the shift from male subject to female object is clearest and most complete, that I shall focus.

In the seventeenth and early eighteenth centuries, the word romance was particularly applied to fictitious narratives, and was associated with unreality as compared with the supposed realism of the emerging novel form. Indeed, the early novelists constantly assured their readers that their works, unlike the romances, were real and true. Clara Reeve, writing a history of the romance in 1785, makes a very clear distinction between the two, and implicitly stresses the modernity of the novel form, as opposed to the traditionalism of the romance:

> The Romance is an heroic fable, which treats of fabulous persons
> and things – The Novel is a picture of real life and manners, and of
> the times in which it is written.[14]

Yet this overlooks the fact that novels themselves often rely heavily on
the elements and structures of romance; it might be nearer the truth to
say that the difference between the two genres is one of degree rather
than kind.

Jane Spencer, in her analysis of Louis B. Wright's uncritical assertion
that 'since women in general have never subscribed to realism, romance
in strange opera lands and love stories with happy endings found favour
with the Elizabethans even as with feminine readers today', brilliantly
demonstrates that the association of women with romance in the sense of
anti-realism depends entirely upon who decides what reality is.[15] In her
study of early women writers, Spencer suggests that the lives of the
women characters about whom they wrote – whose actions were largely
cut off from the world outside the home, and whose concerns seemed
limited to dress, amusements, accomplishments and attracting a husband
– were seen as somehow not serious and not truly real. With a deft sleight
of hand, Spencer neatly overturns the argument and claims that 'What
was "unreal" about romance was precisely women's importance in it';[16]
and in conclusion she encapsulates the essence of the appeal of romance
for women readers: '. . . it offered escape from male-dominated reality
through a fantasy of female power'.[17] In my analysis of Elizabethan
romance I shall suggest that this fantasy was not new, and that elements
of it were present in the romances which men wrote for women over 100
years earlier.

In her shrewd and delightfully personal account of reading, Rachel
Brownstein suggests that the readers of romantic novels are often
women who want to become heroines:

> It is not megalomaniacal to want to be significant; it is only human.
> And to suspect that one can be significant only in the fantasy of
> fiction, to look for significance in a concentrated essence of
> character, in an image of oneself, rather than in action or
> achievement, is historically, only feminine.[18]

The dangers of assuming that the fictional fantasy is a long-term reality
are comically presented in Charlotte Lennox's extremely funny novel,
The Female Quixote (1752),[19] which tells of the adventures of a woman
who has a burning desire to be 'significant'. Like its model, the *Don
Quixote* of Cervantes, it has a protagonist obsessed with a romantic world
and quite blind to the reality of her everyday life. The romances which
have deluded Arabella are the seventeenth-century French romances
with their stories of a romantic heroine who has absolute power over her

lovers. Arabella firmly believes that the romances she reads are true reflections of life – having been brought up in the country by her widowed father, she has no experience of the world – and a series of comic episodes ensue as a result of her application of the expectations and moral standards of the French romances to the incidents of everyday life. So when, for example, one of her father's gardeners is caught trying to steal fish from a pond, Arabella is convinced that he is a young nobleman in disguise who is trying to drown himself out of hopeless love for her. Her imaginary world, however, in which her charms are omnipotent, and in which she completely believes, provides a refuge from the reality that deprives women of power.

In my analysis of Elizabethan romances, I shall suggest that women readers of the sixteenth century might similarly have found in the romance a refuge from a reality of female powerlessness. I shall indicate how a feminist reader-response approach to these texts can increase their accessibility to women reading today, and finally offer ways in which the woman reader can reappropriate the romances, and reread them to her own advantage.

1

The background

Books for women

> I marvel that wise fathers will suffer their daughters, or husbands
> their wives, or that the manners and customs of people will
> dissemble and overlook, that women shall use to read wantonness.[1]

Although this work focuses primarily on woman as construct in male
texts, it will be helpful to show that actual women were indeed avidly
reading the books written for them 400 years ago. The difficulty which
faces any historical study of reading, however, is the scarcity of reliable
documentary evidence. Unfortunately, reading – as process – cannot be
demonstrated, measured or proved in the way that written products – by
their very physical presence – can be, and while some women of the
upper classes did leave written indications of the books they happened to
be reading, there is absolutely no way of finally knowing how many
women below the level of gentry in England learned to read, nor what
their literary preferences might have been.

   The evidence we do have comes mainly in three forms: in references in
the contemporary literature to women reading, in the instruction books
by male writers which assert that women are not to read certain works
(and in some cases, are not to read at all)[2] and, most convincingly, in the
sheer volume of works produced in the period which clearly advertise
that they are written for women.

   Suzanne Hull's study, *Chaste, Silent and Obedient*, usefully identifies the
books printed in English between 1475 and 1640 which appear to have

been directed, at least in part – through titles, dedications or subject matter – to women readers.[3] In that period at least 163 in some 500 editions were specifically directed to, or printed for, women, and 85 per cent of those were published after 1570.[4] Indeed, in the decade 1573–82 the number increased dramatically, and at the same time fiction became a proportionately greater part of the book market.[5] According to Sterg O'Dell,[6] there were 42 prose fiction titles printed between 1563 and 1572; in the next decade, from 1573 to 1582, the number jumped to 75, and rose to 125 in the following decade. Only 24 titles that meet Hull's criteria for women's books were published in approximately the first century of English printing, but between 1573 and 1582 there were 19; the next decade recorded 18, and in the period 1593 to 1602, 24 appeared.[7]

Hull cites further evidence that authors and booksellers were becoming increasingly conscious of women readers, particularly in the 1570s and 1580s: during this time a number of books originally addressed to men or to no specific group at all were redirected or retitled in later editions to include women.[8] Thomas Tusser's rhymed guide to country living, *A Hundreth Good Pointes of Husbandrie*, for example, was first published in 1557. The first edition included two pages called 'A digression from husbandrie to a point or two of huswiferie'; five years later Tusser brought out a second edition and added housewives to the title, which became *A Hundreth Good Pointes of Husbandrie. Lately Maried unto a Hundreth Good Poyntes of Huswifry*; and by 1573 it had become *Five Hundrethe Pointes of Good Husbandry united to as Many of Good Huswiferie*. Twenty-three editions of Tusser's guide giving equal attention to women's duties were printed before 1641.[9] John Lyly's immensely popular *Euphues: The Anatomy of Wit* was published in 1578, and claimed on its title page that it was 'verie pleasant for all gentlemen to reade', and contained further dedications to the gentlemen inside.[10] Two years later the sequel appeared, *Euphues and his England*, and the first general dedication, several pages in length, was to 'the Ladies and Gentlewoemen of England', and in it Lyly declared:

> I would you woulde read bookes that have more shewe of pleasure, then ground of profit, then should *Euphues* be as often in your hands, being but a toy, as Lawne on your heads . . .[11]

And further: '*Euphues* had rather lye shut in a ladyes casket than open in a Schollers studie.'[12]

Women readers were not only increasing in numbers, however; Hull suggests that the many different kinds of books directed to them indicates that they also represented a broader cross-section of the female population.[13] She divides the books into four categories: practical guides, devotional works, books relating to the controversy about women, and fiction and recreational literature.

More than half of all the books for women between 1475 and 1640 were practical guidebooks.[14] Most of them appear to be directed primarily to a middle-class readership, to women who may have had servants but who were nevertheless still very much involved in the daily running of household affairs. Subjects covered include instructions on how to educate young girls, how to write letters, garden, cook, dress, use English correctly, speak French, prepare homemade medications and create fine needlework. However, some of the works do seem to include the poorer classes in their scope. The preface to one of the needlework books, for instance, emphasizes that even maids may make use of it, and indeed it suggests it as a means for their social advancement:

> For many maidens but of base degree,
> By their fine knowledge in this curious thing:
> With Noble Ladies oft companions be,
> Sometimes they teach the daughters of a King:
> Thus by their knowledge, fame, and good report,
> They are esteemed among the noblest sort.[15]

Just 18 of the 163 books for women identified by Hull are classified as devotional, but the few surviving journals and diaries by women that mention reading in this period all indicate that religious works were prominent in their book collections.[16] Lady Anne Clifford's diary records, for example, that she read not only the Bible, but also *The First Booke of the Christian Exercise Appertayning to Resolution* by Robert Parsons, *Supplications of Saints: A Booke of Prayers*, by Thomas Sorocold, a 'lady's book of praise of a solitary life', and a 'book of the preparation to the sacrament'.[17]

The controversy about women generated a prolonged literary debate about the innate goodness or badness of women, and stimulated a flurry of books and pamphlets putting both sides of the argument; among the most common accusations were those of women's excessive jealousy, greed, pride, extravagance, lust and infidelity. Writers on both sides of the question commonly cited classical and Biblical women to prove their cases. These works account for 18 of the books directed to women in this period.[18]

Hull's category of fiction and recreational literature includes one-quarter of her total, and embraces romances, poetry, jests, allegories and biographies.[19] But it was the romance writers in particular who directed their works to women. One of the first was George Pettie, whose *Petite Pallace of Pettie his Pleasure* (1576)[20] carried an epistle to the 'gentle gentlewomen readers' by one 'R.B.', which was followed in 1577 by John Grange whose work *The Golden Aphroditis*[21] was dedicated 'to the courtelike dames and ladielike gentlewomen'. Their example was soon followed by other romancers including Stephen Gosson, John Lyly, Robert Greene, Barnaby Rich, and – most famously – Sir Philip Sidney.

Men wrote nearly all the books for women which were printed before 1640. There was a powerful taboo against women entering the world of print, of assuming the role of author, and the authority which went with it.[22] Translating, on the other hand, was more allowable, and Queen Elizabeth herself, famous for her knowledge of languages, was known to have produced some very fine examples. Margaret Tyler was particularly assertive: she translated one of the most popular romances of the period, *The First Part of the Mirrour of Princely Deedes and Knighthood*, from the Spanish of Diego Ortunez de Calahorra in 1578, and included her own impassioned plea for the rights of women both to translate and to write romantic fiction:

> And if men may and doe beestow such of theyr travailes upon Gentlewomen, then may wee women read such of theyr woorkes as they dedicate unto us, and if wee may read them, why not farther wade in them to the search of truth . . . . But amongst all my ill willers, some I hope are not so strayght that they would enforce mee necessarily either not to write or to write of divinitie . . . . And thus much concerning this present storie, that it is neither unseemely for a woman to deale in, neither greatly requiring a less stayed age then mine is.[23]

She moves smoothly from her first premise, that it is the custom of men to dedicate to women books on many subjects including war, government and religion, to her second, that it was proper and usual for women to read them. Her concluding premise, however, that 'it is all one for a woman to pen a storie, as for a man to address his storie to a woman',[24] would probably have met with little agreement from her male contemporaries.

No such stigma was attached to women patrons, whose activity in the world of letters was limited to financially supporting or encouraging male writers.[25] According to Hull, Franklin Williams' *Index to Dedications and Commendatory Verses in English Books before 1641*[26] reveals that a total of around 1780 books were dedicated to individual women, of which 23 per cent were dedicated to queens. Elizabeth received by far the most, with 219. Other women who had books dedicated to them range from noblewomen like Mary Sidney and Lucy Harington, to obscure friends or relations of the author. Of around 800 different women who were the recipients of dedications, or had books addressed to them in some manner, most were members of the aristocracy: 225 were non-titled women, and another 25 had religious connections. Hull concludes that such a large number of female dedicatees would seem to indicate a broad acceptance of women as patrons of literature.[27]

Any degree of participation in literary culture, however, presupposes at least some degree of literacy; but if it is notoriously difficult to arrive at figures for the spread of literacy in the sixteenth century, that difficulty becomes ten times greater if the sought-after figures relate exclusively to women. J.W. Adamson was one of the first to suggest that the skills of reading and writing were not inseparable parts of sixteenth-century elementary education and, concluding that the number of those who could read was much larger than the number of those who could write, postulates that a large number of these were women.[28] He cites the 1543 Act for the Advancement of True Religion (34 and 35 Hen. VIII c.1.), which clearly forbade the reading of the Bible in English by women, artificers, prentices, journeymen, servingmen of the degrees of yeomen or under, husbandmen and labourers, as indirect evidence for wide-spread literacy among the humbler social ranks irrespective of sex.[29]

R.S. Schofield and David Cressy have developed methods of measuring literacy by comparing the number of people who could sign their names on official documents with the number who made a mark instead, although Cressy admits that this method inevitably underestimates the number of literate women.[30] Cressy's research in documents from the dioceses of Exeter, Durham, Norwich and London leads him to calculate that, as late as the 1640s, 70 per cent of adult English men, and 90 per cent of English women were illiterate, that is, unable to sign their names.[31] The gender difference appears very large, as do the social and geographical variations. Predictably, the greatest literacy was found at the top, among the gentry and professional classes, who were almost wholly literate by 1600. The literacy of those living in London – including servants and apprentices – appears to have been substantially higher than anywhere else in the country.

Serious doubt has been cast on these figures, however, by Keith Thomas, who challenges both the methodology and the results of Cressy and Schofield.[32] Thomas claims that a simple contrast between 'literacy' and 'illiteracy' fails to address the complexity of the subject, and points out that during this period there was a huge diversity of scripts, typefaces, and languages; proficiency in one by no means guaranteed any ability in any of the others. It would be perfectly possible, he argues, for someone to be able to read print fluently, but to be quite incapable of deciphering a written document. This 'elaborate hierarchy' of literary skills makes it very difficult to determine precisely just what proportion was 'literate', and to rely exclusively on one criterion to measure literacy – an individual's ability to sign his or her name – is inadequate. Not only does the inability to sign one's name fail to prove an inability to read – we have seen that they are quite different skills – but, Thomas suggests, it does not even demonstrate an inability to write; the person may have been ill at the time, or may simply have preferred to use the sanctified symbol of the cross, or the traditional device of their trade. And, conversely, someone who could write their name could not necessarily write anything else. Thomas concludes that Cressy's figures for illiteracy in 1640 are not merely an underestimate, but 'a spectacular under-estimate'.[33]

Since much reading was still practised as an oral activity, someone who could not read themselves could still participate in literate culture by listening to others, as Schofield has pointed out:

> . . . it only needs one or two members of normally illiterate groups, who have acquired an ability to read, to read aloud to their friends and neighbours, for a bridge to be thrown across any supposed divide between exclusively literate and illiterate groups within society.[34]

In any household, then, where one member was fully literate, the possibility existed that he or she might read aloud to the others, thus allowing them access to literature. The Bible and prayer-book were obviously used in this way, and Cressy cites the example of clergymen recommending illiterate people to keep a copy of the Bible in their houses, so that when anybody visited who could read, they would not lose the opportunity of hearing it read aloud.[35]

Some women no doubt did experience the books written for them in this way, although – contra Cressy's calculations – there appear to be ample indications that many could read for themselves, even though the facilities for formal education in Elizabethan England were mostly closed to women. Grammar schools and universities did not admit female students, but while daughters of the wealthy classes would probably have private tuition at home, many of the daughters of the lower classes seem to have attended the elementary or 'petty' schools, where they would have learned to read, but rarely to write.[36] Margaret Spufford's account of schooling and literacy in the early seventeenth century focuses almost entirely upon boys, but she usefully develops the important distinction between the skills of reading and writing.[37] Her 'rule of thumb' guide is that children who were able to go to school until they were seven were likely to be able to read; those who remained until eight were likely to be able to write.[38] The age of seven seems also to have been the age at which children could begin to earn significant wages, and Spufford concludes from this that many more children would have been able to read than write:

> It indicates that reading skills, which unfortunately by their nature are not capable of measurement, were likely to have been very much more socially widespread in sixteenth- and seventeenth-century England than writing skills, simply because the age at

which children learnt to read was one at which children of the relatively poor were not yet capable of much paying labour, and were therefore available for some schooling.[39]

There would have been other opportunities to learn to read for even those girls who did not attend petty school. Adamson suggests that girls may have been found in the small classes conducted by parish priests, or parish clerks,[40] and there would also have been informal education networks where girls could have been taught to read by family friends or acquaintances.

Records of women's libraries are quite rare for this period. Sears Jayne, in his *Library Catalogues of the English Renaissance*, provides a checklist of 848 libraries owned in England between 1500 and 1640, usually using inventories of personal wealth as his source.[41] Of the 574 private libraries which he cites, only three belonged to women.[42] Peter Clark has developed and updated Jayne's research, recognizing the limitations of Jayne's decision to list only libraries containing 15 or more different titles and to rely for most of his primary material on lists from the scholastic communities of Oxford and Cambridge.[43] Clark broadens his approach to include all references to books, and takes his sample inventories from three more typical provincial areas, the towns of Canterbury, Faversham and Maidstone in Kent over the period 1560 to 1640. His figures reveal that by 1640 almost every county landowner of note had several shelves of books at home.[44] His calculations for those outside the landed and professional classes are, he concedes, inevitably less complete. In the 1560s, he concludes that fewer than one in ten of Canterbury's inventories referred to a book, but by the 1580s ownership had risen so steeply that well over one in four inventories referred to a book, and the next decade witnessed a further rise, with over one-third listing one volume or more.[45] However, for women's libraries, Clark's figures return to broader speculation:

> Because our female sample is so much smaller, a detailed analysis of book ownership on a similar dicennial basis is impractical.[46]

Instead, he divides the period in half, and calculates that before 1600 a sample of 76 female inventories for Canterbury showed a 14 per cent ownership level; after 1600 the comparable rate was 29 per cent in a sample of 304. And he concludes:

> We would probably not be too far wrong if we said that whereas ownership of books among men in the early seventeenth century reached over forty per cent, among women the overall level was nearer twenty-five per cent.[47]

Many women would, of course, have had access to their husbands' and fathers' books in any case; and some of their own books may have appeared as part of their husbands' collections. Clark omits women's collections from his analysis of the titles which were possessed on the grounds that the numbers are too small.[48]

Our evidence for women reading, then, is inevitably patchy and often anecdotal, but its cumulative effect is a persuasive indication of the prevalence of women using books. The reading of exceptional women of the period has already been well documented, in the accounts of the unusual degree of learning possessed by Sir Thomas More's daughters, by Lady Jane Grey, and, of course, by Queen Elizabeth herself. But we are also able to catch a few glimpses of less exalted figures. Clark cites the example of Elizabeth Baker, the wife of an Otham yeoman who, one night in 1607, according to her maid giving evidence in a law suit, was 'at her book reading as she uses many times to do before she goes to bed'.[49] In another case, the witness tells how one Bartholomew Dann assaulted his wife, and 'when she had been reading and leaving her book in some place . . . he would catch the book out of her hands and tear it in pieces or otherwise fling it away'.[50] In her journal, Lady Mildmay records several references to her reading – in particular, her copy of William Turner's *Herball* – and indicates that her housekeeper could also read, since Lady Mildmay sent written instructions to her.[51] Lady Margaret Hoby, a pious Puritan woman, records many times that she was either reading herself, or being read to by her maids and serving women. Most frequently referred to are her *Herball*, her book of physic, Foxe's *Acts and Monuments*, Perkins' sermons, and similar practical or devotional works.[52] Lady Anne Clifford, more unusually, includes fiction in her diary entries about reading.[53] The works she read, or had read to her, include Spenser's *Faerie Queene*, Chaucer, Ovid's *Metamorphoses*, and Sidney's *Arcadia*; for example: 'The 12th and 13th I spent most of the time in playing Glecko and hearing Moll Neville read the *Arcadia*.'[54]

Women of the lower social orders left even fewer records of their reading habits, but we are given some insight through references in other literature of the period, and through the instructions laid down by men. Although Linda Woodbridge helpfully reminds us that 'the relationship between literature and life is a very slippery subject',[55] and warns against any simple correlation between the two, it would seem not unreasonable to conclude that literary references to women reading at least suggests that some women were thought to be able to read, and to enjoy certain works.

Maids were frequently portrayed as being particularly avid romance readers. A chambermaid described by William Browne in 'Fido, an Epistle to Fidelia' is especially well-versed in the different romances. When she hears her mistress read 'one epistle that some fool had writ' for her,

Her chambermaid's great reading quickly strikes
That good opinion dead, and swears that this
Was stol'n from Palmerin or Amadis.[56]

The confidante in Philip Massinger's *Guardian* declares to her mistress that she not only reads romances, but she also believes in them:

In all the books of *Amadis de Gaul*,
The *Palmerins*, and that true Spanish story
The Mirror of Knighthood, which I have read often,
Read feelingly, nay more, I do believe in't,
My Lady has no parallel.[57]

And a young girl in Wye Saltonstall's *Picturae Loquentes* of 1631 is described savouring vicariously the delights of love:

. . . she reades now loves historyes as *Amadis de Gaule* and the *Arcadia* and in them courts the shaddow of love till she know the substance.[58]

That women of all classes may well have been reading romances is further suggested by the vigour and persistence of men trying to stop them. Edward Hake, for example, bitterly laments that young girls are provided with improper reading matter which prevents them from reading more worthy books:

Eyther shee is altogither kept from exercises of good learning, and knowledge of good letters, or else she is so nouseled in amorous bookes, vaine stories and fonde trifeling fancies, that shee smelleth of naughtinesse even all hir lyfe after . . . .[59]

Thomas Salter has equally clear ideas about what young women should *not* be reading, and in *A Mirrhor mete for all Mothers, Matrones, and Maidens, intituled the Mirrhor of Modestie* of 1574 he condemns fathers in particular who give their daughters:

. . . so sone as they have any understandyng in readyng, or spellyng, to cone and learne by hart bookes, ballades, songes, sonettes, and ditties of dalliance, excityng their memories thereby, beyng then most apt to retayne for ever that which is taught theim, to the same Maner . . . therefore I would wish our good Matrone (who teaches young girls) to eschew suche use as a pestilent infection . . . .[60]

Salter will not allow women to choose their own reading matter. On no account, for example, are they to read Ovid, Catullus, the stories of Dido and Aeneas in Virgil, or 'of filthie love among the Greek poets'.[61] He does, however, make some alternative suggestions:

. . . in steede of suche bookes and lascivious ballads, our wise

Matrone shall reade, or cause her maidens to reade, the examples
and lives of godly and vertuous ladies, whose worthy fame and
bright renowne yet liveth, and still will live for ever, whiche shee
shall make choice of, out of the holy Scripture, and other histories,
both auncient and of late dayes.[62]

He suggests that such works will not only delight women readers, but
also encourage them to follow virtue and shun vice:

... for you shall never repeate the vertuous lives of any such ladies
as *Claudia*, *Portia*, *Lucretia*, and such like were, but you shall kindle a
desire in them to treade their steppes, and become in tyme like
unto them.[63]

Women readers, then, are to read of patriarchal role models, and
fashion themselves in the same mould. This is precisely what we see
many of Robert Greene's fictional heroines attempting to do, and what
Greene himself encourages us, as readers of his romances, to do also.[64]

The educationalist Richard Mulcaster was in favour of women
learning to read, so long as it did not interfere with their household
duties. In his *Positions wherein those primitive circumstances be examined which
are necessary for the training up of chilrden* (1581), he explains further:

Reading if for nothing else it were, as for many thinges else it is, is
verie needefull for religion, to read that which they must know, and
ought to performe .... Here I may not omit many and great
contentmentes, many and sound comfortes, many manifoulde
delites, which those wymen that have skill and time to reade,
without hindering their houswifery, do continually receive by
reading of some comfortable and wise discourses, penned either in
forme of historie, or for direction to live by.[65]

The Spanish humanist and educationalist Juan Luis Vives, who came
to England in 1523 in the circle of Katherine of Aragon, was concerned
with the subject of educating princesses and the daughters of the
aristocracy. He studied the question of what women should read very
carefully, and returns to it many times in the course of his writings.[66]
Romances are at the top of his list of books to avoid at all costs: 'a woman
should beware of all these books, like as of serpents or snakes'.[67] He
objects to them not only on the grounds of their immorality, but also
raises aesthetic objections. For him, romances are full of 'plain and
foolish lies' in their obvious exaggerations, and have no wit in them, 'but
a few words of wanton lust, which be spoken to move her mind with
whom they love, if it chance she be steadfast';[68] women should not be
allowed to touch them, he reiterates vehemently:

And verily they be but foolish husbands and mad, that suffer their
wives to wax more ungraciously subtle by reading of such books.[69]

In order to avoid this unfortunate eventuality, women must ask advice of
men about which books are appropriate for them, and defer to their
superior judgement:

> But as touching some, wise and learned men must be asked counsel
> of in them. Nor the woman ought not to follow her own
> judgement, lest when she hath but a light entering in learning she
> should take false for true, hurtful instead of wholesome, foolish and
> peevish for learned and wise.[70]

The dangers of women reading seem to have been fully recognized by
men, who were clearly anxious to keep women away from books which
could encourage them to step outside the painfully narrow confines of
the role assigned to them during this period. The volume of romances
which continued to be addressed to women suggests that their efforts
were far from successful, however. And even if there were regulations
about *what* women were to read, fortunately it is impossible to legislate
about *how* to read. I shall argue that even though romances written for
women by men are, as products of an intensely patriarchal culture,
oppressive to women in many ways, these texts can be read in a
subversive way which reveals them to be powerful, strongly woman-
centred works which give women a scope and freedom denied them
elsewhere. Perhaps Elizabethan writers and educationalists were dimly
aware of the radical potential of these texts when they warned women
away from them so vigorously.

The politics of romantic fiction

Romantic fiction has, for the past 400 years at least, been associated
almost exclusively with women. Women have constituted its subject
matter, its consumers, and later its producers as well. Romantic fiction
has also, perhaps more than any other literary genre, been ridiculed,
criticised and condemned. These two observations may not be unconnected; indeed, I would argue that romantic fiction has been dismissed
or devalued precisely because of its association with women. Virginia
Woolf pointed out how sexist values are transferred from life to fiction:

> Speaking crudely, football and sport are 'important'; the worship of
> fashion, the buying of clothes 'trivial' . . . This is an important
> book, the critic assumes, because it deals with war. This is an
> insignificant book because it deals with the feelings of women in a
> drawing-room.[71]

Paradoxically, however, critics have inadvertently proved how much power these apparently 'insignificant' books have by their vigorous and prolonged efforts to stop women from reading them.

If power resided in numbers alone, then the sheer volume of romances that are written would give their detractors cause for concern. Louis B. Wright points to the huge number of romances produced at the end of the sixteenth century:

> Romances ... fell from the presses like leaves in autumn, throughout the sixteenth and seventeenth centuries, but the great period of productivity both for translation and original compositions was the last quarter of the sixteenth century, when enough chivalric stories were produced to supply printers with subject matter for the next generation.[72]

Similarly, today, the number of romances produced is a source both of pride and amazement. The Canadian-based publishing firm, Harlequin Enterprises (which in 1972 took over Mills and Boon), after some acrobatic leaps of arithmetic, announced on one of its press releases:

> If placed end to end, Harlequin books sold in 1981 could run along both sides of the Nile, both sides of the Amazon, and one side of the Rio Grande. If all the words of all the Harlequin books sold in 1981 were laid end to end, they would stretch 1000 times around the earth and 93 times to the moon.[73]

Mills and Boon's latest sales figures show a rise from 15 million in 1985 to 20 million in 1987 in the UK, and from 202 million to 240 million worldwide.[74] Mills and Boon, indeed, have become a publishing legend: both the *Independent* and *Guardian* newspapers carried front page stories in 1988 about the phenomenal success of their romances,[75] while Barbara Cartland has become a national institution, with over 400 romances to her name.[76] *Publishers Weekly* estimates that there are over 20 million readers in the United States alone who will buy an estimated half-billion dollars' worth of romances yearly.[77] Harlequins account for 10–12 per cent of all paperbacks sold in the United States, and 28 per cent of the paperback market in Canada; they are published in 12 languages that sell in 98 countries around the world.[78] And, contrary to the popular imagination, romance readers are a widely diffused group of individuals which defies stereotyping. A *Sunday Express* magazine article of 1985, entitled 'Confessions of the blue stocking romantics', set out expressly to challenge the prevailing myth that the romance reader is 'a lonely frustrated spinster who failed her 11-plus and falls into a humble socio-economic group', and to demonstrate Mills and Boon's appeal to high-powered career women,[79] while Peter Mann, who has conducted two

surveys of Mills and Boon readers, one in 1968 with 2788 readers and
another in 1973 with 2000, concludes:[80]

> After nearly five years of contact with romantic novels I now feel
> that it is possible to write with some assurance about their readers.
> If one may sum up in a word, they are 'Everywoman'.[81]

Mann's findings show that a third of readers were full-time housewives,
30 per cent were married women with either full-time or part-time jobs,
and 22 per cent were unmarried women with jobs. The rest were either
retired or full-time students.[82]

The romance readers of the sixteenth century have been analysed
according to class:

> Although lords and ladies and men of letters continued to read the
> romances to some extent throughout the sixteenth century, the
> appeal was made more and more to readers of the less favored
> classes, while academic critics and moralists began to level their
> darts against the iniquity of romance-reading. From the mid-
> sixteenth century onward, the old-fashioned tales of chivalry were
> gradually relegated to the more unsophisticated reader, and
> romances, which had begun as aristocratic works, appeared in
> cheap quartos and at last reached the nadir of their fame as penny-
> chapbooks to be hawked by peddlers at fairs.[83]

Critics, from Renaissance educationalist Juan Luis Vives in 1540 to
feminist Germaine Greer in 1970, have indeed found much to 'level their
darts against' in the practice of reading romances.[84] For Vives, the chief
danger of romances lies in their lewdness; they are responsible for much
of society's immorality, and are too full of 'filth and viciousness' to be
suitable reading material for young women.[85] For Greer, it is the women
themselves who are to be condemned for participating in the production
and consumption of romances which clearly reinforce and perpetuate
oppression, gender-stereotyping and women's subordination to men.[86]
Of a particularly macho hero, Greer acidly comments:

> This is the hero that women have chosen for themselves. The traits
> invented for him have been invented by women cherishing the
> chains of their bondage.[87]

In place of analysis, Greer substitutes blame and recrimination, and
offers no insight into why women should indulge in such an apparently
masochistic activity.

Equally as reductive is the 'conspiracy theory' of romance, posited
most strongly by Shulamith Firestone, which proposes an interpretation
of romance as an all-pervasive manifestation of male ideology, which
increases in its strength in direct proportion to women's increasing

emancipation in order to ensure continued female subordination within a patriarchal framework. This interpretation not only casts all men as guilty and all women as helpless, passive victims, but also fails to account for women's participation in producing romances.[88]

The stereotyped characters of romance, and its clichéd terms, are frequently objects of contempt, but attempts are rarely made to account for them. Romances clearly do fall into the category of formula fiction, which John Cawelti characterizes as a highly standardized, repetitious literature whose primary purpose is reassuring escape and entertainment.[89] The romance publishers themselves make no secret of the formulaic quality of their books, and insist that their authors strictly adhere to them. Harlequin publishers offer the following guidelines to prospective authors:

> Harlequins are well-plotted, strong romances with a happy ending. They are told from the heroine's point of view and in the third person. There may be elements of mystery or adventure but these must be subordinate to the romance. The books are contemporary and settings can be anywhere in the world so long as they are authentic.[90]

Tania Modleski elaborates on the formula, showing even more clearly its rigid specificity:

> Each book averages approximately 187 pages . . . a young, inexperienced, poor to moderately well-to-do woman encounters and becomes involved with a handsome, strong, experienced, wealthy man, older than herself by 10 to 15 years. The heroine is confused by the hero's behaviour since, though he is obviously interested in her, he is mocking, cynical, contemptuous, often hostile, and even somewhat brutal. By the end, however, all misunderstandings are cleared away, and the hero reveals his love for the heroine, who reciprocates.[91]

Mary Wibberley has recently written a guide book especially designed for aspiring romance writers, telling them everything they need to know about the genre, from how to write it to how to get it published. And she should know – a romance writer herself, she has sold no less than 80 million of her books in the last 13 years.[92]

Sixteenth-century prose romances had a formula which, if it was a little less rigid, was none the less equally powerful; almost all involve the history of the course of love between a young and beautiful couple, with the unavoidable obstacles which they face on the way to a happy ending. Some of the most common features include inevitable partings, concealed identities, shipwrecks miraculously survived, wandering in foreign countries, capture and rescue.

But the single most significant difference between Renaissance
romance and contemporary Harlequins lies not in their form or their
content, but in their authorship, for the authors of the sixteenth-century
romances were men, who were self-consciously supplying a female
readership. Over the past ten years, feminists have formulated radical
new approaches to the romance form, approaches which refuse to
dismiss a genre with such huge appeal to millions of women all over the
world. From a brief survey of their findings, I hope to work towards a
methodology for approaching the romances written for women over 400
years ago, but written – crucially – by men.

★ ★ ★

One of the first to put forward a defence for reading romances was Janet
Batsleer, in a *Spare Rib* article in 1981.[93] 'With some trepidation', she
defends them 'from the point of view of the thousands of women who
read the stuff', and postulates that romance reading is one way for
women to cope with their subordination as women. Defining romances
as stories of desire for a happy ending, she remarks: 'If we look for happy
endings in fiction it is because at present it is the only place we can hope
to find them.'[94] More than this, however, she suggests that romance
fiction turns the traditional order of power and history upside down by
making the private sphere of home, family and emotion, central.
Romances, then, are 'celebrations of women's world', of women's
values, and of women's lives.[95] And, more radically, she claims that the
responses of feminism, and of romance reading, are not as unconnected
as some may like to think:

> The conflicts of Cartland's fiction are the conflicts which have
> produced feminism: conflicts *between* the private world of marriage,
> family and home and the world of public decision making and
> conflicts *within* the private world of marriage and patriarchal
> sexuality.[96]

Romances, finally, are manifestations of a longing for a new and better
world in which women, men and children can love without subordination.

Valerie Hey takes up these points and develops them.[97] For her,
romance reading is 'a necessary and rational response to a set of
enormous pressures', and there is something courageous and admirable
about it:

> It is in fact, given the circumstances, a brave effort to hold on to
> some semblance of control over the terms of the exchange of
> female sexuality, in a market place dominated by an equation;
> female equals sexuality equals debasement.[98]

She posits a theory of romance reading which sees romance as a 'survival manual' for women, and recognizes that romances have accorded women a power and significance seldom granted them in any other area of their lives; for in romances, the world of emotion and personal relationships is transformed from a site of female subordination into one of female control. It is both validated and glamorized.

This more complex analysis of romance is shared by Tania Modleski, who agrees that although the romance heroine and the feminist choose utterly different ways of coping with the dissatisfaction they feel within patriarchal society, 'they at least have in common the dissatisfaction'.[99] She interprets romance reading as a form of adaptation to the 'circumscribed lives' that women live in our society and she redirects the negative judgement away from the romances, and towards the conditions which have made them necessary:

> Even though the novels can be said to intensify female tensions and conflicts, on balance the contradictions in women's lives are more responsible for the existence of Harlequins than Harlequins are for the contradictions.[100]

While Modleski argues that the Harlequin fantasy is not always regressive, and that elements of protest and resistance lie beneath highly orthodox plots, ultimately, however, she sees romance reading as a destructive process:

> The energy women now use to belittle and defeat themselves can be rechannelled into efforts to grow and to explore ways of affirming and asserting the self.[101]

Margaret Jensen rejects such pessimistic interpretations, and insists that although Harlequins are indeed heterosexist and ideologically consistent with capitalism, these criticisms can be put to one side in an analysis of romance which sets out to understand the appeal of romances from the perspective of the readers, who take the 'system' for granted.[102] Jensen maintains that the 'new woman' featured in contemporary Harlequins – which have been influenced by feminism to the extent that the heroines are increasingly competent, sexual human beings – gets everything she wants: she is assured economic security, a loving husband, an exciting sex life, and the option of whether or not to pursue a career.[103]

But while the fictional heroine might be getting everything she wants from her world, the actual reader clearly is not from hers, and it is possible to see romance reading as a 'ritual of hope' in which the reader's repeated recourse to romances enables her to tell herself over and over again that a love like the heroine's might really occur in a world such as hers, and that men are able to satisfy women's needs fully.

Evidence that her life does not always live up to that of a romance heroine, and indeed that expectations that it could are detrimental to her real life relationships, was provided in a *Daily Mail* article in 1985 entitled 'Beware of romance', which reported the results of a survey of middle-aged women. It claimed to show that their marriages had broken up as a consequence of the artificially high expectations they had absorbed through reading romances:

> However hard feminists hammer home notions of equality, assertiveness and chore-sharing, most women facing marriage still expect it to be like a Mills and Boon romantic novel. Disillusion sets in when they .find that it is not, according to 27-year-old sociologist Carol Sharp, of Strathclyde University.[104]

A representative from the National Marriage Guidance Council is quoted as agreeing that romantic fiction can damage your marriage, while agony aunt Irma Kurtz has the final word:

> In the past, women's futures were mapped out. They could dream of love but they still behaved like reasonable human beings because they were more realistic about expectations.
> Today's woman dreams too, but her expectations are unrealistic.[105]

Kurtz appears to be rather too sanguine about the effects of romance reading on her female ancestors, however, if there is any factual basis to the descriptions in the contemporary literature. In 1614 we have a perhaps satirical portrait of a chambermaid who was apparently 'so carried way with the *Mirror of Knighthood*, she is many times resolv'd to runne out of her selfe, and become a lady errant',[106] while Gertrude in *Eastward Ho* (1605), having been deserted by Sir Petronel Flash, exclaims: 'Would the Knight of the *Sun*, or *Palmerin* of England, have used their ladies so . . . . Or Sir Lancelot, or Sir Tristram?'[107]

The question of why and how women read romance is the subject of Janice Radway's pioneering investigation, *Reading the Romance*.[108] From a series of interviews, conversations and questionnaires conducted with 42 readers in Smithton, USA, Radway builds up a theory of mass culture which challenges the belief that its ideology is completely dominant and all-pervasive. She refutes the notion that romance readers simply and passively 'consume' an 'objective' text in some complete and programmed way, and makes a plea instead for the recognition of the activity of the reader in the process of producing meaning:

> Because reading is an active process, that is at least partially controlled by the readers themselves, opportunities still exist within the mass-communication process for individuals to resist, alter, and

reappropriate the materials designed elsewhere for their pur-
chase.[109]

This is a crucial statement of power and liberation: by implication, it
reasserts the right of the woman reader to reclaim, at least in part, the
patriarchal form of romance for her own use, and it is precisely in this
way, I shall argue, that we can read sixteenth-century romances.

From a close analysis of the responses of the Smithton women,
Radway concludes that romance reading for them is both combative and
compensatory; it is combative in so far as it enables women to turn their
attention away from the constant demands of others within the
institution of marriage and the family, and it is compensatory in that it
allows them to focus on themselves and their own private pleasure: 'For
them, romance reading addresses needs created in them but not met by
patriarchal institutions and engendering practices.'[110]

One of the most profoundly unsatisfied needs, Radway suggests, is the
need for nurturance. Adapting Nancy Chodorow's theories of mother-
ing, Radway posits an interpretation of romance reading which sees it as
offering women a way of achieving emotional gratification by supplying
them vicariously with the sort of care and attention which they do not
otherwise experience in their day-to-day lives, and which it is normally
their role unstintingly to supply. Because the nurturance is experienced
vicariously, it can only be sustained as long as the reader can displace it
on to a fictional character. Its therapeutic value, then, lasts only as long as
the book, and in order to restimulate it a new romance must be started,
and the cycle of repetitive consumption continues.

If women read romances to satisfy a deep emotional need not satisfied
by patriarchal institutions, Radway concludes, the reading process itself
can be understood as an activity of protest and longing for reform. The
vision at the end of every romance is of a Utopian state where men are
neither cruel nor indifferent, and where they accept, appreciate and
share the values which have been associated with women. It is a vision
which challenges the existing order of things which leaves so many
women longing for genuine affection, tenderness and a sense of self-
worth.

Radway does accept, however, that romance reading can actually be
seen as diffusing the impulse which could lead to real social change,
because it supplies vicariously the very needs which might otherwise be
voiced out loud as demands in the real world, and could potentially lead
to a restructuring of sexual relations. And she remains under no illusion
about the essentially reactionary nature of romance which leaves
unchallenged the institutionalized basis of patriarchal control over
women 'even as it serves as a locus of protest against some of its
emotional consequences'.[111]

Radway's model of the reader actively contributing to the production of meaning is a helpful one to apply to the experience of reading sixteenth-century romances. The sort of reader she postulates is a resisting reader, one who is enabled to 'alter, and reappropriate' what she reads.[112] There are, of course, different degrees of conscious objectivity at work in this resistance. Most of the Smithton women would be no more likely to express their reading experiences in terms of resistance and reappropriation than would the women of the sixteenth century. But objective critical awareness and the language which springs from it are not essential in order to be able to read a work subversively; they are needed, rather, in order to analyse that reading and to build a coherent theory of reading based upon it. We should not assume, then, that either the women readers of the sixteenth century or the Smithton women were unable to 'reread' romances to their own advantage, simply because they did not have the critical tools with which to analyse their activity.

Indeed, Renaissance romances, written by men for women, are essentially double-edged, and the ability to 'reread' in the way Radway envisages is crucial. For the romances offer women a version of themselves as strong, independent, competent human beings, and simultaneously qualify or confine that version, and yet appear to deny the implied woman *reader* those same qualities. In the romance, fictional women are granted a greater degree of autonomy than most Elizabethan women readers would have ever known; their thoughts, feelings, speeches and actions are accorded a worth and significance beyond anything likely to have been experienced by the women reading; the private sphere of family and emotions is transformed from a site of subordination to one of power and importance, and men are transformed into sensitive and affectionate partners who genuinely care for women, and share their values. At precisely the same time, however, almost all the romance writers seek to impose limitations on women, either by drawing back from the radical implications of their own texts, or, as we shall see, by constructing a role for the woman reader which is marginalizing, trivializing and ultimately self-destructive. But the same impulse which enables women to read Harlequins as survival manuals, sources of comfort, reassurance and nurturance, and, indeed, as a form of protest, can operate in a reading of the male-authored sixteenth-century romances; once the reader has become a resisting reader, she can recognize the textual manipulation and, refusing the role offered to her, reread them as the powerfully woman-centred, liberating texts which they can be. Feminist reader-response criticism has formulated theories of reading 'against the grain', and a familiarity with its practice, to be explored in the next section, will offer the basis for a methodology which can be used to reappropriate these romances for our own use.

Ways of reading: feminist reader-response criticism

> Re-vision – the act of looking back, of seeing with fresh eyes, of
> entering an old text from a new critical direction – is for women
> more than a chapter in cultural history: it is an act of survival.[113]

Adrienne Rich's statement demonstrates the degree to which feminist
criticism is a political act which aims not only to interpret the world but
to change it by changing the way we 'read' and understand it in
literature. Feminist criticism does not consist of a single, unified
methodology,[114] but all feminist critical practices share the basic premise
that gender – as social construct rather than a biological given – is a
crucial determinant in the production, circulation and consumption of
literature. No criticism is politically innocent or value-free; it is
inevitably shaped by political, cultural, social and personal factors. The
difference between feminist and non-feminist criticism is not, as Toril
Moi shrewdly points out, that the former is political and the latter is not,
but that 'the feminist openly declares her politics, whereas the non-
feminist may either be unaware of his own value-system or seek to
universalize it as "non-political"'.[115]

Elaine Showalter has divided feminist criticism into two distinct
categories.[116] The first mode is ideological and it is, in essence, 'a mode
of interpretation'. It is concerned with woman as reader – 'with woman
as the consumer of male-produced literature'. Showalter calls this
'feminist critique', and its subjects include the images and stereotypes of
women in literature, omissions and misconceptions about women in
criticism, and the fissures in male-constructed literary history. It is also
concerned with the exploitation and manipulation of the female
audience, and with the analysis of woman-as-sign in semiotic systems.
The second mode focuses on woman as writer – 'with woman as the
producer of textual meaning' – and it examines the history, themes,
genres and structures of literature by women. Its subjects include the
psychodynamics of female creativity, linguistics and the problem of a
female language, and the evolution and laws of a female literary
tradition.[117] Showalter calls this 'gynocritics', and explains the difference
between the two modes thus:

> In contrast to this angry or loving fixation on male literature, the
> programme of gynocritics is to construct a female framework for
> the analysis of women's literature, to develop new models based on
> the study of female experience, rather than to adapt male models
> and theories. Gynocritics begins at the point when we free
> ourselves from the linear absolutes of male literary history, stop
> trying to fit women between the lines of the male tradition, and
> focus instead on the newly visible world of female culture.[118]

In her two key articles about feminist critical theory, Showalter implies that gynocriticism is an area more worthy of feminists' attention than feminist critique. More worryingly, in referring to feminist critique as 'ideological', and 'essentially political and polemical', she seems to indicate that gynocriticism is somehow less ideological and more value-free than feminist critique. Gayle Greene and Coppelia Kahn point to the dangers inherent in this position, and remind us that '. . . if a feminist approach has taught us anything, it is that all critical stances are ideological'.[119]

While Carolyn Allen takes Showalter to task for suggesting that feminist critique examines only male texts, and further, for underrating the sophistication of critical theories of reading,[120] Toril Moi demonstrates that Showalter's critical practice is still predicated on a patriarchal value-system.[121] Showalter claims, for example, that:

> . . . one of the problems of the feminist critique is that it is male-oriented. If we study stereotypes of women, the sexism of male critics, and the limited roles women play in literary history, we are not learning what women have felt and experienced, but only what men have thought women should be.[122]

For Moi, the implication is not only that the feminist critic should turn to gynocriticism, the study of women's writing, precisely in order to learn what women have felt and experienced, but also that this experience is directly available in texts written by women.[123] In this model, the text and language itself have become transparent media which reflect a pre-existent objective reality, 'rather than signifying systems which inscribe ideology and are actually constitutive of reality'.[124] This comes dangerously close to the patriarchal critic's position, for whom the author is the source, origin and meaning of the text. Moi points out that if we are to undo this patriarchal practice of 'authority', we must take one further step and proclaim, with Roland Barthes, the death of the author.[125] Greene and Kahn, quoting Catherine Belsey, warn that feminist criticism should heed the radical implications of post-Saussurean linguistics which, in revealing language as a signifying system, 'implicitly put in question the "metaphysics of presence" which had dominated western philosophy' and, in liberating the text 'from the authority of a presence behind it', released it 'from the constraints of a single and univocal reading', making it 'available for production, plural, contradictory, capable of change . . . unfixed, a process'.[126]

Feminist criticism shares with reader-response criticism a practice which calls into question the objectivity of the literary text. Reader-response theory privileges the role of the reader in the production of meaning; meaning is located in the *process* of reading, in the interaction of text and reader, rather than in the text itself; or, as Schweickart and Flynn's image succinctly has it:

> Reader-response criticism . . . has promoted readers from their previous role as 'extra' to that of 'co-star' with the text in a new script – or, more accurately, scripts – thereby calling attention to the problematical interaction between reader and text.[127]

In formulating a reader-response approach to Elizabethan romance we are doing what Philip Sidney himself perhaps would have expected, since in his *Defence of Poetry* he makes clear that the value of fiction depends on the reader who must read correctly.[128] For him, the purpose of fiction, or 'poesy', is to educate – to figure forth a 'speaking picture – with this end, to teach and delight', as he explains in his *Defence*.[129] And, he elaborates further, 'delight, to move men to take that goodness in hand, which without delight they would fly as from a stranger; and teach, to make them know that goodness whereunto they are moved . . .'.[130] He gives us an example of the positive results of 'right reading':

> Truly, I have known men that even with reading *Amadis de Gaule* (which God knoweth wanteth much of a perfect poesy) have found their hearts moved to the exercise of courtesy, liberality, and especially courage.[131]

His parenthesis, and his use of the word 'even' point, however, to the importance of reading *properly*; that is, of deriving the correct speaking picture from the words on the page. Sidney, then, elevates the role of the reader to co-producer of the meaning of the text, and simultaneously hints at the potential dangers involved. For Sidney, it is possible to read 'wrongly', to misread. Ironically, the *Amadis* was itself frequently cited by Renaissance educationalists to illustrate the lewdness of romances and, in particular, the terrible consequences of romance-reading by young girls. Juan Luis Vives, in his *Instruction of a Christian Woman*, after condemning filthy songs in general, and Ovid's works in particular, adds: 'And this the laws ought to take heed of, and of those ungracious books, such as be in my country in Spain, the *Amadis* . . .'.[132] This underlines the multiple interpretations a text can generate. By implication, if you read the *Amadis* as a woman (or, more precisely, as a man reading as a woman) it is filthy; if you read it as Sidney, it is educative and worthy.

For Sidney, then, believing that the aim of fiction is to teach us to follow virtue and shun vice, it is essential that his readers read correctly, and reading, consequently, becomes as important as writing. He recognizes the potential for misreadings, and admits that poesy's ability to move is by no means automatic: readers may not be moved at all, or

may not translate image into praxis. Gary Waller notes the appropriate-
ness of this kind of critical approach to sixteenth-century poetry:

> In developing a reader-centred cognitive model or pedagogy,
> today's theorists are returning to something of which the sixteenth
> century poets were, at least, dimly aware.[133]

I would add that it is an equally appropriate method of approach to
sixteenth-century romance, once it has been informed by feminist
criticism.

Reader-response criticism does not consist of a single methodology any
more than feminist criticism, but most reader-response critics would
agree that, to at least some extent, the meaning of a text is the production
or creation of individual readers, and that there is no one correct
meaning.[134] Critics differ in their view of the primary factors which
shape a reader's response, at where they draw the line between what is
'objectively' given in a text and the 'subjective' responses of the
individual reader, and in the conclusions they draw about the extent, if
any, to which a text 'constrains' a reader's responses, so as to enable
critics to reject at least some readings as misreadings, even if it is
impossible to demonstrate that any one reading is the correct reading.
    Stanley Fish, in the remarkably candid introduction to his collection of
essays entitled *Is There A Text In This Class?: The Authority of Interpretive
Communities*, offers us a 'rehearsing' of his 'personal history' with respect
to the growth and development of his critical theories of reader-response
criticism, and this rehearsal conveniently summarizes many of the
critical positions within reader-response theory, and simultaneously
demonstrates the extent to which it urgently needed to be informed by
the insights of feminist criticism.[135]
    Fish's initial position was similar to Sidney's:

> ... if meaning is embedded in the text, the reader's responsibilities
> are limited to the job of getting it out; but if meaning develops in a
> dynamic relationship with the reader's expectations, projections,
> conclusions, judgments, and assumptions, these activities (the
> things the reader *does*) are not merely instrumental, or mechanical,
> but essential, and the act of description must both begin and end
> with them.

(pp. 2–3)

Fish met the objection that this would potentially lead to a myriad of
different readings and meanings by positing a level of experience which
all readers share, 'independently of differences in education and culture'

(pp. 4–5). Significantly, he omits gender, and remains unaware of it as a crucial determinant in how we read. The flaw in his argument which Fish does recognize is that it leads once again to the privileging of the text:

> In order to argue for a common reading experience, I felt obliged to posit an object in relation to which readers' activities could be declared uniform, and that object was the text.
>
> (p. 7)

And at that time he went so far as to urge a method of teaching in which students are trained first to recognize and then to discount whatever was unique and personal in their response so that there could be nothing between them and the exertion of the text's control. To feminists, a method so authoritarian and patriarchal in its denial of the unique and personal – that is, of the very political, social, cultural and personal factors which inevitably shape all reading – results in a flawed and ultimately depoliticized interpretation.

The source of the contradiction Fish felt between wanting to allow power to reside with the reader, but also of wanting to constrain totally idiosyncratic interpretations, was, he explains, his unthinking acceptance of the assumption that subjectivity is a constant danger, and that all critical practices must contain a mechanism for keeping it at bay.

To this problem he posits a 'community of readers' who will collectively decide which interpretations to validate, and indeed, which texts to regard as 'literature':

> Thus the act of recognizing literature is not constrained by something in the text, nor does it issue from an independent and arbitrary will; rather, it proceeds from a collective decision as to what will count as literature, a decision that will be in force only so long as a community of readers or believers continues to abide by it.
>
> (p. 11)

The feminist reader would agree with Fish that the production of the meaning of a text is shaped by the interpretive community in which the reading takes place; however, unlike Fish, the feminist would also recognize that the most privileged interpretive communities have been androcentric, and this androcentricity has been absorbed in strategies and modes of thought by all readers, women as well as men.

Fish is led to the conclusion that the claims of objectivity and subjectivity can no longer be debated:

> An interpretive community is not objective because as a bundle of interests, of particular purposes and goals, its perspective is

interested rather than neutral; but by the very same reasoning, the meanings and texts produced by an interpretive community are not subjective because they do not proceed from an isolated individual but from a public and conventional point of view.

(p. 14)

He proceeds from this position to a recognition that there are, in fact, a great many interpretive communities, each with their own interests, and that the business of criticism is not to determine a correct way of reading, but to determine from which of a number of possible perspectives reading will proceed:

This determination will not be made once and for all by a neutral mechanism of adjudication, but will be made and remade again whenever the interests and tacitly understood goals of one interpretive community replace or dislodge the interests and goals of another.

(p. 16)

Fish's notion of interpretive communities is a useful one, so long as we remember that, until very recently, almost all of these communities were determinedly androcentric. The following story of Christine de Pisan's experience of reading the *Romance of the Rose*, related by Susan Schibanoff in 'The art of reading as a woman', demonstrates the dangers of allowing the responsibility of creating and validating interpretation to rest with just one – usually male – interpretive community.[136]

Schibanoff charts Christine de Pisan's progress from reading as a man to reading as a woman. In her *Epistle to the God of Love* (1399), de Pisan attacked both Ovid's *Art of Love* and Jean de Meun's *Romance of the Rose* for their vicious and illogical slanders against women. The ensuing responses, defence and debates became known as the *Querelle de la Rose*, and the central issue became one of interpretation.[137] Jean de Meun's defenders maintained that all readers should interpret the work the way they did, as an ironic discouragement of vice, and furtherance of virtue. De Pisan based her arguments on how, in her opinion, the work could and would be read, and maintained that readers would interpret it however they wished. She illustrates her point with a vivid account of how an actual reader, a married man prone to jealousy, took the *Romance* at face value when he read the passage describing the Jealous Husband, whom Jean's defenders claimed illustrated the enormous irrationality and disordered passion of jealous men:

This was an extremely jealous man, who, whenever in the grips of passion, would go and find the book and read it to his wife; then he would become violent and strike her and say such horrible things as, 'These are the kinds of tricks you pull on me. This good, wise

man Master Jean de Meun knew very well what women are capable
of'. And at every word appropriate, he gives her a couple of kicks or
slaps.[138]

The jealous man, to use Sidney's terms, apparently derived the wrong
speaking picture from the words on the page.

Christine de Pisan repeatedly stressed that readers create their own
meanings and, as Schibanoff points out, her objectors inadvertently
proved her point by insisting that de Pisan herself was misreading the
text.[139] This interpretive community, indeed, attributed her misreading
to the regrettable fact that she was reading like a woman. Schibanoff
brilliantly demonstrates how, in the course of the debate, de Pisan
redefines the charge: she is not reading *like* a woman, but *as* a woman.[140]
As she defends herself, she comes to develop an increasingly positive
view of the way in which she reads, and uses the fact of being a woman as
the source of her authority:

> And it is precisely because I am a woman that I can speak better in
> this matter than one who has not had the experience, since he
> speaks only by conjecture and chance.[141]

She expresses her newly acquired understanding in terms very similar to
the more recent feminist assertion that the personal is the political:
'Nothing gives one so much authority as one's own experience.'[142]
Christine de Pisan's experience, then, should warn us against investing
authority in any one interpretive community, and it demonstrates the
extent to which, as Schweickart observes, reader–response criticism
needs feminist criticism.[143]

Judith Fetterley, in one of the most fully developed accounts of
women reading, claims that despite the literary stereotype of the
emasculation of men by women, the cultural reality is in fact the
'*immasculation* of women by men':[144]

> As readers and teachers and scholars, women are taught to think as
> men, to identify with a male point of view, and to accept as normal
> and legitimate a male system of values, one of whose central
> principles is misogyny.[145]

But is it enough to be a woman, Jonathan Culler asks, in order to read
as a woman?[146] For it is only too clear that women can read, and have
read, as men. Reading is a learned activity, and it is inevitably shaped by
gender. Reading as a woman is both experience and construct; Culler
unravels the complexities in this double, or divided, position:

> To ask a woman to read as a woman is . . . a double or divided
> request. It appeals to the condition of being a woman as if it were a

given and simultaneously urges that this condition be created or achieved.[147]

But at the same time:

> Reading is not simply . . . a theoretical position, for it appeals to a sexual identity defined as essential and privileges experiences associated with that identity.[148]

Maggie Humm takes issue with Culler for implying that, if to read as a woman is to play a role, then critics, male or female, can set up the hypothesis of a woman reader:

> . . . this will not do. A male reading as a feminist, is not a feminist critic because he carries with him the possibility of escape – into masculinity and into patriarchy.[149]

She insists on both parts – biological as well as cultural – for a true feminist reading:

> . . . we are different readers, and therefore different critics, from men because our gendered reading is both essentially different *and* one produced by our agreeing to read 'difference' as a crucial paradigm of cultural construction.[150]

Christine de Pisan had invoked 'essential difference' in her insistence that her authority to interpret works about women had its source in her identity as a woman. In one of her later works, however, she comes to a more theoretical position. Returning once more to Schibanoff's essay, we recognize how, in the first chapter of *The Book of the City of Ladies*,[151] Christine depicts the immasculation of a woman reader, the narrator 'Christine' who, as a result of reading Matheolus' well-known diatribes against women, is suffering from extreme self-hatred, and wishes she had been born male.[152] 'Christine', then, has submitted to reading as a man. However, the allegorical personification of Reason appears to her, and demonstrates a new way of reading as a woman:

> As far as the poets of whom you speak are concerned, do you not know that they spoke on many subjects in a fictional way and that they often mean the contrary of what the words openly say? One can interpret them according to the grammatical figure of *antiphrasis*, which means, as you know, that if you call something bad, in fact, it is good, and also vice versa. Thus I advise you to profit from their works and to interpret them in the manner which they are intended in those passages where they attack women.[153]

As Schibanoff points out, there is a very serious point behind Reason's suggestion, for Reason has taken the methodology proposed by the defenders of the *Romance* – interpretation by opposition – and turned it to women's advantage.[154]

Reading as a woman, then, alerts us to the sexual codes within a text; once aware of them we can, with Reason and 'Christine', deliberately interpret them to mean the opposite of what they apparently say. Or, with the Wife of Bath, we can tear the offending pages from the book, or throw the whole thing in the fire.[155] But the physical destruction of the text, while no doubt extremely satisfying, is scarcely theoretically conclusive. A more sophisticated response is that of Kate Millett, who was one of the first feminist critics deliberately and consistently to read androcentric texts 'against the grain'; by taking an unexpected and 'unauthorized' point of view, her aim is to shock readers out of the comfort of their traditional perspective, and to force them to look from a different direction. With what, in the early 1970s, would seem to be a blatant and provocative disregard for 'authorial intentions', Millett analyses in depth the sexual ideologies of Lawrence, Miller, Mailer and Genet.[156]

Judith Fetterley, developing this practice, proceeds to a theory of a 'resisting reader', whose role is precisely to disrupt the process of immasculation by exposing it to consciousness. Fetterley elaborates on this process:

> . . . the first act of the feminist critic must be to become a resisting reader rather than an assenting reader and, by this refusal to assent, to begin the process of exorcizing the male mind that has been implanted in us. The consequence of this exorcism is the capacity for what Adrienne Rich describes as re-vision – 'the act of looking back, of seeing with fresh eyes, of entering an old text from a new critical direction'. And the consequence, in turn, of this re-vision is that books will no longer be read as they have been read and thus will lose their power to bind us unknowingly to their designs. While women obviously cannot rewrite literary works so that they become ours by virtue of reflecting our reality, we can accurately name the reality they do reflect and so change literary criticism from a closed conversation to an active dialogue.[157]

In my analysis of Renaissance prose romance, I aim to do precisely that: to open up a dialogue with the texts, to interrogate them and to challenge them, and ultimately to give the woman reader a voice with which to name her own reality, to inscribe her own position within the literary discourse. I intend to reread the work of four authors in particular so as to be able to reveal and name the sexual/textual strategies that they use, and by recognizing them, enable readers to resist them. Pettie, Greene, Rich and Sidney all have designs on us, and more explicitly so by constructing an implied woman reader in the text, whose responses and reactions are apparently meant to be consonant with our own. As I shall demonstrate, however, there is a discrepancy between the role the writers create for us in the text, and the role which we may wish, as women readers and feminist critics, to adopt.

Wayne Booth's theory of implied readers is useful here.[158] He posits the roles of implied author and implied reader, and suggests that in order fully to enjoy a literary work, the reader must largely agree with the beliefs of the implied author – the author's second self which is created in the work, sometimes as the narrator.[159] The reader whom the author creates, however, is clearly only one role of the actual reader, for we have seen how the readers can, to varying extents, in fact create their own texts themselves. Wolfgang Iser helpfully draws attention to this:

> The fictitious reader is, in fact, just one of several perspectives, all of which interlink and interact. The role of the reader emerges from this interplay of perspectives, for he [sic] finds himself called upon to mediate between them, and so it would be fair to say that the intended reader, as supplier of one perspective, can never represent more than one aspect of the reader's role.[160]

Booth cites Walker Gibson's remark that a book we reject as bad is often simply a book in whose 'mock reader we discover a person we refuse to become, a mask we refuse to put on, a role we will not play'.[161]

In the romances I examine, the male authors frequently postulate a woman reader – passive, inferior, trivialized, and colluding with male oppression of women – whom we can refuse to become; it is a role we can resist. Fetterley's claim that the texts she studies 'constitute a series of designs on the female reader, all the more potent in their effect because they are "impalpable" ' is likewise true of these Renaissance romances.[162] They, too, have designs on us. And it is by reading as a woman, by naming and demystifying their narrative strategies, by rendering, in other words, their designs palpable, that we can resist the roles we are offered, and reread these romances instead as texts which offer portrayals of strong, determined, resourceful female characters – and, with Janice Radway, 'alter, and reappropriate' the romances for ourselves.

But before moving to a detailed analysis of four romance writers in particular, it will be helpful to explore briefly the history and nature of the Elizabethan romances, and to indicate the limitations of some of the previous critical approaches to them.

2

Out of the literary doghouse:
Elizabethan courtly romance

'[Elizabethan] fiction is thoroughly and . . . deservedly dead', announces John Carey, with complete critical assurance. 'This is not just because it has been superseded by the novel', he goes on,

> but also because it was meticulously superficial. The variegation of the prose surface with stock rhetorical figures was, generally speaking, all it was seriously interested in. Meaning was secondary . . . . Narrative was either reduced to incident or replaced by moral diatribe and debate. These, though, were not purposeful; simply the arrangement and rearrangement of schoolroom-platitudes.[1]

Carey's scarcely concealed contempt is by no means unique; it is only one of the more recent accounts of Elizabethan prose fiction which reveals the widespread critical assumption that fiction should be, in some way, a representation of everyday reality. And although this assumption is completely inappropriate for the fiction of the sixteenth century, it is one which is revealed in almost all critical analyses of the period. Thus J.J. Jusserand, in his anachronistically titled study *The English Novel in the Age of Shakespeare*, judges the romances by the criteria of the novel, and inevitably finds them wanting;[2] Margaret Schlauch's *Antecedents of the English Novel* hunts unsuccessfully for a prototype for the modern novel;[3] while Ernest Baker, in his *History of the English Novel*, indignantly complains that 'verisimilitude is ignored',[4] and indeed comes close to dismissing the whole genre with the withering observation that:

> The Italian novella is a pleasing and sometimes an exquisite thing,

but after all it is only a novella. It is not a novel; it is hardly a short story according to modern standards.[5]

It is with much justification, then, that A.C. Hamilton astutely observes: 'To its misfortune, Elizabethan prose fiction was succeeded by the novel',[6] for the assumption that early prose fiction was trying to achieve the same ends as the novel (and failing) has led to much critical confusion and frustration.

I shall argue that Elizabethan romance has been neglected, dismissed or misunderstood precisely because it has not been approached with an appropriate critical methodology. Hamilton has pointed out that historical criticism could not treat Elizabethan fiction because romance motifs do not belong to any specific historical period, and that the New Criticism wisely chose to ignore it, since there is little or no material in it to be 'interpreted'.[7] There is, indeed, only the experience of reading. Writing in 1984, Hamilton expressed the hope that the increasing interest in popular literature would encourage a more appropriate methodology for approaching the genre:

> . . . when I hear critics argue for the democratizing of our literary tradition and argue against the 'valorizing' or 'privileging' of certain works, I have some hope that Elizabethan prose fiction may finally get out of the literary doghouse.[8]

In coming to these popular texts as a woman reader, calling on the critical tools of feminist and reader-response theory, I hope to indicate that it is indeed high time to reappraise Elizabethan fiction and to recognize its complexity and sophistication.

Romances had made up a large proportion of the output of the early printing presses in England. Caxton translated and published a number of French prose romances, and his successor, Wynkyn de Worde, continued to publish prose romances and also a number of the older metrical romances like *Bevis of Hampton*, *Guy of Warwick*, and *Richard Coeur de Lion*, which were somewhat cheaper than the longer prose romances *Paris and Vienne*, *The Four Sons of Amyon*, *Le Morte D'Arthur*, *Huon of Bordeaux*, and *Valentine and Orson*, for example. Wynkyn de Worde's cheaper publications encouraged a readership among lower-class readers which was continued and expanded by the printers flourishing in the middle of the sixteenth century.

Many of the prose romances were enormously popular: Emanuel Forde's *Most Delectable and Pleasant History of Parismus* of 1598 had gone through 15 editions by 1704 and Lyly's *Euphues*, first published in 1578, was continually reprinted for nearly half a century. Sidney's *Arcadia* was

printed 18 times between 1590 and 1725; it was continued by Gervase
Marcham, and later by Richard Beling; and by 1651 it had a continuation
written by a woman, Anne Weamys. An abstract appeared in 1701 and
the whole story was modernized in 1725 by another woman, Mrs Stanley.
The story of Argalus and Parthenia was separately adapted as a chapbook
in 1672, and was frequently reprinted.

The publication of William Painter's *Palace of Pleasure* in 1566,[9] can be
said to mark the onset of a renewed enthusiasm for prose romances, in
this case the fashion for the novelle translated from French and Italian.
Painter's   sources   included   Boccaccio,   Bandello,   Straparola   and
Marguerite de Navarre, as well as Livy and Herodotus.[10] H.S. Canby is as
dismissive of the genre as many other literary critics, but his condemnation has at least the advantage of indicating the primary characteristics of
this sort of novella:

> It begins, as a rule, with a moral reflection leading on to the plot.
> The idle and courtly hero sees the heroine in church or garden, and
> promptly delivers over all his faculties to love. He writes a lengthy
> letter of declaration, is answered in one quite as rhetorical, and
> finally given an assignation, at which point the story reaches its
> desired path, and now ambles through the intrigue, with abundant
> pauses for confession, discussion, and oration, stopping short at
> certain pleasant gardens wherein is held discourse upon life and the
> metaphysics of love. And then comes deceit which leads to despair,
> despair which brings on the tragedy, and so, with a moral, the jaunt
> concludes. An infinite procrastination of climax; rhetoric which,
> even when brilliant, is fantastic; little individuality of characters;
> and an enormous cargo of superfluous argument . . . .
>   'What's ta good on't?' as Carlyle would say. Not much, it must be
> admitted, for the casual reader.[11]

If the casual reader had been a woman living in the latter half of the
sixteenth century, however, she might have found much good in it: an
opportunity to stretch her horizons – historically, geographically and
mythologically – and to expand her sense of knowledge; a space where
women can argue on the same terms as men, in which their powers of
speech and rhetoric equal, if not surpass, those of men; a romantic
world, in which women's concerns are paramount, and where women's
thoughts, feelings and actions are accorded a significance seldom
granted them elsewhere. Part of Canby's frustration seems to be that the
plot does not lead anywhere – the 'infinite procrastination of climax'; but
that is one of the central aims and features of early romance, to instil awe
and wonder in the reader by one episode, only to redouble it in the next.
Thus the reader's response is crucial to each scene; each episode is there
to be savoured and appreciated for itself, before being surpassed by the

next. Instead of a quest to a preordained goal, there is only wandering; any conclusion may only be temporary. And the 'cargo of superfluous argument' is, of course, only superfluous if one is privileging action and progress in fiction above everything else.

Painter's first volume, consisting of 60 novelle, was followed by a second part in 1567, and by further additions in a volume of 1575. Its immediate popularity is demonstrated by the four editions of the collection which appeared in the space of a decade, and by the imitations which followed. His dedication to the Earl of Warwick in Volume One characterizes his stories as describing:

> ... the lives, gestes, conquests, and highe enterprises of great Princes, wherein also be not forgotten the cruell actes and tiranny of some. In these be set forth the great valiance of noble Gentlemen, the terrible combates of couragious personages, the vertuous mindes of noble Dames, the chaste hartes of constant Ladyes, the wonderful patience of puissaunt Princes, the mild sufferaunce of well disposed gentlewomen, and in divers, the quiet bearing of advers Fortune.[12]

Typically, the women are described in terms of their virtue, chastity, constancy and sufferance, but in fact in many of these tales, the women are strong, determined figures who are active in influencing the world around them.

This is even more the case in Painter's second volume, which focuses more closely on the subjects of love and courtship than on adventure: 'the matter moste specially therin comprised, treating of the courtly fashions and maners, and of the customes of love's gallantise, and the good or yll successe therof', Painter explains.[13] And he goes on to reveal that he designed this volume with women readers clearly in mind by placing the story of the Amazons first:

> The maners and qualities of which nation, bicause they were women of no common spirite and boldnesse, be thought good in the front of this second volume to be described: bicause of divers womens lives plentiful varietie is offered in the sequele.[14]

Painter, indeed, was one of the first Elizabethan fiction writers to realize the great market potential provided by women readers, and to cater for it. Linda Woodbridge suggests that Painter's choice of stories, and his awareness of a female market, were stimulated by the works of the formal controversy about women.[15] In the five years before the publication of his *Palace*, several books about women had achieved success, including the 1560–61 editions of Edward Gosynhill's *The prayse of all women, called Mulierum pean* and *The Schole house of Women*, and Edward More's *Defence of Women*.

Painter intervenes in his text, accompanying the readers through the stories, explaining his purpose and anticipating their reactions in a tone intimate and familiar:

> Pardon me, good Ladies, if I speake so largely . . . . I am very lothe to take uppon me the office of a slaunderer, and no lesse do mean to flatter those, whom I see to their great shame, offende openly in the sight of the worlde: but why should I dissemble that which I know your selves would not conceyle, if in conscience yee were required?[16]

His tone is frequently a mocking one; in the story of 'Faustina the Empresse', for example, after attacking the morals of contemporary women, he quickly attempts to recover the favour of his women readers with flattery:

> But if I list to speake of women of this age, from noble to unnoble, from an Emperors Daughter to a Ploughmans modder, whose lives do frame after Julia hir lore, my pen to the stumpes would weare, and my hande be wearied with writing. And so likewise it would of numbres no doubt in these dayes that folow the trace of Lucrece line, that huswifely and chastly contrive the day and nights in pure and Godly exercise.[17]

His tone of exaggeration and mock penitence are typical of the addresses to the woman reader in these romances.

Geoffrey Fenton continues and develops this practice in his *Certaine Tragicall Discourses*,[18] a collection of 13 stories freely translated from French and Latin sources, which appeared in the same year as Painter's second volume, and was probably influenced by him. Dedicating it to Mary Sidney, Fenton explicitly advertises it as rejecting the marvels of men's worldly achievements in favour of the 'mervellous effects of love'. And, in these stories of love and courtship, Fenton turns to his women readers to comment on the action, and to direct our responses. His collection contains several conventional romance stories. His first tale, 'Salimbene and Angelica', demonstrates how two tragically opposed families are reconciled through marriage, and his final story of 'Dom Diego and Genivera La Blonde' also marks the triumph of love over chaos and disorder. Two of the stories, however, show troubled courtship leading not to happiness in marriage but to disaster, and he includes too a particularly gory tale of an especially vicious woman, the Lady of Milan. As she tries to destroy the evidence of her adultery, the unborn child inside her, Fenton turns to us to underline his horror at her actions:

> Truely I knowe that vertuous Ladyes (sprinkled wyth the dewe of
> pytie) wyll not onely tremble at the remembraunce of the
> inordinate crueltye of this cursed mother, but also open the
> conduits of their compassions, weping on the behalfe of the
> tormente wherin unnaturally she plunged the innocent impe ....[19]

He goes on to explain that his own 'tremblinge feare' at the account he is
giving is affecting his pen, so that he can hardly write the words on the
page. That this is a narrative device employed rather to increase his
readers' anticipation than to reveal his own feelings, is suggested by the
bloody details he appears to revel in as he describes the woman beating
the aborted child against the walls, 'painting the postes and pavements in
the chamber with the blodde and braynes' of the mangled body.[20]

He pretends to anticipate his women readers' responses further when
he explains his reluctance to continue the story of this 'dolorous
tragedye' because '... your eyes (alredy wearyed with wepinge),
methinke I see also your eares offer to close themselves against the report
of this Pandora ...',[21] and he concludes with something of an
anticlimax, by exhorting his women readers to take it as a warning not to
have extramarital affairs: 'Let also the yong Ladyes and lyttel girls learne
to direct the cours of their youth by the contrary of this example.'[22]

The *Discourses* appear to have been popular, and were reprinted again
in 1576 and 1579. The presence of a strong persona speaking to women
readers, in both Painter and Fenton, reaches its climax in George Pettie's
work *The Petite Pallace of Pettie his Pleasure*,[23] published in the year of
Fenton's second edition, 1576, and examined in detail in Chapter 3. The
popularity of Pettie's work took over from Painter's and his *Petite Pallace*
had gone through at least six editions by 1613.

As Fenton's prose was more rhetorically elaborate than Painter's, so
Pettie develops it still further, expanding Fenton's practice of using the
events of a story as a pretext for long soliloquies, debates and rhetorical
display. In the works of all three writers, then, the importance is less in
what happens in the plot than the way in which it is expressed. The
woman reader, who is frequently explicitly addressed, is drawn into the
work as co-producer of the meaning. The ambiguities and complexities
of the relationship between text and woman reader have scarcely been
recognized; Paul Salzman, in his critical history of prose fiction, comes
closest to it when he notes briefly that, with Pettie, 'the reader is left off-
balance, wondering what response is required of him (or, perhaps I
should say, of her)',[24] but his rather patronizing parenthesis indicates his
considerable underestimation of the significance of the specifically
woman reader.

Salzman's dismissal of the role of the reader leads him to dispose of
Barnaby Rich, one of the most sophisticated of Elizabethan writers, in a

few sentences, pointing merely to his skill in manipulating a large range of sources, plots and characters.[25] Rich's *Farewell to Militarie Profession* (1581)[26] is made up of eight tales, five purporting to be Rich's own, and three translations from an Italian source. 'The humour is of the gayest', protests Canby, and characterizes Rich simply as 'a soldier and a courtier of ladies',[27] thereby conflating and neutralizing the most potent source of tension in Rich's work: the dilemma and anxiety he feels as a soldier writing romances for women. The complexities which this generates are explored in Chapter 5.

With George Gascoigne's *Adventures of Master F.J.*,[28] first published anonymously in 1573 as part of a collection entitled *A Hundreth Sundrie Flowres*, we move on to an early example of longer romance works. Since C.T. Prouty's edition, together with a biography of Gascoigne, both published in 1942, the work has been increasingly recognized as complex and skilful. The plot can be summarized in a few lines: F.J. is invited to the home of Count Velasco in the hope that he will form an attachment with, and marry, Velasco's daughter Fraunces; instead, he falls in love with Velasco's daughter-in-law, Elinor, and refuses to believe she has other lovers, despite being confronted with evidence of them. He wins Elinor's favour for a time, then loses it, and lives the rest of his life in dissolute fashion, while Fraunces, who has loved him from the first, consumes away and dies. The plot, however, is the least important part of the work; its interest and sophistication are in the way it is told. Critical histories of this period, which generally limit their attention to plot analysis, are particularly inappropriate, since any plot summary of Elizabethan romance inevitably distorts the experience of the reader because it leaves out the narrative technique, and the important role of rhetorically embellished speeches and debates. A reader-response approach, on the other hand, would focus on precisely these elements which affect the process and experience of reading.

In the case of *Master F.J.*, it might locate skilful artistry in the way the story is presented to us. Our relationship with the story is at three removes – in between, are the printer, A.B.; H.W., who explains to the reader how he delivered the material contained in *A Hundreth Sundrie Flowres* to the printer; and H.W.'s 'familiar friend Master G.T.' who has compiled the collection. Tension and ambiguity are generated by the juxtaposition of the three sources of information we have on F.J.'s affair with Elinor, and our interpretation mediated by them: we are presented with F.J.'s own poems and letters, and Elinor's replies; the events and dialogue reported directly to us by G.T., and G.T.'s own, frequently ironic, commentary on them. Our response to the work depends on our relationship to these different reports of the events of the story; our distance from the central characters slides, and our level of involvement shifts. G.T. himself is frankly cynical over the courtly love convention, and in his explanation of why F.J. should choose Elinor rather than Fraunces – because with her, he is assured of an easier sexual victory – the ideal of courtly love, the elevated affair with a married woman, is reduced to its crudest level.

Gascoigne's friend George Whetstone published two works which drew some inspiration from him, *The Rocke of Regarde* (1576) and *An Heptameron of Civill Discourses* (1582). Although the *Rocke* is dedicated to male readers, Whetstone does advertise the third part for women readers in particular: 'The third is, the Arbour of Vertue, the which I chiefly published, for the delight of vertuous Ladies and Gentlewomen.'[29] The work is made up of poems and stories, most famously the love story of Rinaldo and Giletta. The *Heptameron* purports to be an account of courtly discussions which took place over seven days at Christmas spent at the Italian home of Signior Phyloxenus which, Whetstone assures us, will amuse and edify both men and women readers. The discussions are all concerned with love, courtship and marriage, and include debates over the inconveniences of forced, and of rash, marriages, of marriages undertaken between people of unequal ages, and finally of the excellency of marriage. As in Castiglione's *Courtier*, on which it is partly modelled, the women who take part are witty and articulate, and quite capable of out-arguing the men.

John Grange's *Golden Aphroditis* (1577)[30] is another love story, in which the hero N.O. eventually succeeds in marrying A.O. Hyder Rollins claims it as 'an important novel' which has been 'singularly unfortunate' in English literary history, since it has been 'sadly ignored' by modern critics and historians.[31] He endeavours to make up for this omission by declaring that, absurd though its plot may sometimes be, it is 'far superior to that of Lyly's two dull novels'.[32] Indeed, it anticipates Lyly's *Euphues* in two important respects, its elaborately ornate rhetorical style, and its misogyny. Grange's attitude to his women readers is at once patronizing and antagonistic. In his dedication to Lord Stourton, he hardly bothers to conceal his hostility, and openly attacks women for their vanity, stupidity and lust; while in the epistle 'To the courtelike Dames and Ladielike Gentlewomen' which follows, he addresses women in an outrageously exaggerated fashion, calling them 'the glittering stars and troupes of Venus crew'.[33] These terms are sustained throughout the work with frequent asides to the 'poetical Nymphes',[34] 'my glittering starres',[35] and 'my lovyng troupe'.[36]

But if Grange's work has received little notice, Lyly's *Euphues*[37] has long been the centre of much critical attention. His work was immediately an enormous success. Edward Blount, in the preface to the reader in a 1632 edition of Lyly's plays, exclaims:

All our ladies were then his Schollers; And that Beautie in Court

which could not Parley Euphueism was as litle regarded, as shee
which now there, speakes not French.[38]

By 1636, *Euphues: The Anatomy of Wit* had run to 19 editions, the last 5
including the sequel, *Euphues and his England*. Ernest Baker finds little to
admire in it:

> The thread of story is of the slightest, exciting hardly any interest in
> itself; the characters are not persons, but merely copy-book
> headings, and their doings or mishaps appeal neither to our
> sympathy nor to our sense of humour . . . .[39]

But the source of his criticism is made clear: 'In all this there is manifestly
very little stuff that now goes to the composition of the novel.'[40]

That, of course, is precisely true. The plot can be simply told. In the
first part, a young man 'of more wit then wealth, yet of more wealth then
wisdome, seeing himselfe inferior to none in pleasant conceipts, thought
himselfe superiour to all in honest conditions'.[41] It is a cautionary tale
which tells of how Euphues rejects advice, exploits friendship, and loses
at love. Jilted by the mistress whom he has taken from his friend
Philautus, he comes to see he has abused his little wit with an obstinate
will; he repents, and retiring from the world, takes to moralizing instead.
The second volume gives an account of a trip made by Euphues and
Philautus to England, of the woman Philautus falls in love with, of his
rejection by her, and his greater happiness with another woman. The
way the story is told is crucial to its meaning – indeed, the style is an
extension of the subject matter. It is characterized by lengthy soliloquies
and debates, parallelism in sentence structure, balance and antithesis in
thought and phrase, by examples chosen from nature, classical history
and myth, and from the 'unnatural natural history' of Pliny. Feuillerat
suggested long ago that *Euphues* 'n'est en somme qu'une antithèse
longuement prolongée'.[42] Thus George Saintsbury's formula for dealing
with the work is quite useless:

> . . . if anybody who has the necessary knowledge to understand, and
> therefore the necessary patience to tolerate these knotty, knarry
> envelopes, insertions, and excrescences, will for the moment pay
> no attention to them, but merely strip them off, he will find the
> carcass of a very tolerable novel left behind.[43]

If you strip away everything that makes it 'not-a-novel', you are left with
a novel, he triumphantly declares. For Saintsbury is convinced it is a
novel (for if it is not a novel, what is it?); although with barely concealed
incredulity, he confides to us, in the tone of one uttering blasphemy,
that: 'Some people, it is believed, have denied that *Euphues* is a novel at
all.'[44]

In *Euphues* every action leads to reflection, every character painstakingly examines her or his reactions to situations, and during this process alternative responses are posited and compared. Lucilla, for example, explores her growing affection for Euphues in the following terms:

> O my Euphues, lyttle dost thou know the sodayne sorrow that I sustayne for thy sweete sake; Whose witte hath bewitched me, whose rare qualyties have deprived me of mine olde qualytie, whose courteous behaviour without curiositie, whose comely feature without fault, whose fyled speach without fraude, hath wrapped me in this misfortune. And canst thou, Lucilla, be so light of love in forsaking Philautus to flye to Euphues? canst thou prefer a straunger before thy countryman? A starter before thy companion? Why, Euphues doth perhappes desyre my love; but Philautus hath deserved it. Why, Euphues feature is worthy as good as I; but Philautus his fayth is worthy a better. I, but the latter love is the most fervent. I but Euphues hath greater perfection. I but Philautus hath deeper affection.[45]

It would be quite inappropriate to urge Lucilla to hurry up and decide between them; her final choice is more or less beside the point. It is, rather, the process in which she is involved that is important; the rhetorical eloquence of her words, and the pattern of her thoughts. It offers Lyly an opportunity to display his rhetorical skill, and at the same time women's thoughts and feelings are treated seriously and accorded importance.

At the same time, however, Volume One generally characterizes women as inconstant and unchaste, for which Euphues 'apologises' at the end, with assurances that he did not mean to include all women in his condemnations. In his second volume, Lyly makes more of an effort to appeal to women readers, and includes a preface for them, in which he presents the book as a trifle to be toyed with rather than taken seriously:

> It resteth Ladies, that you take the paines to read it, but at such times, as you spend in playing with your little Dogges, and yet will I not pinch you of that pastime, for I am content that your Dogges lye in your laps so *Euphues* may be in your hands, that when you shall be wearie in reading of the one, you may be ready to sport with the other; or handle him as you do your Junkets, that when you can eate no more you tye some in your napkin for children; for if you be filled with the first part, put the second in your pocket for your wayting maydes; *Euphues* had rather lye shut in a ladyes casket that open in a schollers studie.[46]

His tone hovers between flattery and condescension; he deprecates his work, taking on the role of one who is humble and submissive, and at the same time characterizes his women readers as spoilt and idle.

It was a popular formula, however, and *Euphues* was hugely successful; even when the euphuistic style had passed from being fashionable to being ridiculed, Lyly's fiction continued to be read, and its success led to numerous imitations.

A fresh impulse was given to the art of elaborate plotting and new models made available to Elizabethan writers when the Greek romances of the Hellenistic and Byzantine periods were introduced to English readers.[47] Three texts in particular had a profound influence: the *Aethiopica* or *Theagenes and Chariclea* by Heliodorus; Achilles Tatius' *Clitophon and Leucippe*; and the *Daphnis and Chloe* of a writer known as Longus. The first two are complex and detailed adventure stories, whereas the third is a relatively simple pastoral romance. The episodes in these Greek sources were not themselves new: loved ones are separated by shipwreck or war and go off in search of one another; children are abandoned or stolen; oracles and supernatural interventions generate further confusions, but in the end lost ones are found, recognitions occur, and families are happily reunited. What the Elizabethans did find in these stories were models for diversifying adventurous action with interludes of pastoral tranquillity, and a way of producing heightened intricacy in the plot.

This new style would soon surpass euphuism in popularity; the numerous romances of Robert Greene (he published over a dozen in the decade 1580–90) demonstrate the gradual shift in fashion.[48] In Greene's first romance, *Mamillia*, which came out in 1583, the influence of euphuism is plainly apparent, but by 1589 and the appearance of *Menaphon*, euphuism is being portrayed as both outmoded and affected, and the inspiration for this work comes from the Greek romances instead.

The translations of *Daphnis and Chloe* – in 1559 a French version by Amyot, in 1587 an English one by Angel Day – probably directly influenced the use of pastoral in English prose fiction. Less directly, the same influence was conveyed by foreign imitators of the genre, like Sannazaro's *Arcadia* in Italian and Montemayor's *Diana* in Spanish.

The most famous and most complex English example of an experiment in combining pastoral with chivalric adventure in a complicated plot is, of course, Sidney's revised version of his *Arcadia*, published in 1590.[49] In it we find the complications of a man disguised as a woman and another as a shepherd, together with a long series of adventures – single combats, sieges, wild beasts and rescues, a kidnapping and a long imprisonment. It is a love story which seems destined never to finish; each climax leads to yet another one, and it is interspersed with digressions, flashbacks and stories within stories; indeed, it remains incomplete.

Ernle finds it tedious:

Rambling in structure, unreal in substance, the *Arcadia* owed nothing . . . to beauty of style. Though Sidney protests against the mannerisms of Lyly, his own 'conceits' and tangled sentences are as affected as those of *Euphues*, and, it must be added, at least as tiresome.[50]

Its digressive structure and distance from 'real life' are, of course, traditional features of the romance, and Sidney's style is crucial to the meaning of the text. Ernle's critical assumption that the *Arcadia* should have the qualities of the novel, is clearly both anachronistic and misguided.

Significantly for this study, S.L. Wolff, in his massive work *The Greek Romances in Elizabethan Prose Fiction*, notes that women are superior to men in these romances, 'both in character as persons and in characterization as personages';[51] here was a sphere for women's action, freedom, and power:

both the love and the adventure are such as to take women out of the seclusion of the gynaeceum and make them for a while the companions – sometimes even the leaders – of the men they are to marry.[52]

This no doubt contributed to the popularity of these texts with women readers.

Tantalizingly, Thomas Hägg suggests that the very early Greek romance was also particularly designed for women readers:

If we examine the ideals it expresses, we shall find our theory of a predominantly female audience at least partly confirmed. In several of the novels it is the heroine who is really the main character.[53]

Thomas Lodge's *Rosalynde* (1590),[54] famous as a source for Shakespeare's *As You Like It*, clearly owes much to the Greek romance tradition, despite its subtitle, *Euphues Golden Legacie*, and the heroine of its title is indeed the main character. She is witty and intelligent, and her resourcefulness allows her to utilize the freedom granted by Arden, and by her disguise: thus she is able to woo and win the man of her choice. It was a popular work, and had gone through 11 editions by 1642.

These new romances, deriving from the Greek romance, did not supplant the older chivalric forms popular in the mid–sixteenth century, although they highlighted a shift in the reading public, with the more aristocratic readers preferring the pastoral romances and the middle classes favouring the chivalric romances, especially those infused by the spirit of citizens' ideals and aspirations. The long cycles of *Amadis* and *Palmerin*, and others in a similar vein like *Don Bellianis*, which were first published in Spain and Portugal between 1508 and 1550, were translated into English in the 1590s thanks to the efforts of the seemingly inexhaustible Anthony Munday.[55] Their popularity was highest with the middle classes, and in carrying on the chivalric tradition, it was these works which gradually took over from the chivalric romances of King Arthur and his knights, and of the English worthies, Havelock, Bevis of Hampton and Guy of Warwick.

Their influence can be seen on English writers like the hugely successful Emanuel Forde, while it was Richard Johnson who most effectively made the chivalric romance into a product of the artisan ideology which was beginning to become established in London, and which was characterized by patriotic pride, an emphasis on utility, and on the rewards to be gained by personal effort. These works focused on the hero rather than the heroine, on adventure rather than love, and accordingly I have treated them in less detail. The title page of Johnson's *The Seven Champions of Christendome* (the first part published in 1596, and the second in the following year),[56] which recounts how St George beheaded the champions, summarizes the action and gives a good indication of the nature of these works:

> Shewing their Honourable battailes by Sea and Land: their Tilts, Jousts, and Tournaments for Ladies: their Combats with Giants, Monsters and Dragons: their adventures in forraigne Nations: their Inchauntments in the holie Land: their Knighthoods, Prowesse, and Chivalrie, In Europe, Africa, and Asia, with their victories against the enemies of Christ.

Mary Patchell, who has devoted a whole book to the study of the Palmerin romances and their influence on Elizabethan fiction, writes of the 'monotony and absurdity of the subject matter', and their 'excessive length'. Indeed, according to her, the intrinsic merits of these works is so low that they 'deserve the oblivion into which they have fallen'.[57] Her way of reading the romances is further demonstrated in the following account she gives of their structure:

> In structure the plots of the *Palmerins* are loose and rambling, lacking in order and restraint. Everything seems to be happening simultaneously, the author freely interlacing episodes and dropping one whenever he pleases. Of coherence, in the sense that one episode depends upon another there is little. Each seems to be a separate entity, which could easily be dispensed with. The reader would feel a sense of relief if the conclusion of an adventure advanced the conclusion of the plot. But it does not. It merely frees

a Knight for another adventure more fantastic, and so the episodes run on to the end of the book, whereupon the author adds a sequel by introducing the next generation of heroes, who continue in the tradition of their ancestors.[58]

Patchell identifies the chief characteristics of the Palmerins as a loose structure, and a circular style which emphasizes process above progress towards a preordained goal, with multiple climaxes rather than a single one, together with an unrealistic plot. It will be helpful in this context to look at Julia Kristeva's work on 'women's time', and its more specific application to style and structure in literature by Marilyn French.[59] According to Kristeva, female subjectivity would seem to be linked both to *cyclical* time (repetition) and to *monumental* time (eternity), at least in so far as both are ways of conceptualizing time from the perspective of motherhood and reproduction, rather than to the *linear* time of history. French applies this to her study of 'gender principles' in literature, and postulates that works which reveal the masculine principle are dominated by a male figure; these works are linear, with a narrative progressing chronologically, and a protagonist who has a specific worldly goal.[60] Literature which reveals the feminine gender principle is circular and eternal; it juggles time or ignores it:

> It presents incidents which have no apparent causal (rational) connections. Cause and effect and chronology may be entirely suspended in favor of psychological, emotional, associational links . . . . In 'feminine' literature, there is no great external goal to be achieved because there is no purpose to human life beyond continuation and pleasure.[61]

French indicates the threat this poses to patriarchal order, since it challenges the masculine worldly structures, power and permanence:

> It shows a different side of life: it celebrates flux, the moment, sensation, and emotion. It is likely to be concerned with love and sex rather than power and justice.[62]

The similarities between the style which French identifies as belonging to the feminine principle, and the style of Elizabethan romance are clear, and one might speculate that one of the reasons why critics have found the genre so frustrating and perplexing lies in the challenge which such apparently 'anarchic' literature poses to their critical methodologies. It is tempting to suggest that these popular romance texts have been dismissed or ignored precisely because they defy the sort of analysis and interpretation which patriarchal critical theory – which privileges the 'uniqueness' of a given text above its shared conventions, and its transmission of 'authentic' human experience above its evocation of awe and wonder – generally sees as its purpose and goal.

The demand for romances in the last quarter of the sixteenth century existed at all levels of society, from those who paid shillings for the *Arcadia* to those who paid pennies for *Tom a Lincoln* or *Valentine and Orson*, although the appeal was increasingly made to the middle and lower classes; romances which had begun as aristocratic works appeared in cheap quartos, and finally were relegated to the penny-chapbooks to be hawked by peddlers at fairs. So the *Arcadia*, which was designed for aristocratic circles, found its way into the middle classes, and was frequently reprinted. A cheap edition was published by R. Waldegrave in Edinburgh in 1599 to undercut the more expensive folio edition published by Ponsonby in London. Imitations by later writers who were from the middle classes used the title of the *Arcadia* to attract attention; Gervase Markham, for example, in 1607 published *The English Arcadia, Alluding his beginning from Sir Philip Sidneys ending*, which he describes in the preface as a 'moral historie', and on the first page as 'the Morall English Arcadia'. Similarly, *Euphues*, though designed for an upper-class readership at length became the reading matter and guide for aspiring upstarts, as a remark by Tysefew to Crispinella in Marston's *The Dutch Courtezan* of 1605 suggests:

> . . . by the Lord, you are growne a proud, scurvie, apish, ydle, disdainefull, scoffing, God's foot, because you have read *Euphues and his England, Palmerin de Oliva*, and the *Legend of Lies*.[63]

These readers probably would have read in a way never predicted by the authors, and found in them satisfaction for their own needs and aspirations.

According to Margaret Spufford, chivalric romances were reprinted again and again in the seventeenth century.[64] Tias, the ballad and chapbook publisher, was printing them in 1664, and they figured as chapbooks in Thackeray's trade-list of 1689. Most of them were collected by Samuel Pepys in the 1680s in his *Vulgaria*. Many were simply thumbed out of existence, or did not appear in inventories because they were worth so little.

Interestingly, and appropriately, one of the last glimpses we have of these romances is of a woman reading them. Greene's *Dorastus and Fawnia* (a chapbook version of *Pandosto*, which was the primary source for Shakespeare's *Winter's Tale*) was popular enough to be still appearing in both quarto and small versions in the 1680s; and in Richardson's novel *Clarissa*, the fire at Mrs Sinclair's house was caused by a cookmaid who, sitting up to read *Dorastus and Fawnia* late one night, set fire to the calico curtains at the window.[65]

3

George Pettie and the premature closure of the text

George Pettie's *A Petite Pallace of Pettie His Pleasure* (1576) is a collection of twelve tales, eleven from classical antiquity, and one from the *Golden Legend*, which have apparently been shaped into romances specifically for women's pleasure.[1] Pettie draws in particular from the historians Livy and Tacitus, the mythographers Hyginus and Ovid, and from William Painter's collection of stories translated from the French and Italian whose title is borrowed and adapted, *The Palace of Pleasure*.[2]

In his adaptations of his sources, Pettie's interest is always in the personal lives of his characters, their emotions and relationships. In her examination of Barbara Cartland's romances, Janet Batsleer makes clear that the field of action in romance is determined by the world of women: 'Napoleon is not the director of armies and empire, but the lover of Josephine', she writes.[3] Pettie had mastered the same formula some 400 years earlier; martial heroes are accordingly dragged from the heat of the battlefield and deposited, somewhat out of breath, in women's private chambers, where they display more terror than ever they did in the face of an enemy attack. Douglas Bush finds this exasperating, and complains:

> Pettie's sources are so transformed that they would often be unrecognizable but for the names and the unimportant tragic incidents. Metamorphoses and other supernatural occurrences are freely rationalized or omitted altogether. Character and incidents, dialogue, soliloquies, letters are invented for romantic purposes.[4]

That these 'romantic purposes' were for the benefit of women is first suggested by R.B.[5] in his epistle to 'the gentle gentlewomen readers': 'Gentle readers, whom by my will I woulde have onely gentlewomen, and therefore to you I direct my woords' (p. 3). Further bibliographical information supplied by R.B.'s epistle, and by a letter from Pettie which he prints with it, appears to suggest that the tales were not designed as stories for publication but as discourses for private pleasure (R.B. claims he had them published without Pettie's knowledge or consent, while Pettie's letter asks R.B. to keep them private since some of the characters he draws represent his close friends). The audience in either case is, however, quite clearly female. And if the women who originally heard or read his tales might have excused his over-familiarity with them on the grounds that they knew him personally, his later – perhaps unanticipated readership – might well find his assumed intimacy offensive.

For Pettie teases, bullies, mocks and ultimately woos his women readers. In the narrator's intervention in the text to comment on the stories, he creates a claustrophobically close and oppressive relationship with the readers whom he pretends to know:

> I am heere, Gentlewomen, to admonish you not to suffer yourselves to be caryed away with covetousnesse . . . and as wel for your sakes as mine owne I would wish you who are indued with wealth sufficient to make a man (as they say) & who are at your owne disposition and choice, not to yeeld your selves as a pray to any who hath no neede of your wealth . . . .
>
> (p. 100)

The tone is condescending, and clearly places Pettie in a superior position as moral guide. His pretence that he has a genuine concern for women allows him an apparently intimate confidentiality, and demonstrates his attempt to insinuate himself into the reader's regard. Bush draws attention to Pettie's fawning attitude to his women readers, to the way Pettie 'bows and smirks and rallies them like a Master of Ceremonies in the Pump Room'.[6] But Pettie's attitude is more intimidating than that: he flirts with his readers, but also ultimately sexually harasses them within the text:

> But here hee aptly ended his talke upon her mouth, and they entred into sutch privy conference, their lips beeing joyned most closely together, that I can not report the meaninge of it unto you, but if it please one of you to leane hitherward a litle I will shew you the manner of it.
>
> (p. 137)

Thus he describes the embrace of Admetus and Alcest. His assumed naivety functions to make the sexual innuendo appear more innocent than it really is. His artlessness is part of his role, and only just below the surface of the courteous request of 'if it please one of you' lie violence and cunning.

At the end of his stories Pettie moralizes at length, possibly to appeal to the Puritan minds who could see no virtue in reading romances. Pettie's sententiousness attempts to convince the reader that his stories are useful as examples of virtues and vices, showing what to follow and what to shun. He introduces his tales with an argument which the narrative will illustrate. But whereas the relationship between introduction and story is generally straightforward, his conclusions are often wildly inappropriate to the preceding discourse, most significantly when they qualify or diminish the positive qualities and strength of character displayed by the female protagonist. In his stories, Pettie does expand women's roles, giving them depth of character, allowing them to be active and highly articulate, but his conclusions tend to confine these qualities to certain narrowly defined limits. He gives women power and simultaneously qualifies or undermines it: the text attempts to close off the radical possibilities which it had admitted.

The arrangement of the twelve stories seems to have some internal order and shape. The two middle tales (the sixth and seventh) offer two widely different approaches to a woman proposing marriage; the final story is a complete rejection of women in favour of a religious life of solitude and meditation. Ironically, this is the story which contains the most comprehensive encomium of women's virtues, and appears to answer the diatribe against women in the story preceding it, *Pygmalion's Friend*. These two stories, in fact, posit the opposing sides of the contemporary debate about women. Linda Woodbridge points to the ways in which popular literature fed off the formal controversy:

> In preparing a book for women readers, Pettie seems to have turned naturally to the formal controversy. Not only is his last tale largely a formal defense, but the controversy intrudes at other points as well.[7]

Pettie, indeed, is happy to plead either side of the question, although the diatribes against women tend to outweigh those in their favour. Gollancz, in the preface to his 1908 edition of Pettie's work, confidently asserts that the misogynistic tirades were 'evidently intended to please and amuse the ladies' and maintains that, on 'women's rights', Pettie 'certainly showed no misogyny, though charming banter'.[8] But Pettie cannot be so easily absolved on either count; women are never allowed to forget that they are subordinate. To argue that it is all a game is not to remove its seriousness, but merely to shirk its responsibility.

In the following pages I intend to indicate the dynamics at work between woman reader and text, to show how Pettie adapted his stories for women and thus reveal the basic premises about women from which he worked, and to locate his final inability to allow women to develop freely and fully – his need to qualify, to diminish and to dictate. I shall also indicate ways in which the woman reader can reappropriate the text, and reread it to her own advantage.

Pettie's attempts to confine women takes its most extreme form in the emphasis in his conclusions on silencing women, denying their utterance, and writing out the implications of their reality. On to the actions of his female characters he imposes his own restrictive meaning, distorting and denying their significance; he tries to silence his readers by presuming that his assumed familiarity with us allows him to speak for us, privileging his meaning over ours. Adrienne Rich reminds us of the authority which men have derived from their monopoly on the production of meaning: 'In a world where language and naming are power, silence is oppression, is violence.'[9] By recognizing Pettie's narrative designs, however, we can re-inscribe the legitimacy of our own response and re-interpret his discourse, thus acknowledging the active role of the reader in the production of a text. Pettie's defences against women, his attempts at the suppression and ultimate silencing of his fictional heroines and his female readership, are therefore crucial areas to explore for a fuller understanding of his work. In selecting his tales, I have focused in particular on those which most clearly reveal these strategies.[10]

Pettie's arrogation of a woman's response is nowhere better shown than in his introduction to *Tereus and Progne*, where he informs us that this story, 'though it manifest not our manyfolde misery, yet shall it at least set foorth the frailty of our felicity' (p. 42). The word 'our' in this context may not be the inclusive term it appears to be: Pettie appears to assume that men and women will respond to his narrative in the same way or, less likely since he claims his stories are for women, he is simply not interested in a female reaction. This assumption is an usurpation: it takes away the legitimacy of a woman's response; for a woman, the rape and brutal mutilation of Philomela are clearly 'manyfolde misery'. Pettie's 'our' is as exclusive to the male sex as is the more obvious use of the term 'man', which professes to speak for both sexes, but which in fact again privileges the male: '. . . oh, the sea of sorrow and waves of woe which then overwhelme us, when wee once arrive to mans estate'. (p. 41)

Pettie extends the story beyond the length and depth of any of his possible sources,[11] adding passages to demonstrate his more fully developed characters. We witness, for example, Tereus' hasty wooing of Progne, whose beauty he has seen in a dream. Progne's response to his suit ironically foreshadows the rape which is to take place; the possibility and fear of rape are very real ones, for the threat seldom lies very deeply beneath the suit of a man to a woman in these stories. The woman's response must always contain the knowledge that the man could, if he wished, take by force that which he pleads for by courtesy. This awareness heightens our sensitivity to Progne's measured reply:

> . . . any benefit of my body it is not in mee to bestow on you: for if you do mee that injury to exacte any thing at my handes lasciviously, honesty will not allow it, whose boundes I meane not to transgresse . . . .

(p. 46)

Pettie excludes the omens of ill-fortune that are present at the marriage in both Chaucer's version,[12] and his more probable source, Ovid's *Metamorphoses*,[13] and thus, at the end of the story, allows himself to apportion guilt and responsibility. An anticipation of this is suggested when Progne begs her husband to fetch Philomela from Athens:

> For it fortuned that Progne after they had bene maried together a whyle entred into great desire to see her sister Philomela, and lay very importunately upon her husband to go to Athens . . . .

(p. 47)

'Very importunately' suggests over-zealousness, impatience and inappropriateness, and implies condemnation, as if it were Progne's fault that her sister should meet such a terrible fate. Chaucer, in contrast, stresses Progne's humility in her request:

> She preyde hym that he wolde after hire sende;
> And this was, day by day, al hir preyere,
> With al humblenesse of wifhod, word and chere.[14]

Pettie has chosen to implicate Progne in Philomela's tragedy.

In the analogies of Tereus and Philomela to tiger or wolf, and lamb, Pettie follows the precedent of his sources. His account appears more distasteful, however, since he appears to relish his own descriptions. His verbal puns and alliterative effects argue for a mind conniving in what it apparently condemns: '. . . there was never blouddy tiger that did so terribly teare the litle Lambe, as this tiraunt did furiously fare with faire Philomela' (p. 48). The alliteration of 'f's and 't's, together with the pun on 'fare' and 'fair', suggest a mind callously detached from the real horror of the rape described.[15] The prevalence of animal imagery at this point in the story (in Pettie, and in Ovid and Chaucer) might be seen as peculiarly male. A woman writer describing a rape is more likely to view it in a personal, more direct way, rather than from the standpoint of a detached (male) observer. Pettie's perspective is that of the tiger, not the lamb.

After the rape, Philomela curses Tereus articulately and at length: the power of language is suggested by Tereus' fear of Philomela's discourse, which prompts him to cut out her tongue. She is denied language, locked up, helpless. A mute woman is a powerful symbol of male dominance, which denies the validity of women's experience.

When Progne discovers what has happened, Pettie marvels that she could keep it a secret, a particularly brutal comment when he has just described woman's voice forcibly silenced. It is a jibe deriving more from the traditional male notion of woman's loquaciousness than wonder that anyone could keep such horrifying knowledge to themselves, for he specifically mentions 'a woman':

> Now Progne havinge this cloath convayed unto her, and fully understandinge how the case stoode, notwithstanding her greife were great in the highest degree, yet (a mervailous thing a woman could do so) shee concealed the matter secretly, hoping to be revenged more speedily.
>
> (p. 51)

Compare with Ovid:

> She held hir peace (a wondrous thing it is she should so doe)
> But sorrow tide hir tongue . . .[16]

'She', that is, a person in those circumstances, not 'she', a woman.

Pettie's insensitivity, his relish in the events he describes, is suggested in his insistence that Progne's revenge is so horrific that 'my tungue is not able to tell' what she did (p. 53). His reference to his own tongue, safe in his mouth, and unable to utter only because he chooses for it not to, ironically recalls Philomela's tongue, brutally slashed from her mouth forcibly to render her 'not able to tell'.[17]

He makes clear that Progne's crime outweighs that of Tereus, and attempts to deny our freedom to disagree by his assumption of the right to speak for the reader: 'I thinke your selves wil say her fury exceeded his folly, and her severity in punishyng his crueltie in offendyng' (p. 53). He goes on to weight his argument against the women further by magnifying the crime of a mother killing her son in revenge, and diminishing that of a brutal rapist and mutilator. He omits Ovid's demonstration of Progne's hesitation over killing Itys,[18] and extends the role of the child, making him appear more innocent and vulnerable, and hence the mother's crime all the more evil. He inveighs against her in self-righteous horror in a way he never did against Tereus. In Ovid's account, Tereus' crime is given almost twice as much space as Progne's. Pettie reverses this, characterizing only Progne's as inhumanely and unnaturally cruel.[19] In his summary, Golding indicates that the tale reveals that all are to blame:

The tale of Tereus, Philomele, and Prognee dooth conteyne
That folke are blynd in thyngs that too their proper weale perteyne,
And that the man in whom the fyre of furious lust dooth reigne
Dooth run too mischeefe like a horse that getteth loose the reyne.
It also shewes the cruell wreake of women in their wrath
And that no hainous mischiefe long delay of vengeance hath.[20]

Finally, Pettie twists Ovid's ending to his own design. Ovid, says
Pettie, reports that the two women were changed into birds. Indeed he
does, but that was not, as Pettie suggests, 'meaning they were not worthy
humaine shape or the use of reason, which were sutch cruell monsters
altogether devoyd of ruth and reason', but it is presented rather as a lucky
means of escape from Tereus' 'naked sword and furious heart'.[21] Sandys
confirms this, suggesting that the two sisters were changed into birds 'for
their speedy flight into Athens, by which they escaped the revenge of
Tereus'.[22] As further evidence that Ovid did not mean to imply that
women in particular were so evil that they did not deserve human shape,
it is salutary to observe (as Pettie chose not to do) that Ovid has Tereus
himself change into a lapwing.[23]

In his story of *Icilius and Virginia*, one of Pettie's most radical
departures from his sources is when he allows Virginia to respond to the
threat of rape, but this apparently positive gesture is undermined by the
nature of that response.

It is a story which would not initially seem a likely subject for romantic
treatment. In Livy's version, and for the most part in Painter's which
follows it,[24] it is a history primarily about the way the newly appointed
decemviri in Rome lost their powers, and how the common people were
able to re-establish the plebeian tribunes. The attempted rape of Virginia
in Livy is chiefly of significance in so far as it turned popular support
away from the decemviri, of whom the lascivious Appius Claudius was
one; she is little more than a pawn in a power struggle initiated by
Appius' lust, and she remains mute throughout.

Pettie shifts the focus on to Virginia herself, and stresses her
vulnerability before Appius:

> ... who by the furies of Hell was so set on fire in libidinous lust
> towardes that virgin, that he sought all the meanes possible to
> winne her to his wicked will: but seeyng her so firmely fortified in
> vertue, to bee by consent vanquished by villany, hee determined by
> force to force her to his filthinesse.
>
> (p. 118)

Her helplessness is suggested by the ease with which Pettie suggests this
alternative course of action; if a woman will not do what a man wants,
with an alliterative sleight of hand, he can turn to violence.

But in Pettie's version, she is not mute; she is allowed to respond to his threat, but she does so by pleading with her father for 'honourable death' rather than being given over to Appius' lust:

> And as by your fatherly care I have continued a continent virgin hetherto, so by your further aide, I pray you let mee dye an honest mayde presently: least my life hereafter, contaminate the commendation of my life heretofore: and seeing I can bee no longer suffred to live honestly, good father let mee die honourably[.] For an honourable death is alwayes to be preferred before an infamous life, of evils the least is to bee chosen, and death of body is to bee counted a lesse evill, then destruction of body and soule.
>
> (p. 123)

Pettie departs most significantly from Livy and Painter in having the request for death come from Virginia herself. In the earlier versions it is her father who makes the decision, with which Virginia is in silent compliance. Pettie's change is in keeping with his habit of according more depth and autonomy to his female characters, but ironically he has Virginia use her voice to reaffirm patriarchal order. For it is only male values and male doctrine which dictate that a woman who is raped destroys her soul, and Virginia is forced into a fatal connivance in their values. In his decision to allow Virginia to respond to the threat of rape, in having her choose her own death – an apparently courageous, independent act – Pettie makes her embrace precisely the ideology which oppresses her.

Pettie's story of *Sinorix and Camma* is extended beyond any of its possible sources,[25] allowing more scope for developing character, particularly that of Camma. He gives her personality depth and her actions realistic motivation; she is highly articulate and reasons with more precision and logic than Sinorix does. In their dialogues, she consistently remains in control, while Sinorix is helpless at her mercy. In wit and intelligence she proves more than his equal, reasoning eloquently that he cannot feel the love and goodwill to which he lays claim, or else he would not press her to commit the sin of adultery. She adopts the role of judge and condemns him to perpetual silence in his suit, but offers him instead her friendship, and the second place in her heart. Her action is irreproachable, its balance between sternness and friendliness a fine and delicate one.

Sinorix is persistent in his desire for her body. He writes her a letter, again unsuccessfully pleading his suit, using the traditional but violent military image of besieging a town as analogy to his pressing her to admit him to her heart (and of more pertinence to him, her vagina).[26] His next strategy is to send an old woman to tempt her with gifts. She is another of Pettie's inventions, both helping to prolong the wooing and giving

him a pretext for railing against 'dishonest' women of this sort, as an
antidote to the virtue of Camma. When she has left, Camma experiences
her first doubts; it is one of Pettie's own details not found in his sources,
and while hesitation makes her more culpable in his eyes, it is a fine
stroke of psychological realism. She is not a mere figure-head, or
unchanging Virtue, as in medieval morality plays; she is human, capable
of growth, vacillation and doubt.[27] She engages in searching self-
examination, presenting herself with arguments for both sides of the
question, inclining first to one, then the other. Her final resolve both to
be revenged and subsequently to kill herself, rather than suffer Sinorix to
lie with her after he has caused the death of her husband Sinnatus, is
simultaneously a strong and courageous one, but also one which is
defined by its context within patriarchal ideology, which leaves few
choices open to her.

Pettie is seldom unequivocal. He cannot allow Camma to appear so
completely self-sacrificing and, lest we should think her so, he invents
some little children, 'prety Impes' (p. 36), for her to abandon by her
suicide.

Camma kills herself, then, but Pettie does not leave her at the moment
of her triumph. Instead, he appends his own moral that is violently at
odds with the end of the story, which cannot support it. Were blame to
be apportioned, one might have expected Sinorix to appear most
culpable, but Pettie makes it clear that it is all woman's fault. With
devastating audacity he appeals to his women readers:

> Now I would wish you, blazing starres, which stand upon your
> chastity, to take light at this lot, to take heed by this harme, you see
> the husband slaine, the ruffian fled, the lover poysoned, the wife
> dead, the freinds comfortles, the children parentlesse . . .. But it is
> naturally incident to women to enter into extremities, they are
> either to lovinge or to lothinge, to curteous or to coy, to willinge or
> to wilfull, to mercifull or to mercilesse, to forwarde or to frowarde,
> to freindly or feendly, the meane they alwayes meanely account of.
> Otherwise shee might with reason sooner then rigour have
> repressed his rage.[28]

(pp. 37–8)

The hyperbolic flattery, calling women 'blazing stars', jars with the
mockery of 'which stand upon your chastity', suggesting an over-
preciseness on women's part. His derision is emphasized by the string of
alliterative antitheses which suggest that women simply cannot win.
Camma has been reasoning with Sinorix ever since the story opened, and
it is hard to imagine what else Pettie would have had her do: had she
succumbed to Sirnorix's lust, she would have been roundly condemned,
for Pettie shows himself elsewhere to be a staunch upholder of chastity.

He goes on to commend her for this constancy and chastity, while condemning her for cruelty (any cruelty on Sinorix's part is, typically, unmentioned). This is illogical; if Pettie wants her to be chaste, she must of necessity refuse Sinorix, which she does with tact. If he wants her to be less cruel, then she must succumb to Sinorix, and thus not be chaste.

Finally, in a hideous travesty of judgement, Pettie opens up the case for his readers: 'Therefore Gentlewomen I leave it to your judgements to give sentence, whether be more worthy reprehension, hee or shee' (p. 38). This question cannot be seriously posed. Pettie flatters his women readers by appearing to offer them the position to judge over this (at a time when they were allowed to exercise judgement in few other areas of their lives), but he simultaneously misrepresents the issues, and in fact denies their freedom to inscribe their own meaning. He assumes the role of judge himself, and the readers become a mute, passive jury:

> He had the law of love on his side, shee had the lawe of men and of marriage on her part; love led him, which the goddes themselves cannot resist, chastitie guided her, which the goddes themselves have lost: he killed him whom he counted his enemy, she killed him whom she knew her fleshly freinde: shee with reason might have prevented great mischief, his wings were to mutch limed with lust to fly forth of his folly.
>
> (pp. 38–9)

Pettie arrogates our response, forcing his own meaning on to the text. A woman's reading reveals an alternative one. The story has demonstrated that it was lust, not love, which motivated Sinorix. The successive alliterations appear progressively to weight the argument against Camma. But Sinnatus was no more in fact an enemy of Sinorix than Sinorix himself was a friend to Camma. In the final antithesis in which the rhetorical pattern is reversed, putting 'she' before 'he', Pettie plays his trump card: with a last triumphant twist of logic, Camma is condemned for having reason and apparently not exercising it (of course, the story shows her pre-eminence in reasoning, but not in the services of male desire), whereas Sinorix is apparently 'excused' because he was too consumed by lust to be able to act rationally. It is Pettie's partial judgement which closes the tale.

There is, then, a gross discrepancy between the story and its conclusion, comprehensible only in terms of Pettie's fear of admitting the implications of a woman's dramatic gesture or statement. He appears unwilling to allow too much power and praise to women. For Camma is, in her way, both powerful and praiseworthy, a combination of qualities in a woman to which Elizabethan men could respond with no more complacency than do their twentieth-century descendants.[29]

At the end of *Curiatius and Horatia*, Pettie again appears to offer the subject to his women readers' judgement; and again he inscribes his own verdict, his own meaning. Horatia's lover Curiatius has been killed in battle by her brother; Horatia's grief is overheard by the same brother who, in a rage, draws his sword and kills her: 'Now I would heare your judgementes to whom you thinke this lamentable end of these lovers ought to be imputed' (p. 183). It might have seemed that there would be little doubt that the brother who killed both Curiatius and Horatia would be held responsible for their 'lamentable end'. It appears, however, that Pettie has to compensate for the strength and independence which he has earlier allowed Horatia,[30] and it is to her that he accords most blame, maintaining that were she to have agreed to marry Curiatius sooner, he would have been able to avoid the fatal battle. Pettie's eagerness to shift all responsibility on to the woman leads him to an apparently deliberate misreading of his own text.

Similarly, at the end of *Germanicus and Agrippina*, Agrippina is unreasonably held responsible for the death of her husband whose ambition (prompted, we are told, by his desire to give his wife a comfortable life) leads to his murder by enemies. This interpretation is nowhere in his sources. Indeed, Tacitus' version is very different.[31] History, as Douglas Bush has acidly remarked, is 'not much concerned with the ante-nuptial life of Germanicus and Agrippina',[32] but this is precisely the stuff of romance, and Pettie dedicates himself to the subject with enthusiasm. Well over half of his adaptation focuses on Germanicus' arduous suit for Agrippina's hand in marriage. In Tacitus, the couple are already married; Germanicus is a martial hero, very popular with the common people; his great military successes came in battles against the Germans, to which his wife fearlessly accompanied him. According to Tacitus, this Agrippina was a formidable woman of heroic stature, courageous and independent, and became 'a personage of more consequence in the army than either General or Legates'.[33]

Within the more limited realm of the drawing-room of Pettie's romance she is still a resolute, spirited, witty woman who knows her own mind. In the light-hearted banter and debate in which they engage during their courtship, Agrippina remains triumphantly in control, whereas Germanicus bewails his unworthiness and helplessness. Tacitus would indeed rub his eyes were he to read this, as Bush suggests.[34] In the world of affairs, the traditional 'man's world', Germanicus is supreme. In the world of romance where women have more power and importance, he is insignificant, one suitor among many, vulnerable and fearful. But Pettie is not prepared to allow Agrippina to remain powerful, as his conclusion bears witness: she is guilty of Germanicus' death, and she soon pines to her own death without him. In Tacitus' version, however, she outlives her husband by 14 years and retains an active political life.

Pettie ends his story with a confidential aside to his women readers, admonishing them like young children:

It is your partes also to way your husbandes wealth, and not to decke your heades and neckes with golde when hee hath none in his purse, not to swimme in silkes when hee is drowned in debt, not to abound in bravery when hee is pinched with poverty.

(p. 84)

In a patronizing tone, he uses the story to inculcate a moral lesson upon his female readership.

It is to the unmarried women readers that Pettie addresses *Scilla and Minos*,[35] and his tone becomes provocative as he introduces the subject of sex:

But Gentlewomen bicause most of you bee maydes (I meane at least taken so) I will manifest unto you the mischief of love by the example of a mayde, in that estate (though I hope not every way) like unto your selves, that admonished thereby, you may avoyde the like inconvenience in your selves.

(pp. 147–8)

When he uses the term 'maydes' in the first line, the context in which it is placed suggests the connotation of virginity rather than simply 'unmarried women'; were this not so, his further explanation, 'I meane at least taken so', would be meaningless. The tone appears to be intended as playful and only slightly risqué, inoffensive because generalized. Pettie hints that he knows the actual sexual state of his readers (that the unmarried are not virgins), but is too kind and polite to reveal it. The implication that he could tell more if manners did not restrain him, his apparent tact, and his stance as benevolent teacher, together help to disguise the fact that he is being patronizing and presumptuous. His role of familiar friend almost convinces us, and permits us to allow him an intimacy to which he has no right.

The story is one of unrequited love; Scilla falls in love with her country's enemy Minos. In order to win his affection, she pulls off her father's golden hair 'whereon dependeth the stay of his state, and puissance of his power' (p. 161), and presents it to Minos. She is spurned, however, and as she attempts to swim after his boat, she drowns (Ovid allows her to escape, transformed into a bird).

Pettie's moral is clear. Scilla refused Iphis who was below her (a young suitor whom Pettie invents, to add to the romantic intrigue, and perhaps with the intention of trying to bias our feelings against Scilla for her cruel rejection of him), so she does not deserve Minos, who is above her. Pettie explains the symbolic meaning of pulling off Nisus' hair; for him it is not the traditional symbol of castration, but simply another way of saying that a woman's disobedience upsets her father, especially when it takes the form of wanting to marry someone 'unsuitable'. While this interpretation clearly diminishes the power of the story, it makes it more relevant to his readers' lives. Pettie seems eager to ingratiate himself, to insinuate himself into his women readers' confidence, and he pretends to advocate obedience only when their fathers are in earshot:

> But (Soveraigne) now your father is gone, I will give you more sound advice: I will admonishe you all not to pull of your owne haire, that is not to blinde your selves to the froward fansi of your politique parents, but to make your choice in marriage according to your owne mindes.
>
> (pp. 164–5)

Such a view is clearly welcome to women but allows them just that amount of self-determination that Pettie has shown was the undoing of Scilla. Such contradiction suggests either that Pettie is not in complete control of his material, or that his advice to women is so lightly meant that inconsistency does not matter. Apparently father is returning, so Pettie pretends he is forced back into his former role of lecturing children:

> . . . I must (I say) admonish you that as your parents gave you your bodies, so they may dispose of them. That you requite all their love, care, and cost, at least with obedience. I must tel you that if you honour not them your dayes will bee short on earth: I must tell you that Ravens will put out the eye that blindeth the father, and neglecteth the good instruction of the mother, as Solomon sayd.
>
> (p. 165)

The repeated 'must' implies that Pettie is saying this against his will, and does not seriously mean it. With our experience of his ambiguous attitude towards women, we are unlikely to be taken in however. It is a double bluff: with the young woman he pretends to be playing a joke on the father, but it is in the knowledge that the father's values are, after all, the only legitimate ones in this society. The framework ensures that Pettie's final word is the traditional one; his more 'feminist' polemic is, at best, of doubtful status, and cannot be allowed to stand alone.

With his story of *Admetus and Alcest*,[36] Pettie characterizes his most irreproachable female character. Alcest assumes the role of martyr for her willing death in her husband's place. Her self-sacrifice is treated with unusual subtlety by Pettie, and he unequivocally praises her – 'O loyall loving wife, O wight good inough for god him selfe' (p. 143) – and at the end of the story she is miraculously restored to life by Proserpina, making this the only happy ending in the collection.

In his conclusion, Pettie is eager to explain in practical terms what the mythological passages in his story 'mean'.[37] He is clearly uncomfortable with the idea that a dead person can be brought to life, and seeks to rationalize it: '. . . the meaninge of it is this, that you should die to your selves and live to your husbandes' (p. 145). Alcest is so completely flawless that it would be impossible for Pettie to qualify the virtue of her act (as he did in Camma's story). Instead, he implies that all women should be as self-sacrificing as Alcest; by making her an example to all, he transforms her generous selflessness into an even greater enslavement and oppression.

In this, the story of an independent, spirited woman, who herself proposes to the man she wants, who does not fear parental wrath, who commits the hardest and noblest act on behalf of another human being, Pettie becomes most repressive. In a parody of its true significance, he uses the story to enforce the subordination of women to their husbands:

> . . . you should counte their life your life, their death your distruction . . . you should not care to disease your selves to please them: . . . and so . . . in all thinges you should conforme your selves to their contentacion: so shall there bee one will in two minds, one hart in two bodies, and two bodies in one flesh.
>
> (pp. 145–6)

Lawrence Stone succinctly agrees that, historically, this was the case: 'By marriage, the husband and wife became one person in law – and that person was the husband.'[38]

Amphiarus and Eriphile is a story about a strong and independent widow.[39] Unmarried women of means – usually widows – were the most powerful women in Elizabethan society, and Pettie's transformation of the strong and independent Eriphile into a jealous, trifling flirt who, on being refused by a man for whom she feels little affection, 'in very colorike conceites consumed away and died' (p. 100) demonstrates the threat such women were held to pose. Joyce Youings points to the historical reality:

> Elizabethan men did not have to be Puritans to be persuaded that women, for all their legal disabilities, could, in the domestic context, be wilful, calculating and remarkably self-reliant, perhaps never more so than when they became widows or were deserted, temporarily or permanently.[40]

Pettie's story opens with Eriphile's refusal of Amphiarus' initial proposal of marriage, with its offer of himself as her steward, an offer made with avaricious intent couched in patronizing terms:

> For it is not meete your young yeres should bee tied to any trouble or travaile, but to passe your time in pleasure according to your

bringinge up and callinge, and accordinge to the custome of your
kinde, and sexe.

(p. 87)

He clearly feels uncomfortable faced with an acute business woman.
Eriphile remains unimpressed, and she tells him that she has no wish to
experience again 'the inconveniences and infinite troubles mixed with
mariage' (p. 88) and demonstrates her understanding of the implications
of his suit:

> For where you professe to be my steward and servant, I am sure if
> you were once sure of that you seeke for, you would thinke your
> self good inough to bee my Lord and maister, and you would
> dispose my goods neither at my pleasure, neither to my profite, but
> that which is mine should bee yours, and yours your owne.

(p. 88)

There, in a few words, is the essence of courtship and marriage in the
sixteenth century. To recall Lawrence Stone once again:

> By marriage, the husband and wife become one person in law – and
> that person was the husband. He acquired absolute control of all his
> wife's personal property, which he could sell at will.[41]

Eriphile is a woman of few illusions, whose experience of the world has
taught her prudence and self-reliance.

Later, she decides that Amphiarus is so rich that she might be able to
profit from the union as much as he, and on these startlingly pragmatic
grounds, she agrees to marry him, acknowledging in private that:

> . . . I see not how wee women are bound to love our husbandes so
> mutch, wee are onely commaunded to honour and obay them,
> which I count sufficiente, and more then for my part I meane to
> perfourme.

(p. 89)

She keeps her word, and when Adrastus offers 'great rewardes' if
Amphiarus can be found to take part in the war against Thebes, she
betrays her husband (who later dies in the war).[42] Amphiarus responds
with a lengthy diatribe against women, which is not directed against one
particular woman, but against the whole sex; individual failings become
generic ones:

> Ah fonde foole that I was to repose any trust or confidence in
> women, whose sexe is subtil, whose kinde is cruell, who are
> constant only in unconstancy, who are wytty only in wiles, who as
> Aristotle saith are monsters in nature, altogether imperfect, weake
> vessels, ignoraunt in al things, yea (which we may most lament)

they are naturally indued with baites to allure men, with poyson to infect men, and with charmes to chaunge men from men to beastes, as Cyrces did the servauntes of Ulisses.

(p. 97)

Beneath all this invective, there appears to lie a very deep-rooted fear of women, as the reference to Circe – the woman who had complete power over men – suggests.

After the death of Amphiarus, Pettie has Eriphile 'cast in her head how shee might be sped of any other husband' (p. 99). She feigns repentance for her earlier cruel treatment of a young suitor, Infortunio (an invention of Pettie's to bring about her downfall), and suggests that she would no longer be insensible of his attentions. Infortunio, wiser now, refuses to be drawn. The hasty death which Pettie accords her in reaction to this is at odds with the rest of the story. It is inconceivable that such a strong independent woman would be so affected by a rejection from anyone, much less from one so insignificant as Infortunio. Pettie clearly wished to take his own revenge on this self-reliant woman who threatened male sovereignty. The historian Barbara Todd explores the stereotype of the widow thus:

> the independent widow was . . . an anomaly. English patriarchal society required that, like the state, the household should be headed by a man. The woman heading her own household contradicted the patriarchal theory; the ungoverned woman was a threat to the social order . . . . Yet it was the widow who did remarry who was criticized; for, as men realized, the remarriage of any widow confronted every man with the threatening prospect of his own death and the entry of another into his place.[43]

The most fitting end Pettie can devise for her is to 'consume away' and die from having been repulsed by a man, thereby restoring his own male self-esteem, at the expense of the consistency of his story. His possible sources, Apollodorus and Hyginus, both describe the murder of Eriphile by Amphiarus' son Alcmaeon.[44]

Pigmalions Friende, and His Image is Pettie's most openly misogynistic story in which real women are rejected in favour of one created by a man. It opens with a description of the love between Pygmalion and Penthea, 'a curteous courtly wenche' (p. 230), but one who is married. Pettie marvels that Pygmalion could so control himself that he never seduced or raped her (unwittingly suggesting woman's vulnerability to male lust), and reports that their perfect friendship continued three or four years, before she apparently transferred her affection to a foreign ambassador, newly arrived in Piedmont:

But what perpetuitie is to bee looked for in mortal pretences? What

constancy is to bee hoped for in kytes of Cressids kinde? may one
gather Grapes of thornes, Suger of Thistels, or constancy of
women? Nay if a man sift the whole sexe thorowly, hee shall finde
their wordes to bee but winde, their fayth forgery, and their deedes
dissemblinge. You must not (Gentlewomen) take these words to
come from me . . . .

(p. 231)

Pettie's disclaimer is unconvincing. His grammar and syntax lead us to
read the misogynist comments as if they were his own; they continue
uninterrupted from his description of the couple's happiness, and can in
no way be construed as Pygmalion's utterances, as Pettie would have us
believe – '. . . you must take these speeches to proceede from Pigmalion
. . .' (p. 232). By attributing them to Pygmalion only at the end, it appears
that Pettie deliberately wants us initially to assume the comments are his
own; he is thus able to express anti-woman prejudices without having to
take responsibility for them. He equivocates further by his remark that
he would 'dare not so much as thinke so mutch, mutch lesse say so
mutch' (p. 231). The verb 'dare' suggests his reticence is from fear of
consequences, rather than from disagreement with ideas expressed. He
follows this with some tortuous grammar which increases the ambiguity
of his position:

> for that truth getteth hatred, I meane sutch as tell not the truth, as
> hee in no wise should not doe, which should blowe forthe any
> sutch blast of the most faythfull and constant feminine kinde.

(pp. 231–2)

The complex syntax with so many redundant negatives suggests his
prevarication; the dominant meaning presumably is meant to be that
those who criticize women are liars, but the opposite interpretation –
that such criticism is justified – clearly lies only just below the surface.
The construction seems to lead to the latter conclusion, and then recoils
upon itself.

The unrelieved misogyny continues at length and many of the
arguments are familiar from the formal controversy about women, and
include diatribes against women's lust, greed, vanity, foolishness and
inconstancy. In the following antitheses it is clear that, however they
behave, women are condemned:

> Sutch falsenesse if they be faire, sutch filthinesse if they bee foule,
> sutch wiles if they bee wittie, sutch fondnesse if they be fooles . . .
> such lustinesse if they bee young, sutch lothsomnesse if they bee
> olde . . . sutch often desire of sport if they be healthy, sutch seldom
> quietnesse if they be sikly, sutch unholsomnesse if they be barren,

sutch quesiness if they bee with childe . . . that, to conclude with
scripture, I thinke best for man not to touche a woman.

(pp. 241-2)

His revulsion by women's physicality suggests more about his society's
fear and hatred of women, than it does about women themselves, but
scripture is brought in obligingly to validate his claims.

Pettie appears to offer a palliative to this excess, and tries to excuse it:

Gentlewomen, you must understande this Gentleman was in a
great heate, and therefore you must beare with his bolde blasphemy
against your noble sexe . . . .

(p. 242)

The verb 'must', twice used, is imperious, and the conjunction
'therefore' hides the false logic of the connection between the two parts
of the sentence. Pettie's reference to our 'noble sex' suggests that his
tongue is firmly in his cheek. But his bluff continues:

. . . for my part, I am angry with my selfe to have uttred it, & I shall
like my lisping lippes the worse for that they have bene the
instrumentes of sutch evill, neither shall I think them savory againe,
untill it shall please some of you to season them with the
sweetenesse of yours.

(p. 242)

Thus he follows abuse of women by lewd harassment of them. His tone
is condescending, and self-assured; the intimate familiarity with which
he addresses his women readers, the outrageous suggestion that a kiss
from them will 'make everything alright', and his choice of humour at
this juncture, together point to a numbed sensibility blithely unaware of,
or indifferent to, the emotional and psychological effects on women of
continuous 'woman-baiting'. Linda Woodbridge's assessment here of
Pettie as women's defender who is 'quickly seeking to make amends to
his women readers . . .'[45] is clearly inadequate. Pettie's relationship to the
text is more ambiguous than she suggests; the proportion of space he
allocates to this misogynist tirade, approximately one-third of the total
length of the story, reflects the importance he attributes to it. The whole
of the story so far has been entirely Pettie's invention, added as a prelude
to the Pygmalion story found in Ovid's *Metamorphoses*.[46] Pettie has no
precedent, then, for his approach.

At last Pettie comes to the traditional version of the story, in which
Pygmalion falls in love with a statue of a woman which he has carved and
which subsequently comes to life. Significantly, the only woman with
whom one of Pettie's male characters finds complete satisfaction is one
who has been literally created by him.

Pettie addresses the readers at the end, acknowledging that Pygmalion's 'broad blasphemie' against women was unworthy, but blaming it on 'the ficklenes of Penthea' (p. 245). He advises them that, to avoid further blasphemy against themselves, they should never drop old friends in favour of new; women have to modify their behaviour in order to accommodate men.

He ends pragmatically with what amounts to a threat to women who cast off men:

> It is a daungerous peece of worke, and importeth as mutch as their good name commeth to, for if they shall, without discretion and great cause, disclaime a mans freindship, it is the next way (onlesse his government of himselfe bee very great) to make him proclayme what freindship hee hath had of them in times past.
>
> (p. 247)

His innuendo is oblique and distasteful; the indirectness adds to the tone of voyeuristic suspicion, and implies that the double standard of sexual morality is too well-known to require further explanation. His parting advice to women is to deceive:

> . . . if they cannot frame their fickle nature to sutch firmenes, the best way is, by litle and litle to estraunge them selves from their freindes, to pretend some ernest or honest cause, to professe that never any other shall possesse that place with them, to promise that in hart they wilbe theirs during life.
>
> (p. 247)

Pettie's implication is that women cannot afford to be open and straightforward. It is too much of a risk. They are urged to hedge, to conceal, to compromise.

The story of *Alexius*,[47] which follows *Pygmalion*, appears to posit the other side of the formal debate over women. Alexius overcomes his reluctance to marry, and presents his new wife with a written praise of women. It is highly rhetorical, opening with a long and fulsome encomium of his wife in particular, and then widening to include all women. In a radical tone, Alexius comes to matters of commonwealth administration. Why are women not admitted to it?

> For sooth the malicious spite of men: and I may saye it to my self, it standeth us upon so to do, for if they should be allowed to execute publike offices, whereby their discreet and good government might be generally known, it were greatly to bee feared that wee should be set to the clout and kitchin another while, and they placed in those offices, whiche wee now, not so worthy of them, wrongfully usurpe.
>
> (p. 265)

This is the most thoroughgoing passage of feminist polemic in the whole of the *Petite Pallace*; a welcome, if unenduring, recognition of women's capabilities.

Although Pettie attempts to qualify this praise – 'to speake my fancie freely of the praise which hee hath geven you, . . . his general reasons are altogether sophisticall and full of fallacies' (p. 268) – it remains the most positive view of women in the whole of his work. Against this, we have to place Alexius' complete rejection of women. For he grows tired of his wife, his lust turns to loathsomeness, and he resolves to leave her:

> . . . shall I wilfuly woorke mine owne destruction? Shal I greedely
> devoure the bait, whiche I knowe hath a hooke hidden in it to hurt
> mee? . . . shal I preferre a faire wife before a vertuous life? my
> goddesse before my God? transitory pleasure, beefore eternall
> blisse? . . . first let mee lay up for my self treasure in heaven, and
> then shall I injoy true pleasure in earth.
>
> (pp. 269–70)

The religious veneer of this attempts to conceal its distastefulness; the idea of everything 'for myself' is unashamedly egotistic, and selfishness, under the guise of religion, makes a world of greedy pseudomartyrs. A life dedicated to God might be a noble gesture, but the context in which Alexius makes it, satiated with sex and bored with his wife, renders it suspicious. But this is Pettie's moment of triumph; here his argument appears irrefutable, for within the Christian framework nothing can be compared with Eternity. No matter how good the love of a good woman, Heaven must always be preferable. Alexius' praise of women is radically undermined.

Pettie concludes by admonishing men that they may learn by this to treat women as necessary evils and that, should they be called to follow God, they should leave their wives and wealth. This is in keeping with Pettie's scarcely concealed misogyny which has become typical in his concluding addresses to the reader. But then he turns to the women, and tells them they may learn not to put any permanent pleasure in 'practising with' their husbands, but to use their company only as:

> . . . a solace, to sweeten the sowernesse of this life withal, and to
> thinke that sutch supersticious love towards your husbands, doth
> withdraw you from the true love which you ought to beare towards
> god.
>
> (p. 271)

This sounds uncharacteristically sombre; he realizes he has become preacher-like, and resolves to be more pleasant:

I wil leave this text to maister parson, who while he is unmaried I warrant you will disswade you so earnestly from sutch idolatrous doting on your husbands, that hee will not sticke to tell you beesides that you ought to have no respect of persons, but to love another man or him selfe so well as your husbandes.

(p. 271)

The tone of these final lines has become ironic again. If the Parson will dissuade women from doting on their husbands only while he is unmarried, apparently we are to understand that this is because when he is married himself he will like to be doted upon, but simultaneously the alternative reading (that he can take sexual advantage of women who are not devoted to their husbands) is available. He will preach a Christian lesson, that everyone should love each other, but after Pettie's suggestion of the Parson's lust, the advice that women should 'love an other man or him selfe' so well as their husbands becomes personal and sexual: the Parson wishes to share the woman's body too. This irony undercuts the sombreness of the earlier passage, and reminds us that Pettie is always an unreliable narrator; our terms of reference are always shifting, his tone is constantly altering.

Alexius, then, is Pettie's stooge: his praise of women is shown to belong to a period of illusion, it is set up to be knocked down. Pettie had seemed here to offer women so much, but his greatest gesture to women is undercut by its position: Pettie appears to mean not a word of it. Significantly, in this final story, woman is written out. Alexius' wife is nameless, mute and, ultimately, with all other women, rejected.

If, in *Alexius*, Pettie's most committed and complete encomium of women is demonstrated to be just another pose, radically undermined by the story's conclusion, then Pettie's apparently benevolent attitude towards women in other parts of his text is also called into question. Pettie's benign and sympathetic stance towards his fictional heroines and towards his 'gentle gentlewomen readers' is a posture, a role, and one which paradoxically allows him to attempt to be even more oppressive; for his assumed familiarity with his readers permits him a greater licence to harass us within his text.

But Pettie's work can also be read more subversively, as perhaps his contemporary women readers discovered. For Pettie's attempts to close off the radical implications of his own text are never wholly successful. His female characters, whose roles he has developed and expanded, often defy his urge to contain or confine them. Nearly all the tales revolve around independent women who are able to influence the world around them; their thoughts and feelings are taken seriously, and their actions accorded significance.

Reading as women readers today, we can be alerted not only to Pettie's potentially oppressive narrative strategies, but also to a recognition of the strong and powerful women whom he portrays almost despite himself; and indeed, they continue to dominate his tales despite the fact that, at the very last moment, Pettie withdraws from the consequences of his own discourse and, at the expense of narrative consistency and the work's own internal logic, imposes a repressive closure on the text.

4

Robert Greene: the heroine as mirror

When Thomas Nashe referred to his friend Robert Greene as 'the Homer of Women', he may have had in mind both Greene's prodigious literary output and his peculiar appeal to women readers.[1] The most prolific writer of his time, he produced 23 works of fiction, of which 15 were published between 1580 and 1590.[2] His popularity was enormous, and his name in everyone's mouth, as he acknowledges:

> I became an Author of Playes, and a penner of love Pamphlets, so that I soone grew famous in that qualitie, that who for that trade growne so ordinary about London as Robin Greene.[3]

The attraction of Greene's works for women readers was widely recognized by his contemporaries. A Chambermaid, in Overbury's *Characters*, is epitomized thus: 'She reads Greene's works over and over',[4] and Nashe probably alluded to Greene again in his criticism of the way some authors flatter their women readers:

> Many of them to be more amiable with their friends of the feminine sexe, blot many sheetes of paper in the blazing of Womens slender praises, as though in that generation there raigned and alwaies remained such singulier simplicitie, that all posterities should be enjoyned by duetie, to fill and furnish theyr Temples, nay Townes and Streetes, with the Shrines of the Saints.[5]

In a reference to Greene's work by Ben Jonson, there is a further suggestion not only of Greene's productivity, but of his particular popularity with women. Fastidious Brisk, coxcomb and gallant, boasts of the elegance of his mistress' language:

Oh it flows from her like nectar, . . . she does observe as pure a
phrase, and use as choice figures in her ordinary conferences, as any
be in the Arcadia.

to be taunted thus by Carlo's rebuff:

Or rather from Greene's work, whence she may steal with more
security,[6]

with the implication that Greene wrote so much that her plagiarism will
not be noticed, and that Greene himself 'borrowed' widely.

Louis B. Wright cites a moving tribute to 'the dead laureate of women'
in R.B.'s *Greenes Funeralls*:

He is dead, that wrote of your delights:
that wrote of Ladies, and of Parramours:
Of budding beautie, and hir branched leaves,
Of sweet content in royal Nuptials.
He is dead, that kild you with disdaine:
And often fed your friendly hopes again.[7]

The concluding couplet suggests what was in fact an ambiguous
relationship between Greene and his female readership; it oscillated
between flattery and contempt, often in the space of a few lines. The
uneasy embarrassment which this has caused some of his more
'chivalrous' critics is well illustrated in the tone of Storojenko's
apologetic aside, in his *Life of Robert Greene*:

We are ignorant of the causes that could have influenced Greene to
change his front so suddenly, and to send the shafts of his wit
against the very sex which he had always so highly lauded.[8]

However, in what is still the most comprehensive study of Greene, René
Pruvost persuades us not to take this ambivalence too seriously for, he
argues, Greene constantly altered the guise under which he presented
himself to his readers.[9] Indeed, Pruvost is inclined to overlook Greene's
misogyny completely, in favour of his portrayal of fresh, strong,
independent female characters:

La plus grande originalité des jeunes filles de Greene leur vient
d'ailleurs du caractère naïf et spontané de l'honnêteté qu'elles
savent allier à la vivacité de leur ésprit et à l'indépendance de leur
allure ... Greene ... a surtout mis en scène des jeunes filles
parfaitement maîtresses d'elles-mêmes et surtout étrangères à tout
calcul et à toute reticence.[10]

Others have noticed the strength of Greene's characterization of
women. John Clark Jordan claims that 'Whether in novel or in play,
when Greene had a theme centering around a heroine rather than

around a hero, he was at his best',[11] while Storojenko speculates about Greene's readership, surmising that 'women in general were charmed by the exalted opinions of female perfection' which they found in his works, although apparently 'ladies of fashion and professional beauties admired them for the exquisite mannerism of their style'.[12]

But it is Samuel Lee Wolff who, in a passage designed to absolve Greene from the charge of misogyny, almost unwittingly realizes the essence of Greene's treatment of female characters, when he describes their often masochistic loyalty to their menfolk: 'Most of Greene's female characters suffer and are true',[13] he writes, and earlier draws attention to 'Greene's predilection for a suffering heroine'.[14] It is more complex than that, however: Greene's heroines become martyrs, in fact, to his ideal of perfect womanhood.

Despite these passing recognitions of the strong female characters in Greene's works, and the importance of a female readership, no critical study has posited this as a basic premise. Many of the earlier studies were deflected by the attractions of Greene's colourful personality, and devote more energy to hypothesizing over his life history than to evaluating the works which he left. Storojenko has a whole theory based on the completely unknown personality of Greene's wife;[15] lack of evidence is enough to sadden him, but not to suppress his vivid imagination. A more recent work concludes that Greene's place in literature is finally secure 'through the personality of the man himself':[16]

> About the idea of him in his green cloak, his hair a little over-long, his reddish, pointed beard 'whereat you might hang a jewel' – perhaps a slightly fantastic figure if we judge him closely – about this picture, we gather the characteristics which Greene had, and we endeavour to recreate him in our mind's eye.[17]

For just enough is known about Greene's brief life (c. 1558–92) to stimulate the imagination, fuelled as it is by tantalizing glimpses of the man from Nashe, to whom we are indebted for a vivid picture of Greene at work:

> In a night & a day would he have yarkt up a Pamphlet as well as in seaven yeare, and glad was that Printer that might bee so blest to pay him deare for the very dregs of his wit.[18]

When they are not hypothesizing about 'the man himself', nearly all critical works on Greene have focused on his sources, influences or contribution to the development of the novel. Wolff's massive and painstaking study charts the precise influence on Elizabethan prose fiction of Heliodorus' Æthiopica, Longus' Daphnis and Chloe, and Achilles Tatius' Clitophon and Leucippe,[19] while Jordan traces further influences from Sidney, Lyly, translations of Italian novelle, and from the conduct

books of Castiglione, Guevara, Elyot and Ascham.[20] None of these
critical approaches treat Greene's texts on their own terms, however, and
I shall suggest that it is only through approaching them as a woman
reader that their complexity and sophistication can be appreciated.

Greene confronts the woman reader with a gallery of paragons of
feminine virtue and insists that she live up to them, that she subordinate
herself in all things, that, if necessary, she become a patient Griselda, like
his Barmenissa of *Penelope's Web*.[21] His female characters are usually
strong, resolute women, often independent and resourceful, but these
qualities are exercised to effect women's own subordination. Mamillia,
Publia, Susanna, Philomela, Cratyna, Barmenissa, Fawnia, Bellaria,
Isabel: all these willingly accept the most brutal cruelty on the part of
their lovers, husbands or fathers – and indeed from Greene who
contrives this – and they are praised for their submission. The implied
reader is encouraged to emulate these impossible, self-abnegating roles;
Greene's manipulation of the mirror-metaphor, his asides and implications, generate in the woman reader a sense of dissatisfaction for failing
to achieve such heights of self-sacrifice herself.

Greene's 'predilection for suffering heroines', then, is deeply disturbing: by making his heroines, his models, those who accept suffering,
indeed often seek and embrace it, he limits the positive implications of
these women. His characters are turned into ciphers of virtue, constantly
watching themselves, and being watched by others. As readers, we too
are encouraged to watch and judge them, measuring the discrepancy
between their action and our own. The metaphor of the mirror becomes
the means by which Greene effects this 'splitting' of the female character,
self-watching and watched; by referring not only to the book but to the
heroine herself as a mirror, he sets in motion a complex process of self-
evaluation and judgement for fictional character and reader alike.

Herbert Grabes' work on mirror-imagery provides a comprehensive
history of the use of the metaphor in titles and texts of the Middle Ages
and Renaissance, revealing that in the second half of the sixteenth
century the number of mirror-titles rapidly increased.[22] The study's
breadth of scope, however, precludes it from grasping the complexities
and ambiguities which the mirrors frequently generate. Grabes cites two
works by Greene, *Mamillia* and *The Myrrour of Modestie*, and classifies
them as writings 'in a heroic and eulogistic vein'.[23] While this suggests
the nature of Greene's works as exempla, it fails to account for the
peculiar and oppressive process involved in making the heroine herself a
mirror.[24] John Berger's theories of visual perception are more helpful; he
suggests that, within patriarchal society, woman is encouraged always to
watch herself, and is almost continually accompanied by her own image:

And so she comes to consider the surveyor and the surveyed within

her as the two constituent yet always distinct elements of her
identity as a woman.

She has to survey everything she is and everything she does
because how she appears to others, and ultimately how she appears
to men, is of crucial importance, for what is normally thought of as
the success of her life.

. . . Women watch themselves being looked at. This determines
not only most relations between men and women *but also the relation
of women to themselves.* The surveyor of woman in herself is male: the
surveyed female. Thus she turns herself into an object [my
emphasis].[25]

Greene creates a series of multiple projections; when he holds up the
mirror of his virtuous heroine for his female readers to look into, they
see a 'perfected' image of womanhood which, in its complete self-
sacrifice and martyrdom, they themselves are unable to attain. The
heroine is conscious of her role as mirror, as exemplum; she watches
herself being watched, and moulds herself completely into that object
role. It is ultimately prescriptive, oppressive and dehumanizing. When
Greene's male readers look into the mirror they see, in a fashion almost
voyeuristic, images of suffering and beautiful women; their response is
likely to be a more disinterested one than women's, for these figures are
not being offered as models for men; the prospect of male power
exercised over women might tend also to be gratifying.

Greene's heroines sometimes recognize their dilemma. In *Perimedes*,
Melissa explains to her suitor the constrictions such a role imposes:

For Ladyes honors are like white lawnes, which soone are stayned
with everye mole: men in their loves have liberties, that soare they
never so high nor stoope they never so lowe, yet their choice is little
noted: but women are more glorious objects, and therefore have all
mens eyes attentivelye bent upon them.[26]

In turning now to a closer analysis of individual romances, I shall focus
on five in particular: *Mamillia*, Parts One and Two (*Works*, vol. 2),
Penelope's Web (*Works*, vol. 5), *The Myrrour of Modestie* (*Works*, vol. 3), and
Philomela (*Works*, vol. 11). These are the works which seem most
particularly directed to women readers, and in which Greene's narrative
strategies can be most clearly detected and exposed.

That Greene deliberately shaped his first work *Mamillia* for women can
be seen by a comparison with the work it most closely imitates, the first
part of Lyly's *Euphues*.[27] Greene's romance opens with Mamillia having
just returned to her father's house in Padua, following a letter from her
friend Florion, advising her departure from the vicious Venetian court.
In Padua, Pharicles falls in love with her and wins her affection, then

meets Mamillia's cousin Publia, woos, and wins her too. Thus engaged
to both women, fearing the outcome of such inconstancy, he travels to
Sicily. The women remain faithful in his absence; in the Second Part,
Publia enters a convent and there dies, leaving all her goods to Pharicles;
Mamillia saves Pharicles from death in Sicily, and marries him. In his
study of Greene, Jordan draws attention to the similarities between
Mamillia and *Euphues*, and while he discovers that 'the fundamental
theme of infidelity is the same with the sexes reversed',[28] he fails to
develop the proposition further, in relation to Greene's female readership. For it is clear that Greene intends to praise women's constancy,
where Lyly denigrates their fickleness, that Greene's focus is on his
female characters, where Lyly's is on Euphues and Philautus. In *Euphues*
there are two faithful male characters, one faithless female; in *Mamillia*
women are stronger, more virtuous, and more prominent, and there are
two faithful female characters, and one faithless male. Further parallels
have been noted.[29] Corresponding to Euphues' departure from Athens,
we have Mamillia's departure from the court to Padua; Euphues returns
home to gain worldly experience, Mamillia to avoid the temptations of
such experience; on arrival in Naples, Euphues haughtily rejects the
advice he is offered, Mamillia accepts advice given to her, and tries to
follow it; Philautus introduces Euphues to Lucilla as Mamillia introduces
Pharicles to Publia; as Euphues retires to Silexdra, so Publia enters a
convent; and corresponding to Euphues' letters are the letters of
Mamillia to Lady Modesta.

Pruvost's comment in 1938 has met with little opposition:

> Imitateur de Lyly dans son premier roman, Greene introduit
> pourtant dans celui-ci une peinture idealisée de la femme, et des
> aventures romanesques, dont son aîné ne lui offrait guère le
> modèle.[30]

But this is not the whole truth. A close reading of *Mamillia* shows it to be
far more than a reversal of *Euphues*, and more complicated than a
straightforward encomium of women.

Significantly, its subtitle reads:

> A Mirrour or looking-glasse for the ladies of Englande. Wherein is
> deciphered, howe gentlemen, under the perfect substaunce of pure
> love, are oft inveigled with the shadowe of lewde lust: and their
> firme faith, brought asleepe by fading fancie: until wit joyned with
> wisdom, doth awake it by the helpe of reason.
>
> (*Mamillia*, p. 3)

The suggestion is that the book is a mirror for women to see reflected the
lust and inconstancy of men. However, when the metaphor is used again,

in a passage of self-examination by Mamillia, its implication slides, to
refer to Mamillia herself as a mirror:

> Shal they, who deemed thee a mirrour of modestie, count thee a
> patterne of lightnes? shal thy staied life be now compared to the
> Camaeleon that turneth himselfe into the liknes of every object?
>
> (*Mamillia*, p. 24)

Her first reaction to feeling affection is to worry about what other people
will think of her, how they will see and judge her. Her recognition of her
role as exemplum has begun.

Greene's narrator sets himself up as a friend to women, warning them
of men's designs on them which are covered with a cloak of flattery. But
we cannot forget that the narrator is himself a man, and one who flatters
women. Our suspicions of his trustworthiness are aroused in the first few
pages of the book when we are informed that Florion has been deceived
by the 'lightnesse' of one Lumina, and knew well that:

> there was little constancy in such kites of Cressids kind, whose
> minds were as foule within, as their faces faire without: . . . yea hee
> had beene so deepelye drenched in the waves of womens wyles,
> that every sodayne sight was a sea of suspition, as he made a vowe in
> the way of mariage to abandon the company of women for ever,
> and to a solemne oath, since he had wonne againe the fieldes of his
> freedome, never by the leawdnes of love to enter into bondage.
>
> (*Mamillia*, pp. 16–17)

But the narrator hastens to add that Florion avoids complete misogyny:

> Yet he would not altogether (although hee had cause with
> Euripides to proclaime himself open enemie to womankind) seeme
> so absurd a Sophister, to inferre a general conclusion of a particular
> proposition, nor be counted so injurious, to condemne al of
> lightnesse, for ones leawdnes, . . .
>
> (*Mamillia*, p. 17)

The apparent reasonableness of these last lines confuses/diffuses the
sense of frustration which the first part generated, and we might be
tempted to dismiss it. A closer reading, however, reveals that Florion is
guilty of precisely the misogyny from which the narrator attempts at
such length to absolve him; in his decision to avoid women, he
manifestly *is* inferring 'a general conclusion of a particular proposition',
and with the narrator's approval, for did he not have 'cause with
Euripides' to be an enemy to all women? With such an unreliable
narrator, we feel radically insecure.

This unreliability is further demonstrated in a passage where the

narrator is apparently criticizing Italian gentlemen for being so blinded
by self-love that they cannot make a wise choice among women:

> for if she be faire, they thinke her faithfull: if her bodye be endued
> with bewtie, they judge she cannot but be vertuous. They are so
> blinded with the visor of Venus and conceite of Cupid, as they
> think all birdes with white fethers to be simple Doves: every
> seemely Sappho, to be a civill Salona: every Lais to bee a loyall
> Lucreece: every chatting mayden to be a chaste matrone.
>
> (*Mamillia*, p. 35)

As the passage progresses, it becomes increasingly clear that Greene's
narrator only appears to be on the side of women. He is certainly
condemning men – but their fault is to have failed to recognize that
women are not as virtuous as they might appear. The 'joke', in fact, is
against women.

Mamillia's position can be seen as hedged about with threats. When
she considers a single life, her nurse conjures up the terrible vision of the
'unseemely' form of 'an old wrinkled maid', apparently the logical
conclusion for life as an unmarried woman (*Mamillia*, p. 42). For the
nurse, under orders from Mamillia's father, must urge her to marry,
while Florion exhorts her to choose the right mate, for many are not
what they appear to be: lust abounds. It is a treacherous arena for
women, encompassed by dangers, poised between the two poles of
ruined maiden and old maid. At the same time, her primary concern
must be her reputation, her role as mirror.

The ambiguity of Greene's relationship with his women readers is
confirmed in the following passage of unmitigated and unprovoked
misogyny on the part of the narrator when he intervenes in the narrative
to commend Pharicles' view of marriage. In fact, Pharicles claims only
that those who marry in haste often repent at leisure. Greene the narrator
goes further with an aside to male readers:

> And surely Gentlemen . . . there is no such hinderaunce to a man,
> as a wife . . . for she is that burden that Christ onely refused to take
> from mans shoulders: yea some have called a wife, a heavy Crosse,
> as a mery jesting Gentleman of Venice did: who hearing the
> preacher command every man to take up his Crosse, and follow
> him, hastily took his wife on his shoulders, & said he was ready with
> the formost.
>
> (*Mamillia*, p. 54)

Thus in this 'mirror for the ladies', we as women readers are supposed to
identify against ourselves, to find ourselves in accord with the 'mery
jesting Gentleman'. It is a particularly unpleasant passage, mutually
reductive for both Biblical reference, and for women.

Greene will not let us alone; he is a chameleon, changing colours and loyalties when it suits him. In a further aside to gentlemen readers, he adopts again the role of women's defender, apparently reproving men – whom he characterizes as fickle and lukewarm in love – for writing against women:

> . . . where doe we see any writing of love, or of any such matter, but they must have one fling at women? dispraysing their nature, disciphering their nurture, painting out their polliticke practises and subtil shiftes, declaring their mutabilitie, comparing them to the Polipe stone, that chaungeth colours every houre; to the Weathercock, that wavereth with the wind; to the Marigolde, whose forme is never permanent, but chaungeth with the Sunne: and yet they themselves a great deale worse.
>
> (*Mamillia*, pp. 76–7)

In the light of our understanding of Greene, this passage must be heavily ironic, for who better than he at having 'flings' at women? And here, when he is apparently arguing in favour of women, the length and layers of his similes, the enthusiastic alliteration and vigorous tone, tend to weight his argument in the opposite direction. Examples against women are heaped up one on top of another, against which Greene balances with only a few words: 'and yet they themselves a great deale worse'. The final impression of the passage is that, contrary to his avowed intention, he is writing against women. Either he is losing control of his material, or trying to pull off a double bluff; the quantity and tone of his diatribes against women lead one to suppose the latter.

Part Two is more clearly set up as a defence of women, as its full title suggests: 'Wherein with perpetual fame the constancie of Gentlewomen is canonised, and the unjust blasphemies of women's supposed fickle-nesse (breathed out by diverse injurious persons) by manifest examples clearly infringed' (*Mamillia*, p. 139). Its superlative language might arouse doubt as to its sincerity, however. Richard Stapleton, in his prefatory poem, advertises that this is a work that women should read. He calls upon the 'curteous and courtly ladies of England' to:

> come heare your passing fame
> Displaide abroad with golden trumpe

and to witness the praise of their virtues of faith, constancy and loyalty (*Mamillia*, pp. 146–7). And the story does indeed celebrate women's constancy. Publia remains loyal to Pharicles until her death, and Mamillia forgives his fickleness; learning of his imprisonment, she goes to his rescue in Saragossa, and eloquently pleads his innocence. Greene's narrator draws attention to her virtue thus:

Where I cannot passe over without some speech, gentlewomen, of the incomparable constancie of Mamillia, which was so surelie defenced with the rampier of vertue, as all the fierce assaults of fortune could no whit prevaile as prejudiciall to such professed amitie.

(*Mamillia*, p. 162)

Virtuous women must still act as mirrors, however, and her father, in his dying words, reminds her that the most important thing in her life is her good name (*Mamillia*, p. 29).

At the end of the work, she takes on a new and surprising freedom; she suddenly becomes much more active in influencing her own destiny. Resolving to obey her father only so far as the law of Nature commands, and to keep truth with her love, she furnishes a ship and arrives disguised in Saragossa the day before Pharicles is to be executed. She obtains a copy of the letters which passed between Pharicles and Clarynda, the courtesan who falsely betrayed him, and finally intervenes in his trial with a competence foreshadowing that of Shakespeare's Portia, explaining the truth and revealing the letters.[31] The work ends triumphantly with their marriage. Mamillia has proved to be independent, resourceful and successful. It is she who has dominated the romance; her actions have been accorded great importance, and her faithfulness is rewarded. Her final power and freedom would no doubt have been as attractive to Greene's contemporary female readership as they are to women readers today.

At the end of Part Two there is appended 'The Anatomy of Lovers Flatteries', letters between Mamillia and the Lady Modesta, corresponding to those at the end of *Euphues*. Instead of a man's writing, however, it is a woman's words and woman's authority which are being inscribed. And yet it is more complicated than this, for Greene has obviously contrived this situation, and the difference this makes to a woman's response is hard to calculate precisely. We no longer trust Greene as a narrator, and feel correspondingly uneasy. But it is here that Mamillia is made to come closest to a feminist statement.[32] She recognizes that women's legitimate voice has been silenced, usurped by a male voice speaking for us (but can we forget that Greene is writing this too?). She condemns Ovid as 'lascivious', a 'foe to womankind' who in *De Arte Amandi* prescribes:

a most monstrous Method to all men, whereby they may learne to allure single women to the fulfilling of their lust, and the loosing of their owne honor . . .. Yea Juvenall, Tibullus, Propertius, Callimachus, Phileta, Anacreon, and many other authors have set downe

caveats for men, or armours of proofe to defende themselves from
the alluring subtilties of women.

(Mamillia, pp. 254–5)

She deplores the fact that none before her have left any guide to protect
women from men's flatteries. Her recognition of the oppressiveness of a
male tradition of authority recalls the Wife of Bath, who similarly
struggles under the weight of men's writing against women:

> By God! if wommen hadde writen stories,
> As clerkes han withinne hire oratories,
> They wolde han writen of men moure wikkednesse
> Then all the mark of Adam may redresse.[33]

Mamillia proceeds to identify the sort of men to avoid, including
flatterers, hypocrites and lechers. This reaches a climax in a demystifica-
tion of the implications of marriage for women, in which she claims it is
folly for a woman willingly to marry, to become a 'perpetual slave to
another man' if she has the choice *(Mamillia*, p. 262). Her plea is a moving
and liberating one, and in answer to a final question over whether or not
to accept advice in choosing a husband, she answers categorically: 'to live
we must follow the advice of our friends, but to love, our own fancie'
(Mamillia, p. 267).

It is in *The Myrrour of Modestie* that Greene's mirror metaphor reaches
its fullest expression. The subtitle suggests this exemplary focus:
'wherein appeareth as in a perfect Glasse howe the Lorde delivereth the
innocent from all imminent perils, and plagueth the bloud thirstie
hypocrites with deserved punishments. Shewing that the graie heades of
dooting adulterers shall not go with peace unto the grave, neither shall
the righteous be forsaken in the daie of trouble' *(Myrrour*, p. 3). It is the
story of Susanna and the Elders, expanded from the Apocrypha,
supposedly at the request of Lady Margaret, Countess of Derby, to
whom it is dedicated. Greene makes explicit the story's moral intention,
'to profit all by Susanna's chastitle' *(Myrrour*, p. 7). [He makes clear the
connection between 'modesty' and 'chastity' when he later calls the work
'this Mirrour of Chastitie' *(Myrrour*, p. 8); for him the terms are
interchangeable.] In the course of the work, Susanna herself becomes the
mirror in which women can see chastity assailed, and finally triumphant.
Critics have traditionally found little of significance in the story, and
Storojenko's comment is typical: the work 'does not afford any interest,
either from a biographical or a literary point of view'.[34] But he adds:

> It is impossible to read without a smile the long tirades which the
> old men exchange with Susanna, on penetrating her bathing-
> house, where she is discovered robed in the classical costume of the
> Venus de Medici.[35]

I would argue that for a woman reader it is very hard to smile, for the image in the mirror reflects the male threatening of a vulnerable woman. Storojenko's pedantic language, furthermore, hints at his own voyeuristic impulse.

The story tells of how the happily married Susanna is about to bathe in the privacy of her garden when she is accosted by two elders, who use their honourable reputations as a screen for their evil intentions. They try to persuade her to have sex with them, but she refuses despite their intimidation, refuting their arguments with passion, logic and religious dignity. Their threats first suggest, by implication, rape, and then finally death:

> . . . Helias counsell did litle prevaile to persuade Ahab from enjoyeng the vineyarde of Naboth, but that he both obtained his desire, and rewarded such an obstinate subject with cruell death. Barsabe could not witholde David both from sacking hir honor and honestie and also from murdering cruelly hir loving husbande Urias: neither shall these painted speeches prevaile against our pretended purpose, for he is a cowarde that yeeldeth at the first shotte, and he is not woorthie to weare the budde of beautie that is daunted with the first deniall: we have the tree in our hande, and meane to enjoye the fruite, we have beaten the bushe, and will not nowe let the birdes escape, and seeing we have you here alone, your stearne lookes shall stande for no sterling, but if you consent be assured of two trustie friends, if not hope for no other hap but death for your deniall.
>
> (Myrrour, pp. 24–5)

The threatening of Susanna is undertaken with relish; for the elders do not in fact attempt rape, although each of the examples so lovingly lingered on above posit the man 'obtaining his desire'. After the words 'hope for no other hap but' we anticipate a reference to the forcing of her chastity, but what they in fact offer is death. An even greater evil than either death or rape, however, is loss of reputation, as the elders are not slow to point out:

> Tis a sayeng not so common as true, that a womans cheefest treasure is hir good name, and that she which hath crackt hir credite is halfe hanged, for death cutteth off all miseries, but infamie is the beginning of all sorrowes.
>
> (Myrrour, p. 25)

Again, woman is observed and judged.

John Berger, commenting on paintings of Renaissance nudes in which the subject is very frequently aware of being watched by the spectator, observes:

> Often – as with the favourite subject of Susannah and the Elders –
> this is the actual theme of the picture. We join the Elders to spy on
> Susannah taking her bath. She looks at us looking at her . . . . In
> another version of the subject by Tintoretto, Susannah is looking at
> herself in a mirror. Thus she joins the spectators of herself.[36]

Berger clearly explains the real function of the mirror in painting: 'it was
to make the woman connive in treating herself as, first and foremost, a
sight'.[37] A literary form of this device is precisely what is produced by
Greene. The mirror-metaphor makes woman into an object to be seen
and judged, not only by others, but also by herself. She is split in two, the
surveyor and the surveyed. It is a complex process. To be fair to Greene,
he does not over-emphasize the voyeuristic element: we do not even
know if Susanna is naked, for there is no reference to her body. He seems
to be more concerned with the power dynamics which the situation
generates, in which a woman's whole identity (and very nearly her body)
are violated by the power and authority invested in men. It is significant
that two men threaten her, not just one – the overpowering and
intimidation are very real. She is put in an intolerable situation: physical
adultery, a sin against God, but which will not be made public, if she
consents; open accusations of adultery, and the accompanying shame for
herself and her family, if she refuses. Greene the narrator appears to
enjoy watching her struggling, like a butterfly caught on a pin, as the
relish of his alliteration suggests:

> . . . seeing that they had so laide the traine that she could no waie
> escape the trappes but either she must incur the daunger of the
> bodie, or the destruction of the soule, was perplexed with such
> doubtfull passions, and cumbered with such carefull thoughts that
> shee burst foorth into trickling teeres, sorrowfull sighs, and wofull
> wailings, which poore soule she blubbred fourth in this wise.
>
> (Myrrour, p. 26)

In fact, her reply is not 'blubbred' at all, but precise, logical and
intelligent.

She is saved from the penalty of the law by the holy spirit in the person
of the child Daniel, but the reaction of her family, praising God, 'seeing
that there was no dishonestie found in hir, but that she was without spot,
and their stock unstained' (Myrrour, pp. 41–2), suggests that they, too,
regard her as a mirror, one in which their own good name is reflected.

The story of Philomela shows what happens when a woman surveys
herself too intently; as Berger indicated, the logical conclusion is for her
to turn herself into an object. In Greene's dedication to Lady Fitzwaters,
Bridgit Ratcliffe, he maintains that it was written 'at the request of a
Countesse in this Land to approve womens chastitie', and he has

dedicated it to her as an appropriate gift for one whose mind 'is wholy
delighted in chast thoughts' (*Philomela*, p. 110):

> so that seeing there hath few led more chaste then an Italian
> Philomela, I thought none only more fitt to patronyse her honors
> than your Ladyship, whose chastety is as far spred as you are eyther
> known or spoke of.
>
> (*Philomela*, p. 111)

We begin to have the impression of being in a hall of mirrors; Greene's
Philomela not only mirrors in her chastity the original Philomela of
Ovid's tale, but also reflects Lady Fitzwaters' own chastity.[38]

Ovid's version of the *Philomela* story, which Elizabethans would have
known through Golding's translation, is one of rape and violence, and
our awareness of this informs our expectations of Greene's narrative. It
describes a woman's response to her husband's 'rape upon reality', as
Walter Davis terms it.[39] Against all evidence to the contrary, Philippo
convinces himself of his wife's infidelity. Obsessed by the idea, he forces
his own image on to reality, and when his trials of her chastity prove her
faithfulness, he suborns two slaves to swear they saw her in an act of
adultery. She is thus divorced and cast out. When the truth becomes
known, Philippo is banished in his turn. In a dramatic denouement,
Philomela selflessly saves him from death, and while she is honoured as a
paragon of constant chastity, he kills himself 'in an extasie' (*Philomela*, p.
203).

From the first, Philomela is presented as a paragon, and 'Italie held hir
life as an instance of all commendable qualities' (*Philomela*, p. 116), in
particular chastity, silence and modesty. Indeed,

> . . . she never would goe abroad but in the company of hir husband,
> and then with such bashfulnesse, that she seemed to hold hir selfe
> faultie in stepping beyond the shadow of hir owne mansion: thus
> was Philomela famous for hir exquisite vertues . . . .
>
> (*Philomela*, p. 116)

But what Greene sees as virtue we might justly term symptoms of a
pathological neurosis; it is no surprise that she is afraid to go out when
she has so much to live up to. Her virtue remains flawless; in the face of
her husband's cruelty, she resolves to win him back to her through
'obedience, love, and silence' (*Philomela*, p. 122). Lutesio, under
instructions from Philippo to attempt Philomela's chastity, is firmly
refused with an explanation of her values: 'A woman's honestie is her
honour, and her honour the chiefest essence of her life' (*Philomela*, p.
130), she insists, for:

> A Ladie Lutesio that regardeth her honour will die with Lucrece
> before she agree to lust, she will eate coales with Portia before she

prove unchast, she will think everie miserie sweet, every mishappe
content, before she condiscend to the allurementes of any wanton
leacher.

(Philomela, p. 132)

A woman's celebration of the constrictions of patriarchal values reveals
the extent to which she has imbibed them, with their resulting fatal
distortions.

Simon Shepherd's exploration of Lucrece's suicide offers a further
dimension to the process in which Philomela is involved:

The dignified suicide must be deliberate, and so, too, martyrdom
need not be simply passive. Lucrece has to make herself into a
martyr, she has to link her sexual 'death' with physical death . . . *she
herself has to make her chastity a cause worth dying for* [my emphasis].[40]

The exalted vision of chastity which patriarchy enshrines, and Philomela's
embrace of it, and absolute self-dedication to it, function to transform
her into an Idea of Chastity. The consequent distortion of values and
dehumanization are apparent in the reasons Philomela adduces against
telling Philippo about Lutesio's advances:

Least if hee should kill Lutesio she might be thought the occasion
of the murther, *and so bring hir unblemisht honour in question* [my
emphasis].

(Philomela, p. 145)

Not a moment is spared for a thought of her friend Lutesio's death; her
honour, her reputation, her role as chaste exemplum are more important
than his life.

After the false accusation, she cannot bear to remain in the same
country 'sith her honour so famous through Italy, was now so highly
staind' (*Philomela*, p. 171), so she and her page secretly hire a passage on a
ship to Sicily. She disguises herself, and takes the name Abstemia. Once
again the focus is immediately on her chastity, for the ship's master,
Tebaldo, lusts for her: he resolves to keep her as his paramour if she will
consent, or to force her by rape if she will not. His purpose is prevented
by his overhearing her laments. Her mind, meanwhile, revolves only on
her reputation; her dishonour becomes more than an individual plight,
and grows to universal significance:

Once Abstemia thou wert counted the fairest in Italy and now thou
art holden the falsest: thy vertues were thought many, now thy
dishonors are counted numberles: thou wert the glory of thy
parents, the hope of thy friends, the fame of thy country, the
wonder of thy time of modestie, the peragon of Italy for honorable
grace, & the patern wherby women did measure their perfections.

(Philomela, p. 175)

Women in the process of looking at themselves through men's eyes must logically compare themselves with other women.

   Her awareness of her sexual vulnerability (all the more pronounced for the reader, for we know Tebaldo is listening outside her door, contemplating rape) is suggested in her anticipation of sexual violence. She lives in constant fear of rape (we think of Ovid's Philomela), and has accordingly equipped herself with a poison in the seal of her ring. Significantly, however, it is not for her assailant, but for herself:

> So, before any leacher shall force to satisfie his passion, I will end my life with this fatall poison. So Abstemia shalt thou die more honorablie, which is more deere than to live disgraced.
>
> (*Philomela*, p. 177)

Her dedication to her role as exemplum, and identification with it, makes death preferable to 'dishonourable' sex, even though as an unwilling victim of rape, the guilt should not be hers. But in the ode she sings subsequently, she suggests a view of women's guilty collusion in rape:

> Jove could not hide Ios scape
> Nor conceale Calistos rape.
> Both did fault, and both were famed,
> Light of loves whome lust had shamed.
>
> (*Philomela*, p. 178)

By implication, then, women are at fault for being raped. That Greene can give such words to a woman with approbation is profoundly disturbing, suggesting both his own moral confusion and a deep misogyny. When Tebaldo recognizes her virtue, his immediate transformation from desire to reverence, from affection to honest devotion, implies that if all women were sufficiently virtuous they would not be raped, clearly a ludicrous proposition.[41] Ovid's story functions as a counterpoint to Greene's; the tension generated between them leads to a fuller understanding of Greene's narrative strategies. The original Philomela stands raped and disfigured, a mute emblem of ravished innocence. What Greene does to *his* Philomela is unforgivable, for he has her connive in man's guilt. He takes away from her the legitimacy of a response; he writes out her anger and revenge; he makes her as dumb as did Tereus.

   When Philomela learns that her name has been cleared, and that her husband lies in prison awaiting death (having admitted to a murder he did not commit, so weary of life has he become), at first she rejoices in what she sees as God's justice:

> . . . now maiest thou triumph in the fall of thy Jealiouse husband,

and write thy chastitie in the characters of his bloode, so shall he die
disgraced, and thou returne to Venice as a wonder.

(*Philomela*, p. 197)

But Greene has her change her mind about triumphing in Philippo's
death; her role as exemplum cannot allow it. He thus takes away
woman's response while simultaneously rendering her a more acceptable mirror for other women. By taming the story, he diffuses the threat
of woman's legitimate anger. For at this politic moment, he has her
reiterate the duty of wives, in order to atone for her momentary
forgetfulness:

Knowest thou not that the love of a wife must not end, but by
death: that the tearme of marriage is dated in the grave, that wyves
should so long love and obey, as they live and drawe breath: that
they should preferre their husbands honor before their owne life,
and choose rather to die, than see him wronged.

(*Philomela*, pp. 197–8)

The woman reader is thus confronted by a model of absolute and
unconditional self-denial, against which she is invited to measure herself.
Philomela goes on to dismiss the memory of her husband's intense
cruelty to her with the devastatingly casual remark: 'And what of all this
Philomela? hath not everie man his fault?' (*Philomela*, p. 198). Her
motives for forgiving Philippo are dictated by her role. She has to 'show
herself' virtuous, as she has earlier been regarded as honourable, to
'heape coales on his heade' (*Philomela*, p. 198), by showing him favour:

. . . for rather than hee shall die in the sight of Philomela, I wile
justifie him with mine own death, so shall my ende bee honorable,
as my life hath beene wonderfull.

(*Philomela*, p. 199)

She is willing to sacrifice her life to the imperative of having the 'show'
of her life consistent and complete.

Accordingly, she interrupts the trial proceedings and herself claims
responsibility for the murder. The case is resolved and the truth revealed.
While the onlookers rejoice at her 'woondrous vertues', Philippo ends
his life, so moved has he been by his wife's self-sacrifice. But Philomela
'fell into extreame passiones' (*Philomela*, p. 206) on hearing of his death,
and despite an offer of marriage from one Arnaldo Strozzo, she returns
to Venice:

and there lived the desolate widdow of Philippo Medici al her lyfe:
which constant chastety made her so famous, that in her lyfe shee
was honored as the Paragon of vertue and after her death solemnely

and with wonderfull honor intombed in S. Markes Church, and her
fame holden canonized until this day in Venice.

(Philomela, p. 204)

And thus her last scene is played out; she could not have had a better
script. What more convenient than that Philippo should die, leaving her
the moving role of 'desolate widdow'? (It has not been suggested earlier
that his death would render her in the slightest bit 'desolate'; indeed,
only a few pages earlier she was triumphing in the anticipation of his
death.) What more engaging than that she should also have a suitor to
repulse for the sake of her husband's memory? It is a truly exemplary
part, and she plays it to the full. The price she pays for it is high. She
sacrifices herself to the Idea of Chastity, but it is one that has been
imposed on her by patriarchal society and, more specifically, by Greene
himself. And, almost paradoxically, in that very sacrifice, Philomela's life
is given significance. If every single action a wife makes and every
thought she has are magnified into something of great significance – as
we have seen is the case in Philomela's story – then the role of wife
becomes hugely important. As women readers, we are left finally to
celebrate Philomela's virtues and her strength, while abhorring the
abnegating ends to which they are put.

With *Penelope's Web* we are given an insight into a woman's world of
female community, in which a group of women talk with one another
with familiar ease, telling stories and exchanging thoughts. It is an
unusually warm and intimate scene, the tone relaxed, bantering and
friendly. The title suggests where the focus of Greene's interest in this
classical tale lies; Ulysses is still abroad, and the story revolves around the
way Penelope spends her time without him in the company of her old
nurse, colloquial and matronly, and her sprightly, eager, young maids.
Penelope herself is charming, dignified and witty; she is presented as a
model of wifely obedience and fidelity. They are a learned gathering; all
can cite Greek and Roman authorities, with strains of euphuistic
imagery. Over three nights, as Penelope unravels the portion of web
which she has woven during the day,[42] she tells three tales. They are
'instructive', illustrating the three virtues requisite in every woman –
obedience, chastity and silence. The scene has been likened to that of an
Elizabethan sewing circle;[43] but while this effectively suggests the
relaxed and intimate industry they undertake, it does not do justice to the
underlying tensions that a woman's reading reveals.

The mirror-image – familiar by now – first occurs on the title page:

Wherein a Christall Myrror of faeminine perfection represents to
the viewe of everyone those vertues and graces, which more
curiously beautifies the mynd of women, then eyther sumptuous

Apparell, or Jewels of inestimable valew: the one buying fame with
honour, the other breeding a kynd of delight, but with repentance.

(Web, p. 139)

Greene clearly intends to instruct women by the example of Penelope
and the tales she tells, for the syntax suggests that it is Penelope herself
who is to be identified with the crystal mirror. The work is dedicated to
two women, Lady Margaret Countess of Cumberland, and Lady Anne
Countess of Warwick, whom he celebrates as famous for their virtues:

For if trueth be the daughter of tyme ... the report that the
Gretians made of the Princesse of Ithaca, may seeme but a fiction
compared with the fame of your Ladyships vertuous resolutions.

(Web, p. 142)

The woman reader is overwhelmed by models to emulate, and
examples against which to measure herself. For it is clearly a woman's
story, 'womens prattle',[44] as Greene confides to his gentlemen readers, in
a deprecatory tone (*Web*, p. 145). In his epistle 'To the Courteous and
Courtly Ladies of England' he claims a more serious moral purpose: to
have set down the duty of a wife.

At the same time as Penelope instructs her maids, so she instructs the
women readers. But the virtues which the heroines of her three tales
display and which, it is suggested, all women should possess, involve
extreme subordination, and masochistic self-sacrifice. The tales are
prescriptive, reiterating patriarchal values, oppressive in their insistence
on female subservience. In her preface to the first one, Penelope relates
with approval the tale of Aristides, 'the true and perfect Justiciarie of his
time' (*Web*, p. 163), who ordered brides to be shown a portrait of a
woman on her knees so as to remind them of their new role of obedience
and submission to their husbands. It is particularly insidious to have a
woman celebrate her own shackles in this way. She follows this with
another version of the mirror-metaphor:

As a looking glasse or Christall though most curiously set in
Ebonie, serveth to small purpose if it doth not lively represent the
proportion and lineaments of the face, inspicient, so a woman
though rich and beautiful, deserveth smal prayse or favour, if the
course of her life be not directed after her husbands compasse.

(Web, p. 163)

A wife exists not for herself but for her husband, then. Her first tale, a
variation of the Griselda story, bears this out. Barmenissa, obedient wife
of Saladyne, remains patient and forgiving despite being cast out and
replaced by the concubine Olynda, and is finally reinstated. The story has
none of the ambiguity of Chaucer's *Clerk's Tale* in which the narrator's

tone and attitude shift, and from which multiple meanings can be extracted, including one which suggests that women should never be tried so far. Greene's narrator quite clearly expects complete submission from women.

The subject of the second night's discourse is chastity. Penelope quotes the male authorities, all of whom regard it as woman's most important attribute. Euripides, for example, claimed it is the cause of 'such greate glorie and honour amongst women' because:

> it sheweth the feare she oweth to the Gods, the love she beareth to her Husband, the care she hath of fame, the small desire to inordinate affections, and maketh her of a woman, a very patterne of supernaturall perfection.

> (*Web*, p. 200)

To have to attempt to become 'supernaturally perfect' must be impossible, yet this is the standard set for women. The story of *Philomela* has shown the distortion of values which it involves, the way which it prescribes and confines. To further her argument Penelope gives examples of men whose lust has been bridled by woman's chastity, but the unfortunate implication is that if a woman fails to withstand male lust which is forced on her, she herself could never been chaste.

As illustration, she tells of the shifts which the honest Cratyna and her husband Lestio are put to, in order to avoid the lust of the nobleman Calamus. Cratyna refuses all Calamus' bribes and temptations, and reveals wit and resourcefulness in her determination to remain chaste. Margaret Schlauch has found her a particularly attractive character, especially when, disguised as a youth to escape from Calamus, she joins her husband as worker at a coal-pit:

> Greene envisaged his heroine in reduced circumstances as none of his others are shown. She steps forth 'whistling with her cart' and 'having her lether coate all dustie, and her sweete face al besmeared with coales,' thus increasing the effectiveness of her disguise and at the same time placing herself in a category quite apart from arcadian and euphuistic nymphs with their unvarying complexion of lily and rose.[45]

At the end of the story, when Calamus realizes how devoted and chaste a wife she is, he miraculously reforms, thus apparently proving the effective consequences of women's chastity.

Several times in the tale Greene has women explicitly speak against themselves: of Lestio, Penelope remarks, 'when he sawe that womens thoughts are aspyring and gape after preferment . . . he began to frowne' (*Web*, p. 212). Later, in a parenthetical reference to Cratyna's natural desire to reveal her true identity to her husband, we read that 'womens secrets oft hang at the tip of their tungs' (*Web*, p. 214). Most clearly, here, Greene is appropriating women's discourse and attempting to use it to oppress other women.

The last story tells of a king dividing his kingdom according to the virtue of the wives of his three sons; the kingdom is given to the youngest, who is not only obedient and chaste, but also silent.[46]

Chastity, silence and obedience: these are the qualities which Greene enshrines in his heroines. Nor is he alone in this. During the sixteenth century, religion and education everywhere reiterated the importance of these virtues in women. But at least in the romances, with their emphasis on love and personal relationships, women are accorded a significance and a (limited) power seldom granted them in any other area of their lives. In *Mamillia*, *The Myrrour of Modestie*, *Philomela* and *Penelope's Web*, women are dominant; their lives are taken seriously, their thoughts and feelings given importance. Their roles are both validated and glamorized. On many occasions, Greene flatters women but, as it has been pointed out, 'violence lies on the other side of flattery',[47] for both treat women as objects. Greene's treatment of women is violent also; it forces them to sacrifice themselves to his, and his society's, ideal of womanhood. Greene's use of the mirror-metaphor functions to involve the implied reader in the same process. We are encouraged to look into his mirrors, and to compare ourselves with the perfected image reflected. When faced with the discrepancy between Greene's version of womanhood and our own experience, women are encouraged to reconcile the difference in terms of their own deficiency. By demystifying these narrative intentions, however, we can recognize Greene's oppressive strategies, and resist them. We do not have to become the reader he postulates. Instead, we can reclaim the romances as one of the few areas in the sixteenth century in which women's lives were given value and significance, and speculate that Greene's contemporary women readers were drawn to them largely for that reason.

5

Barnaby Rich, reluctant romancer

Alone among the romance writers, Barnaby Rich gives us a very clear testimony as to what it feels like to be a man writing for women; to him, it is effeminate, frivolous, embarrassing, and foolish – but also, regrettably, the only way of winning popular ty and credit in 'the abuse of this present age'.[1] The title of his collection of eight romances, *Riche his Farewell to Militarie Profession* (1581), might alert the reader to his uneasiness about this new 'profession', despite the further elaboration of the dedication which makes clear their particular appeal:

> Gathered together for the onely delight of the courteous Gentle-women, bothe of Englande and Irelande, for whose onely pleasure thei were collected together, And unto whom thei are directed and dedicated.[2]

For Barnaby Rich (1542–1617) was primarily a military man, entering service at 21, serving at first in France and in the Low Countries, and later in Ireland,[3] and continuing in service until he could be justly described, in 1616, as 'the eldest Captain of the Kingdom'.[4] He was also the most prolific military pamphleteer in England during Elizabethan and early Jacobean times, and 5 of the 26 works[5] he composed between 1574 and 1617 were directly connected with army affairs.[6] Indeed, one critic's opinion of these works is high enough for him to suggest that Rich's contributions to military literature are 'historically speaking, every bit as important as Shakespeare's contributions to drama'.[7]

But however reluctantly the *Farewell* might have been written, it was a great success; and while we may feel a little suspicious of Thomas Cranfill's rapturous praise, his work clearly was popular:

Not only were Rich's tales unquestionably best-sellers in his own
day, but they evidently continue to delight scholars, critics, and
even casual readers today [1959], if we may judge from the praise
they still inspire.[8]

Demand for the *Farewell* was strong enough to exhaust the first edition in
2 years, and sufficiently sustained to justify a fourth edition 25 years
later.[9] And Cranfill is not alone in his commendation of it; it has been
heralded by one editor as 'a landmark in Elizabethan short-story
writing',[10] and the author of a history of the short story in English
pronounces it 'one of the pleasantest story-books of the period'.[11]

The sophistication of the work has been largely overlooked, however,
and its female readership ignored. Easily three-quarters of the critical
debate about Rich's works has been devoted to a painstaking hunt for
sources, analogues and influences, with critics divided between feeling
the frustration of a John Lievsay who regards Rich as guilty of nothing
less than 'petty larceny',[12] and who grimly accuses him of being 'beyond
doubt . . . one of the most persistent, most repetitious, and most abject
literary thieves that his age produced',[13] and the approval of a Cranfill
who, in his concern to restore Rich's reputation, makes a virtue out of a
necessity by hailing him as a genius at patching together other people's
writing, and by finding positive skill and proficiency worthy of
commendation in Rich's manipulation of such a 'formidable lot of
sources'.[14]

But if there is a dilemma in analysing a text purporting to be Rich's
own but which, on closer examination, bears a striking (and often
verbatim) resemblance to the work of other writers, there is a still greater
one in relating to the dizzying variety of tones which the narrator uses,
and to the poses which he adopts. In the *Farewell*, Rich immediately
strikes up a relationship with his women readers; he addresses them first
in the title, then in the first preface, and subsequently at many intervals in
the text he appeals to them in terms of confidential intimacy. But the
ambiguity of this posture is apparent from the beginning, as an
examination of the prefatory material demonstrates.

For the *Farewell* is actually introduced by three distinct prefaces: the
first, 'To the right courteous gentlewomen' (p. 3); the second, 'To the
noble Souldiours' (p. 9); and finally a non-gender-specific one, 'To the
Readers in generall' (p. 19). Each fashions a different sort of reader,
suggesting that Rich did not, in fact, anticipate a readership of women
alone.

In his relationship with the gentlewoman reader of the opening
preface, Rich adopts the role of the awkward but honest soldier, blunt
and gauche, incompetent in social affairs, and more at home on a
battlefield than in a boudoir.[15] He starts by anticipating women's

surprise that he has exchanged his loyalty to men and war for a devotion to women and peace, and explains:

> ... I see now it is lesse painfull to followe a fiddle in a gentlewomans chamber: then to marche after a Drumme in the feeld. And more sounde sleapyng under a silken Canapie cloase by a freend, then under a bushe in the open feelde, within a mile of our foe. And nothyng so daungerous to be wounded with the lurying looke of our beloved Mistres: as with the crewell shotte of our hatefull enemie, the one possest of a pitifull harte, to helpe where she hath hurte: the other with a deadly hate, to kill where thei might save.
>
> (pp. 3–4)

But while this appears to flatter women, the reversal of the familiar topos that a mistress's glance is more deadly than the wounds of war in fact ironically serves to deflate the rhetoric of power which traditionally surrounds women in their literary role of beloved mistress, and is more bluntly realistic.

He appears to lament what he sees as his lack of credentials for being welcomed into women's company: he is unable to dance or play musical instruments, he cannot sing, and is not witty enough to talk well. Characterizing himself as clumsy and unskilful, he apparently humorously admits his own ineptitude:

> Our Galliardes are so curious, that thei are not for my daunsyng, for thei are so full of trickes and tournes, that he whiche hath no more but the plaine Sinquepace, is not better accoumpted of then a verie bungler, and for my part, thei might assone teache me to make a Capricornus, as a Capre in the right kinde that it should bee.
>
> (p. 5)

But as he goes on to catalogue his inadequacies, his criticisms shift from being solely self-directed, to being a half-concealed contempt for the dancers themelves:

> A Rounde is too giddie a daunce for my diet, for let the dauncers runne about with as muche speede as thei maie: yet are thei never a whit the nier to the ende of their course, unlesse with often tourning thei hap to catch a fall. And so thei ende the daunce with shame, that was begonne but in sporte.
>
> (p. 6)

For a moment the dancers are themselves shown to be slightly ridiculous. But the narrator quickly regains his humble persona, and admits:

> But my capacitie is so grosse, my wittes bee so blunt, and all my
> other sences are so dulle: that I am sure you would soner condemne
> me for a Dunce, then confirme me for a Disciple, fit to whisper a
> tall in a Gentlewomans eare.[16]
>
> (p. 7)

He concludes with the hope that his zeal and devotion will make up for
his shortcomings, and offers these 'fewe rough heawen Histories' (p. 7)
to demonstrate his commitment. And he signs off with a flourish: 'And
thus (gentlewomen) wishyng to you all, what your selves doe beste like
of, I humbly take my leave. Yours in the waie of honestie, Barnabe
Riche' (p. 8). Despite this jesting innuendo (for 'honesty' often meant
'chastity' to Elizabethans),[17] the woman reader whom he addresses
appears to be one whose approval he seeks, and whose judgement he
apparently respects.

A reading of the preface to the soldiers radically undermines this
impression, however, since in it Rich savagely derides those very skills
which, moments before, he had appeared sorry not to possess himself. In
order to demonstrate the way folly is better rewarded than wisdom, he
criticizes precisely the qualities and occupations which he has associated
with pleasing women:

> . . . flatterie shall be welcomed for a guest of greate accompt, where
> plaine Tom tell troth, shall be thrust out of doores by the shoulders:
> and to speake a plaine truthe in deede, doe ye not see, Pipers,
> Parysites, Fidlers, Dauncers, Plaiers, Jesters, and suche others,
> better esteemed and made of, and greater benevolence used
> towarde them, then to any others that indevuours themselves to the
> moste commendable qualities.
>
> (p. 9)

The need to justify his romance-writing to his fellow soldiers is very
strong, and he remarks apologetically:

> Then seeyng the abuse of this present age is suche, that follies are
> better esteemed then matters of greater waight. I have stept on to
> the Stage amongst the reste, contented to plaie a part, and have
> gathered together this small volume of Histories, all treatyng (sir
> reverence of you) of love.
>
> (pp. 9–10)

The parentheses underline his embarrassment. He had wanted to write
about the discipline of war, but recognizing that it is no longer valued,
has turned to romances instead. The player metaphor strengthens the
reading which interprets Rich's second preface as ironic, by implying
that romance-writing is simply a role he has adopted, and that his true
calling is that of the soldier. He continues with more irony:

And it pleased me the better to doe it, onely to keepe my self from
Idelnesse, and yet thei saie, it were better to be Idle then ill
occupied. But I truste I shall please Gentlewomen, and that is all
the gaine that I looke for.

(p. 10)

His 'compliment' is derisory: the word 'yet' implies that to write for
women is indeed to be ill-occupied, and his last phrase suggests that in
writing for women he has lowered his ambitions, for the most he can
hope for now is women's praise, which is worth little to him.

A lengthy description and criticism of men who dress in an effeminate
fashion is used, with irony, to demonstrate that some men go as far as
trying to look like women in order to please them, and Rich draws a very
clear parallel between a man who dresses like a woman, and a man
(himself) who writes for women; both activities are apparently equally
contemptible.[18] And with bitterness, he advises his fellow soldiers to
follow his example as the only way to win credit, since the military
profession has been so devalued:

... laie aside your weapons, hang up your armours by the walles,
and learne an other while (for your better advauncementes) to Pipe,
to Feddle, to Syng, to Daunce, to lye, to forge, to flatter, to cary
tales, to set Ruffe, or to dooe any thyng that your appetites beste
serves unto, and that is better fittyng for the tyme.

(p. 12)

According to the second preface, then, Rich's humble courtesy to his
women readers has been simply for his 'better advauncemente'; his
earnest desire to please them has been purely expedient, his flattery,
irony and his humility, a sham. The tension generated by the ambiguous
tone and status of the prefaces makes the reading experience an
unsatisfying one. It is impossible that Rich cannot have intended women
readers to read the second preface – although we are left with a sense of
having fallen upon something we were not meant to see, and it leaves an
unpleasant taste – so we must conclude that either Rich did not care, or
that the second preface was not, after all, serious. This is precisely how
Robin Hood chooses to read it:

So Riche explains his title with the teasing dedication that since the
sympathies of the age have turned from military affairs to love, he
has decided to achieve advancement by joining 'Venus bande'.[19]

And Cranfill similarly remarks that Rich has been 'teasing the ladies
unmercifully'.[20] Neither Hood nor Cranfill seem open to the text's
ambiguities and multi-layered structure, and they seem unaware of any
other readings.

In his final preface, 'To the Reader in generall' (p. 19), Rich does not define his readership by sex. But if that leads us to expect some kind of explanation for the first two prefaces, or some indication of how the 'reader in general' might respond to Rich's tales, then we will be disappointed. For it is a remarkably short preface (just one page, compared to the ten pages devoted to the preface to the soldiers, and six to the gentlewomen readers), and gives very little away. If Rich were deliberately aiming to override the first two prefaces with this one, if they had been, in some sense, a 'false-start', then one would expect a far more detailed preface in their place. Instead we have simply an apology for causing any offence by any indecent words or terms, and a version of the traditional formula of disclaiming any desire or intention to publish the work (thus contradicting his stated purpose in the earlier prefaces). We must conclude, then, that all three prefaces are meant to co-exist, and that Rich's meaning rests in their interaction.

Our experience of Rich's prefaces – the unresolved ambiguities in which they hover, the internal unreliability within them and the contradictions between them – prepares us for the sustained ambivalence towards women throughout his work.[21] And while it would be possible, of course, to argue that Rich's position throughout is purely a role, a stance or game (the vehemency of his self-disgust on several occasions leads me to believe otherwise), that would serve only to make Rich an even more sophisticated craftsman, and would not fundamentally change our experience of reading the *Farewell*. Reading as a woman reveals a set of tensions and disjunctions within the text which otherwise remain hidden. Thus Robin Hood is able unproblematically to write:

> The addresses promise that the collection will include both humour and seriousness . . . . *They win the reader's confidence and shape his expectations* . . . [my emphasis].[22]

A feminist reading demonstrates that if the reader is reading as a woman, the very last thing 'she' can experience is confidence; the prefaces are profoundly disturbing, but the tension generated between the first two, and their uneasy co-existence, is completely missed by Hood.

There seems to be some internal structure in Rich's arrangement of his eight tales. The first one picks up the second preface's theme of the rejection of the military profession in peace-time; he includes two comedies, and ends – perhaps significantly – with a story which makes the strongest call for women's rights. The context in which it is made, however – by a man dressed as a woman, intent on persuading a woman to sleep with him – undermines its more serious implications, just as Pettie's final story, *Alexius*, simultaneously offers apparently the most committed and complete encomium of women, and most thoroughly undermines it.

Five of the eight tales he has 'forged'[23] himself, and three are translations of Italian histories by Master L.B.[24] All of them deal with courtship and marriage. Rich focuses on women's roles within these institutions, and emphasizes women's virtue and loyalty, as well as their strength and independence. Only in his original stories does Rich address his women readers directly, and accordingly I have treated these in most detail.[25]

One of the paradoxes of Rich's romance writing lies in the discrepancy between the type of fictional woman he describes in his stories – the spirited, resourceful and courageous heroine – and the type of implied woman reader he fashions, the qualities of foolishness and weakness he often attributes to her and his trivialization of her anticipated responses.

His first story, *Sappho Duke of Mantona*,[26] relates how the worthy Duke Sappho and his family are unjustly exiled, for in a time of peace and idleness Sappho's military skills and austerity have become unpopular. Those now in favour are:

> . . . Dauncers, Pipers, Fidlers, Minstriles, singers, Parisites, Flatterers, Jesters, Rimers, Talebearers, Newes cariers, love makers, suche as can devise to please women, with newe fangles, straunge fassions, by praisyng of their beauties, when sometymes it is scarce worthie, by commendyng of their manifolde vertues, when God knowes thei have fewe or none at all.
>
> (p. 24)

We have heard this list before. It is the familiar catalogue from the preface to the soldiers, and the culture of peace-time, associated with women, is treated with similar scorn. His immediate apology to his women readers, however, marks the difference. This time he is self-conscious, aware of his women readers, and he apparently seeks to make amends:

> But see I praie you how farre my wittes beginne to square, I pretended but to penne certaine pleasaunt discourses, for the onely pleasure of Gentilwomen, and even at the first entrie, I am falne from a reasonable tale to a railyng rage, as it maye seeme. But I praie you Gentilwomen beare with my weaknesse, and as the Preacher in the Pulpit, when he is out of his Texte, will saie for excuse: Good people, though this bee somethyng degressyng from my matter, yet it maie very well serve at this present: Take this I praie you for my excuse in like case.
>
> (p. 24)

But this 'apology' in fact addresses itself to his awareness of having digressed from his story, rather than of having offended women by his derision. The status of the apology is further complicated by the

ambiguity of the word 'pretended'; it means both 'intended' and
'feigned', and Rich's own meaning is left hovering between the two.[27]
The reader appears not to be credited with fully understanding the
'game' Rich is playing here, and is left uncertain of the role she is being
invited to adopt.

The heroines of the story, Messilina and Valerya, are treated less
ambivalently. Messilina is celebrated as an ideal wife who, through her
devotion and loyalty, preserves and restores her marriage to Sappho;
Valerya is a younger woman, who independently chooses her own
husband, proposes to him, and finally elopes with him. The narrative
focuses on the way the women respond to the struggles they must endure
before they reach their ultimate romantic fulfilment, and in doing so,
demonstrates these women to be courageous and independent as well as
loving and virtuous.

The woman reader is credited with no such strength, however. In
summarizing the cunning lies told against Sappho, his fall from favour
and subsequent exile with his family, Rich implies that his readers will be
overwhelmed by the tragedy of it all: 'I beseche you gentelwomen, yet to
comfort yourselves. I knowe your gentill hartes, can not endure to heare
of such ungentill partes' (p. 25). The discrepancy between the qualities
he attributes to his fictional heroines, and to his women readers, is
sustained and broadened in a further aside, where he vows not to reveal
the 'pitifull plight' of other soldiers:

> . . . because right courteous Gentilwomen, I rather desire to drawe
> you into delightes, then to drowne you in dumphes, by revealyng of
> suche unnatural factes, as I knowe your gentle Natures is not able to
> digest.
>
> (p. 26)

The tone of these two asides, the rhyming of the first one, and the
repetition in both of the word 'gentle', suggest an exaggerated concern
for his readers' finer feelings which, while it is not wholly serious,
conveys a disparaging and patronizing attitude. This seems particularly
ironic in a story which demonstrates so clearly the virtue, discretion and
courage of Messilina, who is able to deal with adversity so much more
ably than her husband.

Rich is indeed capable himself of putting forward a very strong
argument for greater freedom for women, even if it does owe much to
other sources.[28] Valerya, falling in love with Sappho's lost son, bewails
the fact that, as a woman of high degree, she is constrained to sue, where
other women of lower class are sought after with importunate insistence.
In a remarkably powerful analysis of contemporary sexism, she makes a
vigorous appeal on behalf of women:

... what strictnesse is this prescribed to our sexe, that we should be
bereved of our libertie, and so absolutely condemned of lightnesse
in seeking to satisfie our lawfull and honest desires, with what
trampe bee wee tempered withall more then menne, whereby wee
should bee able to withstande the forces of the fleshe, or of power
to resiste the concupiscences which Nature it self hath assigned,
wee bee tearmed to bee the weaker vessells, and yet thei would
have us more puissaunte, then either Samson, or Hercules, if
manne and woman bee made of one mettall, it must needes followe
by consequence, wee bee subject to like infirmitie, from whence
commeth then this freedome, that menne maie aske what thei
desire of us, bee it never so lewde, and wee maie not crave any thing
of them, that tendeth to good and honest pretence: it is termed to
bee but a mannes parte that seeketh our dishonour, by lewde and
lawless luste, but to a woman it is imputed for lightnesse, to firme
her lawfull likyng, with pure and loyall love, if menne will have
preheminence to dooe evill, why should wee bee reproved for
doyng well.

(p. 41)

Her rigorous, flawlessly logical argument answers the contemporary
charge of the insatiable lust of women, and explores the paradox
whereby women are told they are weaker than men, and simultaneously
are demanded to be stronger than men by denying themselves the
freedom to pursue and fulfil their love. And, in fact, Valerya refuses to be
governed by these constraints and, in a very sensitively rendered passage,
she woos Sylvanus, and wins him.

When war breaks out, Sappho's fortune begins to change: the
Emperor recalls him from exile, and repents having neglected valiant
men with military experience in favour of cowardly fools: 'Simple sottes
that were more fitter to waite in Gentlewomans chambers, then to be
made Captaines, or leaders in the warres' (p. 49). The complaint against
peace-time effeminacy continues, the syntax making it unclear whether
Rich is supposedly reporting the Emperor's own thoughts, or developing
his own:

... and those that had braved it up and downe the Courte in the
newe cuttes ... lookyng with suche grisly and terrible counten-
aunces, enough to make a wiseman beleeve thei were cleane out of
their wittes, now in tyme of warres, were glad to runne under a
Gentlewomans Farthingall to hide them.

(p. 50)

Again, a clear, and possibly causal, connection is made between the
culture of peace-time which focuses on women and women's values, and

the effeminacy of men. And, by extension, romances – an important part of women's culture – are associated with the effeminacy Rich experiences as romance author.

The story ends with the reunion of Sappho's family, and it is clear that it is Messilina's resourcefulness and constancy which have led to the restoration of her marriage: she has been able to earn enough money to look after her daughter and herself, and she has sufficient courage to set off in search of her lost husband; she has outwitted the importunate suitors who have threatened her, and remained loyal throughout to Sappho. It would seem that, for Rich, she shares none of the qualities which he typically sees in women which lead to effeminacy in men; nor does she show the weakness and foolishness which Rich attributes to his women readers. Rich's heroines are the exception to his own rule.

Rich's paradoxical attitude to women is sustained in his second tale, *Of Apolonius and Silla*, which further develops the theme of women initiating courtship and independently pursuing their own choice in love. Silla, vivacious, young and idealistic, and Julina, more experienced and sexually mature, both exert their freedom in pursuit of the men they desire, but respond to the consequences of that independence in very different ways. Rich shows an unusual sympathy with their ideals, and demonstrates an understanding of their dilemmas.

The plot, familiar from Shakespeare's *Twelfth Night*, tells of how Silla falls in love with Duke Apolonius and of how, when he remains obdurately unaware of it, she is faced with a dilemma similar to that faced by Valerya in *Sappho* – of how to let him know of her affection without seeming immodest. Rich appears to describe her difficulties with sensitivity, but his attitude towards his women readers continues to hover between flattery and condescension. When Apolonius, still ignorant of Silla's love, sets sail for Constantinople, Rich leans forward with a confidential air to comfort us:

> Gentlewomen . . . I will heare for brevities sake, omit to make repetition of the long and dolorous discourse recorded by Silla, for this sodaine departure of her Apolonius, knowyng you to bee as tenderly harted as Silla her self, whereby you maie the better conjecture the furie of her Fever.
>
> (p. 69)

Tender though Silla might be, however, she is also enterprising and courageous; she secretly follows Apolonius by sea to Constantinople, and escapes rape by a timely shipwreck which, miraculously, she survives.

Disguised as a serving-man and using her brother's name, Silvio, she obtains service with Apolonius, who grows to trust and value her; and when he falls in love with the widow Julina, it is natural that he should

choose Silla to be his messenger. At this point, Rich appeals to the
women readers for their sympathy for Silla's unhappy situation:

> Now gentilwomen, doe you thinke there could have been a greater
> torment devised, wherewith to afflicte the harte of Silla, then her
> self to bee made the instrumente to woorke her owne mishapp, and
> to plaie the Attorney in a cause, that made so muche againste her
> self.
>
> (p. 74)

The narrator, indeed, appears to treat the episode more sentimentally
than Silla herself does; for she, we are told, cared only to please
Apolonius, and did as she was requested with as much good will 'as if it
had been in her owne preferment' (p. 74). Silla, loving and loyal, works
diligently in her new role, and is greatly distressed to discover that Julina
has mistakenly fallen in love with her.

The plot is complicated further by the arrival of the real Silvio, when
Julina confuses him with the Silvio she already knows; they sleep
together, and when he disappears the following day, Julina is left
distraught. When she later discovers she is pregnant, she becomes even
more distressed. The painful scene in which she accuses a bewildered
Silla of betraying her is very sensitively rendered, and Rich makes her sad
but dignified confrontation with Apolonius and Silla appear both brave
and pathetic.[29] And it is precisely here that Rich radically alters the tone
by interrupting his story with a tongue-in-cheek aside to the women
readers which both trivializes the narrative episode and calls into
question his apparent sympathy with Julina:

> I praie you Gentilwomen, was not this a foule oversight of Julina,
> that would so precisely sweare so great an othe, that she was
> gotten with childe by one, that was altogether unfurnishte with
> implementes for suche a tourne. For gods love take heede, and let
> this bee an example to you, when you be with childe, how you
> sweare who is the Father, before you have had good proofe and
> knowledge of the parties for men be so subtill and full of sleight,
> that God knoweth a woman may quickly be deceived.
>
> (p. 84)

The opening bawdy rhetorical question breaks our sympathy with
Julina as we are invited to share the narrator's joke at her expense; she is
momentarily shown to be ridiculous. The joke is then turned against the
woman reader, who is ironically warned not to act as Julina has done.
Rich seeks our approval for his first comments, and then undermines it
by his subsequent remarks.

The plot is resolved when Apolonius, overcome by Silla's selfless
devotion when her true identity is revealed, falls in love with her, and the

true Silvio returns and marries Julina. Rich allows his heroines to achieve
their ends, and does not strive to contain the implications of their
independence as Pettie has done. As readers, however, we are encouraged to approve of the strength and independence of these women, and
simultaneously denied these qualities ourselves. The role which Rich
offers us is one which calls for no such characteristics – we are to share
his jokes, follow his directions, and passively accept the scorn he
sometimes turns towards us – because we, as women readers, are
associated with the peace-time effeminacy which he despises.

In none of his three stories from Cinthio, does Rich attempt to
establish a direct relationship with the reader, and nowhere does he
address us within the text. They share a common theme, as each
demonstrates in different ways how the virtues of chastity and loyalty in
women restore relationships and, indeed, save lives.

The first one, *Of Nicander and Lucilla*,[30] focuses on a troubled courtship
in which the devoted lovers are prevented from marrying by Nicander's
mercenary father who demands a more lucrative match. The plot is
complicated further when the Duke's son, Don Hercules, falls in love
with Lucilla, and persuades her mother to act as a bawd. A happy ending
is secured only by a change of heart in Hercules, as he is diverted from
his aim of forcing Lucilla to sleep with him by witnessing her virtuous
and steadfast chastity, and he rewards her by giving her a sufficient dowry
to enable her to marry Nicander. Where Cinthio's version ends in
extravagant praise for Hercules' exemplary restraint and bounty, Rich
appends an extra paragraph of his own, in which he chooses to moralize
the story by focusing on Lucilla's chastity:

> And thus this honeste Damsell Lucilla, by the meanes of her
> Chastitie, the vertue and excellencie whereof, did winne and
> maister the harte of that yonge Prince, muche more then the
> perfection of her bodily beautie had dooen before, obtained the
> thyng she most desired and joyed in, whiche was to have Nicander
> to her housbande.
>
> (p. 105)

Rich makes it clear that, for him, Lucilla's virtue has enabled Hercules to
find and exercise his own, and thus she restores goodness to the world
around her. It is a limited power, leaving authority firmly in the hands of
men, but it is sufficient to win her own happiness.

The second translation, *Of Fineo and Fiamma*,[31] operates in a similar
framework: a dissenting father again prevents two lovers from marrying,
and their relationship is restored (and their lives saved from the angry
and vengeful King of Tunis) only by Fiamma's following her lover across
the seas, and by her eloquent expression to the King of her constant and
devoted love. Her demonstration of love and virtue carry the same

sincerity and conviction as Lucilla's did with Hercules, and has the same effect of securing her happiness.

For his final translation, Rich chose a story extolling the virtues of a woman who is already married. *Of Gonsales and his vertuous wife Agatha*[32] celebrates the unwavering constancy and love of Agatha for her husband, even after he has attempted her murder, and taken a courtesan to wife in her place. After Gonsales has been sentenced to death for her supposed murder, she comes back to him, pleading his innocence and begging his release. She saves his life, and their marriage is restored. This story only sharpens the politics of the preceding two, and the message is clear: to be a heroine in these stories one need only exert one's chastity and constancy in the face of all adversity. It is here that Rich comes closest to Greene and his use of heroines as exempla,[33] for the logic appears to be that personal chastity wins personal happiness (and its more sinister corollary: unhappiness points to unchastity). We are urged towards finding personal rather than political solutions to male violence and authority. Strong as Lucilla, Fiamma and Agatha undoubtedly are, they lack the dynamism and independence of the heroines which Rich draws himself, and as readers we are not invited to enter into a relationship with them.

Of Aramanthus[34] is the other story in which Rich makes no address to his reader. It is a story of military strategy and martial cunning, seemingly calculated to appeal more to Rich's readership among the 'noble souldiours' than to his women readers. Aramanthus was born a leper as a result of poison his pregnant mother, Isabel, was given by his jealous uncle, who wanted to wrest the throne from his father, and to be unhindered by heirs. The baby Aramanthus is shipwrecked on a journey to a healer in Crete, and he is brought up by a fisherman in Turkey. He grows to be very courageous and cunning in military affairs, and ultimately unwittingly uses his best military strategy to capture his own town and family.

While much of the story develops Aramanthus' brilliant scheme to capture Tolosia, the narrative also celebrates Isabel's courage, forgiveness and resourcefulness. Even after her husband has banished her in the mistaken belief that she has committed adultery, she remains loyal to him: when she hears that he has been captured and is starving in prison, she disguises herself as a servant and gets into the service of the jailer, and keeps her husband alive for, in a variation of the Roman Charity motif,

> She would leane her self cloase to the grate, and thrusting her Teate betwene the Irons, the kyng learned againe to sucke, and thus she dieted him a long season. (p. 175)

Thus woman's life-giving qualities are celebrated, and Isabel's devotion to her husband vividly demonstrated.

As the plot is resolved, with identities revealed and errors made good, it is significant that the last scene is Isabel's, and it is one which demonstrates again the virtues which have informed her role in the story throughout:

> The Queene Isabell, not forgettyng the great goodnesse she had received by these Outlawes, which before had saved her life, and with whom her daughter yet remained, so dealt with the Kyng her housbande, that thei were althogether sent for, and verie joyfully receivyng his daughter: restored the Outlawes againe to their libertie: bestowyng of them for recompence, roomes, and offices of credite and estimation.
>
> (p. 179)

Although it is clearly a world of male authority, and has focused primarily on the traditionally male pursuits of battle, Isabel has informed this world with her own values: those of virtuous love, forgiveness and constancy.

Both Isabel and Agatha, then, suffer wrongly by their husbands, both remain constant and forgiving, and initiate the process back to reconciliation and a new happiness.

If *Of Aramanthus*, by its primary subject matter, would seem to be designed to appeal to Rich's readership among the soldiers, his comedy, *Of Two Brethren and their Wives*,[35] focuses uneasily in two different directions. It contains direct addresses to the woman reader, and at the same time gives clear indications that it is intended for men. For the purpose of the story, as Rich explains it, is to explore whether it is better to marry a beautiful and wise harlot or a chaste but 'foolishe overthwarte and brauling woman' (p. 120).

The question is clearly being posed from a male point of view, but Rich makes clear his anticipation of a female readership in his very first words, and attempts to pre-empt the objections by immediately appealing to women's patience, which seems to be expected as a typical female response:

> Gentlewomen, before I will proceede any farther in this Historie, I must desire you to arme your selves with pacience in readyng herof, that if you finde any thing that might brede offence to your modeste myndes, take it in this sorte, that I have written it onely to make you merrie, and not to sette you a snarrying or grudgyng against me, for although I meane to present you with a Chapter of knaverie, yet it shall be passable, and suche as you maie very well permit . . . .
>
> (p. 120)

Despite the light-hearted tone, Rich is in fact assuming the right to make our judgements for us; while he acknowledges that part of the story may be offensive, his simultaneous statement of good intentions appears to absolve him of responsibility. He is himself in no doubt as to which sort of wife to choose: '. . . to speake my mynde without dissimulation of bothe those evilles, I think the first is least, and therefore is to be chosen' (p. 120). But in case we are not convinced, he will set down the story of two brothers, each of whom chose a different sort of wife, 'for your better confirmation' (p. 121). The issue of why women should want to know which is best is left unaddressed.

It is a richly comic narrative, 'as hilarious as the best of the French fabliaux', as Cranfill admiringly remarks.[36] At the centre of it stands Doritie, resourceful, witty, attractive and unfaithful. The success with which she outwits her two jealous lovers, a doctor and a lawyer, testifies to her remarkable power within the terms of the story. She is confident and skilful, divining their motives immediately, and anticipating their manoeuvres.

When the doctor outrageously suggests that she should sleep with him out of kindness to her husband, since he is her husband's friend, and when Rich turns to his women readers to develop the joke, we are happily aware that Doritie is doing precisely what she wants to do, and that she is triumphantly in control:

> How thinke you gentlewomen, bee not these gentle perswasions to bee used by a Doctor. Marie he was no Doctor of Devinitie, and therefore you neede not followe his doctrine, unlesse you liste your selves, but this pitifull gentlewoman, seyng Maister Doctor at such desperate poinctes, for feare of damning of her owne soule, that so deare a freende to her housbande as Maister Doctor was, should perishe and bee so wilfully caste awaie through her default, she received hym for her freend, and so I praie God give them joye.
>
> (p. 126)

Rich's irony is not against Doritie, but at himself in his assumed role of naive narrator, and indeed at the doctor who, in his belief that he is tricking Doritie, fails to realize that he is being equally used by her.

When the doctor and lawyer grow jealous of each other, they lose more dignity, and our sympathy is again with Doritie in her resolve to cure them of 'ungratefulness'. At the same time, Doritie is wooed by a soldier who, typically in Rich, is blunt and plain, but sincere and honest. He asks her to judge him by his actions not words, since learning fine words has not been part of his training. Doritie recognizes him as a soldier, 'for she knewe that thei had little skill in the courtyng of Gentlewomen' (p. 130), but finding the vehemency of his love and his directness attractive, she leads him into a chamber, where, remarks Rich mock-innocently:

other speeches were passed betweene them in secrete, which I
could never yet understande, and what thei did farther when thei
were by themselves, gentlewomen I praie gesse you, but this I must
advertise you of, that before thei came forth of the chamber againe,
the Souldiour had pleased Mistres Doritie so well, that both
Maister Doctor, and Maister Lawyer, were put quite out of
conceipt.

(p. 130)

Rich again draws his women readers into sharing his joke at the expense
of the naive narrator he sets up.

This soldier proves to be the best lover, while the doctor and lawyer
grow increasingly jealous. They convey their anger and bitterness to her
in letters, the one from the doctor unpunctuated so that it can equally
well be read in her praise as dispraise, and the lawyer's, railing bitterly at
the nature of womankind. And after a page and a half of the lawyer's
misogynistic invective, in which he accuses all women of inconstancy, of
dissimulation, lewdness and cunning, Rich interposes with an apparently
earnest plea to his women readers:

Gentlewomen I beseche you forgive me my fault, in the publishyng
this infamous letter, I promise you I did but signifie it accordyng to
the copie, whiche this unhappie lawyer sent to Mistres Doritie, and
when I had well considered the blasphemie that he had used against
your sexe, I cutte my penne all to peeces, wherewith I did copie it
out, and if it had not been for the hurtyng of my self, I promise you
I would have cutte and mangled my owne fingers, wherewith I held
the penne while I was writyng of it: and trust me accordyng to my
skill, I could well have founde in my harte, to encountred hym with
an aunswere in your defence, but then I was interrupted by another
as you shall well perceive.

(p. 133)

But Rich's apparent concern is undercut by its tone and context; he
clearly did not have to include the text of the letter (indeed, he did not
have to write it); his flamboyant exaggeration suggests that he does not
mean a word of it. He would have cut and mangled his own fingers, he
assures us, were it not for the pain it would cause; but such a gesture
depends upon willingness to endure pain – that is precisely the point.
The joke he is enjoying this time is one at the women readers' expense.

A defence of women – over two pages long – is in fact delivered by the
soldier. Rich has already encouraged identification between the type of
honest and blunt soldier, and himself, and he continues to do so here.[37]
For after this eulogy of women's goodness, purity and virtue (culled from
Pettie, Painter and Lyly),[38] Rich turns to his women readers with a self-
satisfied flourish, as a performer looking for applause:

But I pray gentle women how like you by this Souldiour, doe you
not thynke hym worthie a Sargantes fee for his aunswere: in my
opinion, you ought to love Souldiours the better for his sake.

(p. 136)

Rich's comments reinforce the idea of the speech as rhetorical perform-
ance rather than sincere testimony, and his arch reference to women
loving soldiers (and hence himself) better because of this speech further
undercuts its seriousness.

Doritie's cunning scheme to humiliate her unwanted suitors is a comic
success, but she has little time for enjoying the soldier afterwards, for he
is soon called to the King's wars where he spends the rest of his life,
leaving Doritie sorrowing for the loss of so loyal a friend. That Rich has
the soldier, with whom he has encouraged identification with himself,
return to the military profession is surely significant: Rich is able to
demonstrate that soldiers can succeed in the women's world of love, but
even so prefer the masculine realm of war. Doritie's husband has
remained entirely ignorant of all her affairs, and continues to love her
dearly until his death.

Rich then turns quickly to the course of the second brother's marriage
to a chaste scold. It is predictably miserable, and concludes with the
brother forcibly dressing her in the guise of a madwoman, scratching her
arms until they bleed, fixing a great chain around her leg, and
imprisoning her in a dark house. Calling neighbours to witness her
'lunacy', he pretends to be heartbroken at the spectacle. When it fails to
'cure' her, he leaves her and travels abroad.

It is a profoundly disturbing story, even in its brevity; violence and
hatred of women are inextricably linked, and the wife's punishment is far
from humorous. Rich appears to expect us to respond to it in a way
similar to Doritie's tale, however, and there is no apology appended to it.
This may be partly resolved by Rich's closing words:

Thus to conclude, besides the matter that I meane to prove *menne
maie gather example here*, when thei goe a wivyng, not to chuse for
beautie without vertue: nor for riches without good conditions.
There be other examples if thei be well marked, worth the learning;
both for men and women, which I leave to the discretion of the
reader [my emphasis].

(p. 147)

Rich makes clear here that the morals to be drawn from his story are
quite specifically for men; and the unspoken audience of the story is
male. The brutality of the second brother's treatment of his wife is there
to prove his point about the dangers of marrying ill-tempered women.
The hero of the tale has been the soldier, and the heroine, the wise and
witty Doritie; all the other figures appear to be treated with equal

contempt by Rich, and he hardly bothers to give them any substantial
characterization at all. We are now clearly in the world of the fabliau,
where coarseness and brutality are as common as farce. The underlying
seriousness is in the literal and painful enactment of what Foucault calls
the hystericization of women; Foucault has shown that societies define as
mad whatever challenges the dominant (almost always male) definition
of rationality, and during the fifteenth and sixteenth centuries, close
associations were made between hysteria, madness and sorcery, and the
perceived disruptive potential of women.[39] Her husband's solution to
her talking too much is to empty her words of meaning – as a
'madwoman', her words are interpreted as nonsensical babble, and her
meaning denied.

Rich's second comedy and last story, *Of Phylotus and Emelia*,[40]
generates a similar ambiguity. On the surface, it is a very amusing
demonstration of mistaken identities and comic reversals. More seriously, it
articulates a plea for greater understanding for women who are forced to
marry against their will. Significantly, however, the champion for
women's rights is a man dressed as a woman, and male self-interest
governs his successful reappropriation of freedom for women. Hood
finds the story unproblematic:

> It is a final triumphant demonstration of Rich's ability to combine
> playful humour and seriousness, and to provoke his gentlewomen
> readers without losing a genuine sympathy with them.[41]

But on closer examination, it becomes clear that the sympathy Rich has
is for his women characters, not his women readers.

The story opens seriously enough with speculation about the impar-
tiality of love, which can draw people to friend and foe alike, regardless
of wealth and age. So it happens that a rich old man Phylotus falls in love
with the beautiful young Emelia: 'or rather I maye saie in his olde yeares
beganne to doate after this young maiden' (p. 182). Rich hastily corrects
himself, showing his vigorous contempt for Phylotus:

> for it can not bee properly called love in these olde men, whose
> dotage if it were not more then outragious, either their greate
> discretion would represse it, either their many yeares would
> mortifie it.

(p. 182)

Emelia's father Alberto, knowing of Phylotus' wealth, readily agrees to
marry her off; and Rich leaves us in no doubt about his own opinion of
him, borrowing words from Pettie to demonstrate his scorn for one who:

> accordyng to the custome of parentes, that desires to marie their

daughters, more for goods, then for good will betweene the parties, more for lucre then for love,

(p. 182)

and who never remembers

> what strifes, what jarres, what debates, what discontentment, what counterfaityng, what dissembling, what louryng, what loathyng, what never likyng, is ever had where there is suche differences betwene the maried, for perfecte love can never bee without equalitie, and better were a married couple to continue without livyng, then without love.

(p. 182)

Rich goes even further, showing himself capable of a stout defence of women, and a sensitive perception of their dilemmas: 'and what are the occasions that make so many women to straie from their housbandes, but when thei bee maried to suche as they cannot like of' (p. 182). And finally he addresses women personally with some advice about keeping away from 'these olde youthes' (p. 182):

> for besides that thei be unwildie, lothsome, (and sir reverence of you) very unlovely for you to lye by, so thei bee commonly inspired with the spirite of jelousie, and then thei will looke to you so narrowly, and mewe you up so closely, that you will wishe a thousande tymes the Prieste had bin hanged that maried you, but then to late.

(pp. 182–3)

With some relish, but not without understanding, Rich describes the perils of marrying old men. And although he is unable to resist a familiar jibe at women's supposed love of mastery ('to desire superioritie, it is commonly every womans sicknesse', p. 184), Rich's account of Emelia's desperate attempts to force herself into a liking of Phylotus is sympathetic and moving, and its frank acknowledgement of the needs of youthful sexuality is sensitively honest; for no matter how much she can think favourably of what she will be able to do with his wealth during the day, her mind must always return to the events of the night, when 'she must goe to bedde to be lubber leapt' (p. 185), the vigorous phrase resoundingly expressing her physical repulsion.

Much of the humour revolves around a set of mistaken identities; in order to escape the prospect of marriage with Phylotus, Emelia disguises herself as a man and escapes to live with a younger, more attractive suitor, Flanius. Phylotus and Alberto, alerted to her disappearance, come across her brother, Phylerno, whom no one has seen for many years, and mistake him for the disguised Emelia. He plays along with their error, and soon finds himself betrothed to Phylotus, and left alone for the night with the old man's daughter, Brisilla, with whom Phylotus has suggested 'she' sleep until their wedding day. Phylerno preys on Brisilla's credulity by pretending that he is a woman who, through the grace of the gods, is suddenly transformed into a man. Afraid that she will face a similar fate to Emelia's, and be forced to marry Alberto (as Phylerno has cunningly suggested), Brisilla is only too happy to find the sex-changed Phylerno in bed beside her. As part of his strategy to persuade her to sleep with him, Phylerno – in the guise of Emelia – delivers a lengthy analysis of the iniquities of forced marriages, especially between those of unequal ages. His eloquence and conviction engage our sympathy and understanding, and there is a genuine pathos in what would have been the real Emelia's fate:

> But consideryng the inequalite of our yeres, I can not for my life frame my self to love hym, and yet I am forced against my will to marie him, and am appoincted to be your mother, that am more meete to be your companion and plaie felowe.

> (p. 190)

As soon as Phylerno (as Emelia) is duly married, 'she' insists on quickly establishing which one of them will have the authority in their marriage. Phylotus only takes it seriously when they come to blows and he loses. Completely shamed, humiliated, and at Phylerno's mercy, he is forced to accept the conditions on which his 'wife' insists. First, that she may go out with friends, wherever and as often as she likes, and with whom she likes, and with no questions asked when she returns. And further, that she will sleep with him only when she so wishes; for the first year, to be once a month if he deserves it, and once a quarter thereafter.[42]

When identities are finally revealed, Phylerno marries Brisilla, and Emelia, Flanius. Rich has shown himself able to put forward the argument in favour of greater freedom of choice for women, and his final words reveal his sympathy for the happily married couples, together with his delight at the outwitting of old Phylotus: 'And so I praie GOD give them joye and every old dotard so good successe as had Phylotus' (p. 203). The story triumphantly offers a spirited defence of a woman's right to choose her own husband, and calls for a far greater degree of freedom for women within marriage. But that these demands have been made, not by a woman, but by a man disguised as a woman, and used as part of his plan to trick a woman into sleeping with him, inevitably qualifies our response to it. We cannot be completely sure of Rich: his tone is ambiguous and his design unclear.

In his conclusion he delivers his strongest expression of reluctance about writing for women. The disgust and vehemence with which he admits that he has simply been following the fashion, as young men who wear outrageous clothes do, would seem to persuade us to resist discounting his comments as the traditional modest disclaimers typical of the period. He rails at their excess at length, as he has done in his prefaces, and then draws the parallel with himself:

> Lette this then suffice likewise for myne excuse, that my self seeyng trifles of no accompt, to be now best in season, and such vanities more desired, then matters of better purpose, and the greatest parte of our writers, still busied with the like. So I have put forthe this booke, because I would follow the fashion.
>
> (p. 205)

While Hood dismisses these remarks as unserious, he does helpfully draw attention to a comment made by Rich in a work on military affairs written three years earlier, where Rich looks forward to the *Farewell* by grimly noting that he would have earned more profit and credit had he produced

> some conceite according to the time, some pleasant discourse, some strange novell, some amorous history, some farre fette or unknowen device.[43]
>
> (*Allarme to Englande*, 1578; sig. A₁ᵛ)

It seems that even in 1578 Rich was anticipating that economic pressure would soon force him into following the fashion which he most despises.

Significantly, he chooses to end his collection of love stories by repeating a story he had heard which will illustrate the foolishness of following fashion: 'And now freendlie Reader, because I have entred thus farre to speake of fashions: I will conclude with a tale that maketh somethyng for my purpose' (p. 205).[44] And it is in this anecdote that Rich is at his most hostile towards women: the devil Balthazar marries a beautiful young woman, Mildred, but becomes so frustrated by her constant addiction to new fashions that he leaves her. He travels instead to Scotland, where he possesses King James and causes him terrible fits.[45] Mildred's father, a doctor, cures the king by making Balthazar believe that Mildred has come to Edinburgh on purpose to find him. The devil's response is immediate:

> ... then I shall be sure to be troubled with new fashions; naie then farewell Scotland, for I had rather goe to hell: and thus leavyng the kyng he departed his waie.
>
> (p. 211)

Rich draws the moral of the story thus:

> ... if a sillie woman were able to wearie the Devill, that troubled

hym with newe fashions but once in a moneth, I thinke God hym
self will bee wearied with the outrages of men, that are busied with
new fangles at the least once in a daie.

(p. 211)

If Rich's aim is indeed to excoriate male fashion, it is curious that he
should choose to do so by telling a story against women; for despite the
moral which he apparently means to convey, it is the incessantly nagging
Mildred that we remember, rather than the evils of male fashion which
her story is supposed to illustrate. Cranfill might be able to refer amiably
to this 'delightful tale',[46] and other critics debate whether its source is
Machiavelli's 'Belphegor' or Straparola's *Le piacevoli notti*, but its essential
oddness has been left unexamined.[47] The strangeness of this story,
reminiscent of the second part of *Two Brethren*, might lie in their being
the two examples of Rich's hostility to female *characters* in the collection,
while his final words could almost be taken as the ultimate indication of
his position throughout:

> I can no more, but wishe that Gentlemen leavyng such superficiall
> follies, would rather indevour themselves in other exercises, that
> might be much more benefficiall to their Countrey, and a greate
> deale better to their owne reputation, and thus an ende.

(p. 211)

It is remarkably strange to conclude a collection of love stories written
for women by urging men to stop wearing outlandish clothes. The two
would appear to be utterly unconnected, but for Rich's belief that both
writing romances and wearing the latest fashions are expressions of the
peace-time culture, associated with women, which Rich makes clear that
he despises. Without this explanation, his constant criticism of men's
fashions would seem both irrelevant and out of proportion to its
significance. In his last words he goes so far as to suggest that fashion is
preventing men from doing something more 'beneficial' for their
country; fashion, for Rich, means the weakness and effeminacy caused by
the decline of the military profession in times of peace.

I would suggest that Rich's ambivalent attitude towards women
sustained throughout the work is a consequence of the dilemma Rich is
in: he despises 'women's culture' and at the same time he is dependent
on it to make a living. This dual response generates much of the tension
within and between his prefaces and his eight tales. It would appear that
the motif of men dressing as women or dressing in 'womanish' fashions
occurs when the text is most anxious about the decorum of a man
writing romances for women. It is a motif which ultimately challenges
male authority; for while romance sanctions women dressing as men
(there are numerous examples, of which Shakespeare's Rosalind in

As You Like It, Viola in *Twelfth Night*, and Julia in *The Two Gentlemen of Verona* are among the most well-known), it becomes far more problematic and worrying when men dress as women. When, for example, in Spenser's *Faerie Queene*, the victorious Radigund dresses Artegall in 'woman's weedes', it is seen as a moment of complete shame and humiliation, and Britomart's first words to him on freeing him from Radigund express her horror at this 'lothly uncouth sight':[48]

> Ah my deare Lord, What sight is this (quod she)
> What May-game hath misfortune made of you?[49]

But while Britomart reads the 'speaking picture' before her of the noble Artegall dressed in women's clothes as an image of disorder and mortification, its literal equivalent for Rich – men writing romances for women – might, in fact, be far less problematic for women readers than for men. Rich's anxiety over 'becoming like a woman' by writing romances for women could generate a similar anxiety in men who might be reading them: a woman reader is far less likely to be faced with this dilemma. Indeed, there is much for women to value in Rich's romances: his fictional women have mostly been characterized by strength, independence, resourcefulness and wit, as well as loyalty, and virtue, and they have acted in a context of freedom which would have been seldom available to Rich's contemporary women readers.

6

Sir Philip Sidney:
woman reader as structural necessity

In Sidney's *Old Arcadia* the role of the woman reader in sixteenth-century prose romance reaches its culmination, for here the woman reader becomes structurally essential to the author's narrative theme and design. The role which the text encourages her to adopt is one which becomes increasingly difficult to sustain, until in the final part of the work the woman reader finds her position so incompatible with the story's own internal logic, that she is forced to try to negotiate her way towards an alternative one; and it is only Basilius' miraculous resurrection at the very end of the book which saves that negotiation from completion. This process generates confusion for the reader, together with a sense of radical insecurity. This is Sidney's intention, I would argue, for it is only through experiencing the contradictions inherent in Sidney's theme that we are able to come to a fuller understanding of them.

It is a work which appears to have appealed to women from the time that it was first written, and the version which was finally published remained one of the most popular books in England for over 150 years.[1] The plot revolves around two young princes, Pyrocles and Musidorus, who disguise themselves as an Amazon and a Shepherd to gain access to the princesses Philoclea and Pamela, whose father has them guarded in a solitary place to avoid the dangers foretold by an oracle. The first version, the *Old Arcadia*, was written for a particular woman, Sidney's sister Mary, Countess of Pembroke, and in a letter prefaced to the beginning of the text, Sidney writes:

Now it is done only for you, only to you; if you keep it to yourself, or to such friends who will weigh errors in the balance of goodwill, I hope, for the father's sake, it will be pardoned.[2]

This is clearly an exceptionally specialized readership. Sidney imagines his sister reading the work among a small gathering of sympathetic friends; he addresses her in her semi-public persona, however, not anticipating the sort of intimacy in which Wordsworth, for example, wrote to and for his sister Dorothy. Mary Sidney was, in fact, the sixteenth century's most significant woman poet, but it is only recently that critical studies of the period have begun to treat her works as seriously as those of her more famous brother. Not only a fine poet, she was also a distinguished patron of poetry, a competent translator, and the editor of her brother's works. Indeed, she devoted most of her adult life to promoting his cultural ideals, and during the last 20 years of the century her home at Wilton was a kind of salon for many Elizabethan writers and intellectuals.

The *Arcadia* did not retain the restricted readership which Sidney appears to have envisaged, of course, and there is much evidence to suggest its popularity among a far wider readership. The learned Anne Clifford was painted at the age of 13 with a copy of the *Arcadia* beside her, and when Richard Lovelace addresses a poem to women, he pictures them reading Sidney's romance: 'Pray Ladies breath, awhile lay by Celestial Sydney's Arcady'.[3] Charles Cotton finds his beloved similarly engaged:

> The happy object of her eye
> Was Sidney's living Arcady
> Whose amorous tale had so betray'd
> Desire in this all-lovely maid,
> That, whilst her cheek a blush did warm,
> I read love's story in her form:
> And of the sisters the united grace,
> Pamela's vigour in Philoclea's face.[4]

Its appeal crossed classes as well as centuries. A young girl in Wye Saltonstall's *Picturae Loquentes* is shown vicariously savouring the gratifications of love: '. . . she reades now loves historyes as *Amadis de Gaule* and the *Arcadia*, & in them courts the shaddow of love till she know the substance'.[5] That such amorous reading was frowned upon, and regarded as a bad influence on young women who were likely to be distracted from their duties, is made very clear in a passage on the education of women in *Tom of All Trades, Or the Plaine Pathway to Preferment* (1631), where author Thomas Powell counsels severely:

In stead of Song and Musicke, let them learne Cookery and
Laundrie. And in stead of reading Sir Philip Sydney's *Arcadia*, let
them read the grounds of good huswifery. I like not a female
Poetresse at any hand.[6]

Powell finds fault with the *Arcadia* for filling young girls' heads with
romantic ideas (and, apparently, for encouraging them to write themselves); and when, in later centuries, it suffered a decline in popularity, its
'faults' of length and style are still described in terms of its special interest
to women. Horace Walpole in 1768 called it 'a tedious, lamentable,
pedantic, pastoral romance, which the patience of a young virgin in love
cannot now wade through'.[7]

In 1820, William Hazlitt not only characterized it as 'one of the greatest
monuments of the abuse of intellectual power upon record', but also,
more specifically, he remarks:

It no longer adorns the toilette or lies upon the pillow of maids of
honour and peeresses in their own right (the Pamelas and
Philocleas of a later age), but remains upon the shelves of the
libraries of the curious in long works and great names, a monument
to shew that the author was one of the ablest men and worst writers
of the age of Elizabeth.[8]

Since the time of its first publication, readers and critics have
attempted to fit author and text into a coherent schema which,
stubbornly, they appear to resist; the debate is further fuelled by the
confusion which surrounds the genesis and publication of the work. The
text exists in three major versions, none of which was published by
Sidney himself. The first version, now known as the *Old Arcadia*, may
have been started as early as 1577, and was probably completed by 1580.
Some time between 1582 and 1584 Sidney engaged in a revised and
hugely expanded version, the *New Arcadia*, which he never finished.
Although there were manuscripts of the *Old Arcadia* in circulation after
Sidney's death, it was the incomplete *New Arcadia* which was published
by William Ponsonby in 1590, under the supervision of Sidney's friend
Fulke Greville. Three years later Sidney's sister Mary published the
'composite' text which joined the last three books of the *Old Arcadia* on
to the incomplete revision, and made some vital changes. It was this
version which became known as *The Arcadia* until the beginning of this
century, when Bertram Dobell discovered long forgotten manuscripts of
the full text of the *Old Arcadia* in 1907.[9] And since that time, critics have
come increasingly to compare the *Old* and *New* Arcadias in efforts to
explain Sidney's intentions, quite disregarding C.S. Lewis' earnest plea
that critical analysis should concentrate on the second version as 'the text
which really affected the English mind'.[10]

Sidney's own words about his compositions seem only to have added to the confusion which surrounds them. In a letter to his brother Robert in 1580, he refers to his work as a 'toyful book',[11] and in his tantalizing letter to Mary he writes of it as 'this idle work of mine' which is not for severer eyes, 'being but a trifle, and that triflingly handled'.[12] R.W. Zandvoort takes Sidney's disclaimer at face value, and declares that the *Old Arcadia* is 'at best the immature work of a young man of great promise who is trying his hand at romance writing',[13] while Richard Lanham dismisses Sidney's words as typical sprezzatura – that 'careful craftmanship and . . . amateur pose, which Castiglione sees as the crowning glory of the courtier in life and in art' – and suggests that the *Arcadia* in both its versions is far more crafted and complex than Sidney indicates.[14]

Sidney's contemporaries could not agree either. Gabriel Harvey weights his appreciation of the *Arcadia* in favour of its entertainment value:

> Will you needes have a written Pallace of Pleasure, or rather a printed Court of Honour? Read the Countesse of Pembrookes Arcadia, a gallant legendary, full of pleasurable accidents and proffitable discourses,[15]

whereas Sidney's more earnest friend Fulke Greville insists that:

> His end was not vanishing pleasure alone, but moral Images, and Examples, (as directing threads) to guide every Man through the confused Labyrinth of his own desires, and life.[16]

For Greville, both versions are primarily serious political and moral allegory, and Sidney's intention was 'to turn the barren Philosophy precepts into pregnant Images of life'.[17] More recently, Kenneth Thorpe Rowe confidently asserts that 'There can be no doubt that Sidney aimed at an ideal presentation of love and marriage in the *Arcadia*.'[18] To Rowe, the princes are 'models of virtue in their function of lovers as well as in their chivalry and prowess'.[19] But by way of complete contrast, Franco Marenco finds them 'most evident examples of moral disintegration, and it is in them that the forces of rebellion find closest parallels', and, for him, the work's primary purpose is not to extol virtue but to condemn vice: '. . . it is a gloomy, almost desperate book, mocking and not glorifying the worldly hero', he concludes.[20]

It is a pastoral romance, a tragi-comedy, a sustained allegory of Elizabethan politics, a psychological exploration of Sidney's troubled mind – like the repertoire of the Players at Elsinore, it is 'tragical-comical-historical-pastoral'.[21] We must be alert to an important distinction to be made, however, if we are to deduce that the diversity of critical opinion about the *Arcadia* points to the work's own multivalence.

Annabel Patterson warns us: 'There is a difference . . . between arguing
that Sidney was himself responsible for the divisions among his readers,
and that he had not himself made up his mind.'[22]

The following pages make the case that Sidney was very well aware of
the multiple and contradictory voices in the *Arcadia*, and that it is
precisely through the examination of the roles of narrator, his many
voices, and the woman reader, that we can begin to understand Sidney's
text.

It can, of course, make for frustrating reading:

> Sidney is always getting up from his seat in the audience, climbing
> on stage to act a scene, turning to comment on it in an aside,
> arranging his characters in specific poses and facial expressions, and
> then going back to his seat for the next scene. Much as we would
> like him to stay put, he will not.[23]

Richard Lanham's scarcely concealed exasperation at Sidney's insistent
participation in his own text, and his charge against Sidney as an
'untrustworthy narrator' who can never be guaranteed to sustain one
voice, or one pose, or a fixed distance from the events which are
described, lead him to condemn the unstable narrative voice as an
inadequacy in the work's structure.[24] But it is in the very instability of the
text, and the discomfort which it causes the woman reader, that its
meaning resides.

As mentioned earlier, Gary Waller has convincingly suggested that in
developing a reader-centred cognitive model, we are returning to
something of which the sixteenth-century writers were themselves at
least dimly aware.[25] The arguments of Sidney's own *Defence of Poetry*
(1595) depend absolutely on the notion that the reader must take up her/
his part in a dialogic process:

> . . . part of the poet's training was always to have his readers in
> mind, continually to be aware that the power of poetry resided in
> the forcefulness to a reader of the image that was presented to what
> Cicero termed the mind's eye.[26]

Sidney's definition of poetry as 'an art of imitation . . . with this end, to
teach and delight' (p. 25), and his conviction that its true worth lies in its
ability to move readers to virtuous action, depend wholly upon the
reader's 'right reading' of a given text. Thus reading a text becomes
equally important as writing it.[27]

I have concentrated my analysis almost entirely on the *Old Arcadia*; the
implied reader of the *New* is an ungendered one, since the woman
reader's role is no longer necessary to the narrative design. In his
revision, Sidney abandons all his personal addresses to the reader, and
for the multiple voices of the *Old Arcadia*'s single narrator, he substitutes

the multiple narratives of diverse character-narrators who tell stories to each other, and to the reader, in the *New*. If in the *Old*, Sidney demonstrates what he saw as the inevitable collision of reason and passion by causing the dual roles of the implied reader to become incompatible, in the *New* he offers multiple narrators and multiple viewpoints on the same subject and, setting them all side by side, leaves it for the readers, as for the princes themselves, to weigh and assess each of them. The implied reader within the text has a single, coherent role: to read rightly the speaking pictures which make up the narrative episodes. While the *Old Arcadia* leads the reader to measure the discrepancy between the action of the princes and the moral code put forward first by Philanax and later by Euarchus, the revision requires the reader to compare the sub-plots with the activity of the main characters. As Susan Gubar observes, perception of analogies replaces consciousness of discrepancy.[28]

The implied reader of the *Old Arcadia* is a woman whom the narrator addresses with a confident intimacy, seemingly assured that he can predict her feelings and anticipate her responses. The asides are constantly on the subject of love and the tender emotions of the female reader. His assumption that her judgements match his own draws her into a collusive contract with him, in which his praise for her is dependent on her agreement with him. Thus his first persuasive aside comes when he is apparently seeking approval for referring to the disguised Pyrocles by the name of Cleophila:

> and thus did Pyrocles become Cleophila – which name for a time hereafter I will use, for I myself feel such compassion of his passion that I find even part of his fear lest his name should be uttered before fit time for it; which you, fair ladies that vouchsafe to read this, I doubt not will account excusable.

> (p. 25)

Here the narrator very clearly identifies his own sympathies to be with Pyrocles, and draws the woman reader into a similar involvement. Sidney's treatment of Pyrocles dressing as a woman is complicated, and the choice of an Amazon disguise an important one. Musidorus, on hearing of his friend's feelings and intentions, is horrified, and reveals a similar fear of effeminacy to that which we have met before in Rich's *Farewell*:

> And this effeminate love of a woman doth so womanize a man that, if you yield to it, it will not only make you a famous Amazon, but a launder, a distaff-spinner, or whatsoever other vile occupation their idle heads can imagine and their weak hands perform.

> (pp. 18–19)

The effeminacy Musidorus anticipates has a very literal manifestation in Pyrocles taking on women's clothing, but a clear distinction is made between becoming a famous Amazon – a woman who possesses all the martial skills and qualities of a man – and becoming weakened and humiliated as Hercules, the 'distaff-spinner', was under Omphale's direction.[29] Pyrocles' motive further reduces male anxiety over his transformation; for, as he announces with some bravado:

> Neither doubt you, because I wear a woman's apparel, I will be the more womanish; since, I assure you, for all my apparel, there is nothing I desire more than fully to prove myself a man in this enterprise.
>
> (p. 21)

The innuendo is as good as a nod and a wink. Pyrocles' disguise is acceptable among men because it is in the (male-sanctioned) pursuit of sex, just as Phylerno's was in the last story of Rich's *Farewell*; and the woman reader is inclined to feel sympathy for Pyrocles since he defends women against the charges of idleness, weakness and 'peevish imperfections' (p. 18) which Musidorus, in his attempts to dissuade Pyrocles, has brought against them.

This initial aside to the reader is followed by ten further asides in Book One, each one designed to predispose the woman reader to a close and sympathetic response to the love intrigues. Commenting, for example, on the speed with which passion for Cleophila strikes both Gynecia and Basilius, the narrator defers to us:

> But you, worthy ladies, that have at any time feelingly known what it means, will easily believe the possibility of it. Let the ignorant sort of people give credit to them that have passed the doleful passage, and daily find that quickly is the infection gotten which in long time is hardly cured.
>
> (p. 44)

He assumes his female readership to be specialists in the finer points of feelings and emotions, and to have experienced at first hand the 'doleful passage' of love, and he compares them favourably to the 'ignorant sort of people' who have not. The woman reader is encouraged to include herself in this more exalted company, and to mould her responses accordingly. He is particularly courteous to these readers, and flatters them by suggesting that they are as courtly as he is; and so he saves them from listening to the incoherence of the frightened shepherds: 'I think it best not to trouble you, fair ladies, with their panting speeches; but to make a full declaration of it myself' (p. 41). Indeed, he becomes increasingly gallant:

It were a very superfluous thing to tell you how glad each party was
of the happy returning from these dangers, and doubt you not, fair
ladies, there wanted no questioning how things had passed; but
because I will have the thanks myself, it shall be I you shall hear it
of.

(p. 46)

His gallantry, however, is limited to recounting the story of the more
active heroic gallantry of Pyrocles and Musidorus. While the princes win
the gratitude and admiration of the princesses by rescuing them from
wild animals, the narrator's hope is to be granted the same by the women
readers by delivering them the story of it. The distinction which is made
between pleasing women and winning merit and respect by traditional
masculine heroics, and pleasing women by writing stories for them
recalls the anxiety of Barnaby Rich, the military man writing romances
for women.

As the love between the two couples becomes visible, the narrator
again turns with intimacy to the woman reader, and shares with her his
private observations:

Whereof seeking the cause that they which were most bound said
least, I note this to myself, fair ladies, that even at this time they did
begin to find they themselves could not tell what kind of inclination
towards them.

(p. 49)

He seems here to be priding himself on having made the sort of
particularly perceptive observation about the inception of the love
between the young couples which only a connoisseur of love and
romance would have. His concern to win the women readers' approval
and admiration for this – and to show, perhaps, that he is a worthy
member of the circle of women readers which Sidney at first envisaged –
is suggested by the obvious contradiction of the statement 'I note this to
myself', which is immediately followed by an account of the observation
made to all his readers.

Even apparently insignificant asides which seem only to make sure
that we are following the story, have the effect of strengthening the
shared intimacy between the narrator and the woman reader, and
reinforces Sidney's control over guiding her responses, moulding her
attitudes, and firmly associating the growing passion of the young people
with her sympathy and approval.

These references become fewer as the work progresses, with five in
Book Three, and none at all in Books Four and Five.[30] The very last one
comes, significantly, as Pyrocles and Philoclea consummate their love.

This act, which becomes critical in the judgement scene in Book Five, is treated here by Sidney with sympathy and satisfaction and we are drawn into a similar attitude. Twice in that crucial last paragraph, he appeals to the woman reader, explaining that the prince, making love,

> . . . gives me occasion to leave him in so happy a plight, lest my pen might seem to grudge at the due bliss of these poor lovers whose loyalty had but small respite of their fiery agonies.
>
> (p. 211)

There will be no need of further asides to women, for now Sidney has completed the association of the woman reader with the passion of the lovers. By moulding an implied woman reader who will favour the princes, Sidney ensures her sympathy for them throughout the *Old Arcadia*, and leads her to take their side during the trial in the final book.

The text, however, becomes more complicated. For there is another role for the implied reader: the role of ethical judge, who will respond to the judgements of Philanax and, even more so, of Euarchus. In the first part of the work, the touchstone for wisdom is Philanax, Basilius' friend 'not only in affection but judgement, and no less of the duke than dukedom' (p. 5). His love for Basilius shows itself chiefly in direct and fearless advice, even when it goes against the Duke's will. He berates him freely, for example, for ever consulting the Delphic oracle, pointing out that such 'soothsaying sorceries' are either fancies, and therefore not to be respected, or inevitable, and therefore not to be prevented. He uses both political and moral arguments in order to try to persuade him not to abdicate his responsibility to his subjects by hiding with his family in seclusion. But Philanax's love for the Duke becomes also his weakness when it leads him to prejudge the guilt of the four lovers in plotting to kill Basilius: he assumes Philoclea's innocence is a pretence, or at best an attempt to hide guilty lust, and when he sets eyes upon Pyrocles, 'compassion turned to hateful passion' (p. 261). He unfairly conceals the letters of Pamela and Philoclea during the trial, and treats the accused with sarcasm and derision. Gynecia sums up the way his excess of zeal clouds his judgement when she expresses the paradox: 'It may be truth doth make thee deal untruly, and love of justice frames unjustice in thee' (p. 330).

At this point, Euarchus takes over as ethical touchstone. He is presented from the first as one whose wisdom is absolute, and is introduced as '. . . a prince of such justice that he never thought himself privileged by being a prince, nor did measure greatness by anything but goodness' (p. 9), and his fitness to be king is demonstrated by his attitude of humility when Philanax goes to ask him to act as judge, and finds him '. . . taking his rest under a tree with no more affected pomp than as a man that knew, howsoever he was exalted, the beginning and end of his body was earth' (p. 308).

The narrator's very clear approval of him elicits support from the reader for the values which he upholds; but at the same time the reader has also been drawn into a close and sympathetic relationship with the lovers. We are, then, involved in two sets of values, those of Euarchus and 'reason', and those of the lovers and 'passion': for as the princes become more enamoured of Pamela and Philoclea, and more under the sway of passion, so their passionate and unreasonable actions grow (Musidorus' attempted rape, his offer of bringing an army to help Pyrocles escape with Philoclea, his 'abduction' of Pamela, and finally Pyrocles' consummation of his passion). We are encouraged both to judge them harshly with Euarchus, and to feel approval and support for them. I am indebted to Susan Gubar for the following analysis of the reading process:

> This means that the two responses of the reader become increasingly incompatible, until they are contrary: as the intensity of the lovers increases, the 'faire ladyes' become more eager to see their passion achieve its goal, but as the lovers become more irresponsible, the judging reader becomes convinced of their guilt and the necessity of their being punished.[31]

Sidney uses the dilemma of the dual role of the implied reader to demonstrate the central dilemma of the *Old Arcadia*: whether or not reason and passion can be reconciled. This dilemma reaches its climax in the final book during the trial scene. The process of reading this part of the *Arcadia* is a profoundly disorienting and distressing experience for the woman reader, for it is here that the two sets of reader responses are brought most violently into opposition and, ultimately, into collision. At precisely the time when we are convinced of the princes' virtue and worthiness, Euarchus is introduced as the work's ethical judge, whose wisdom is given out as absolute. It becomes impossible to hold the claims of both principles as co-equals, although this is exactly what the narrator encourages us to do.

Helgerson identifies this process, without recognizing the significance of the gendered reader, or of her dual role:

> ... the *Arcadia* makes of sympathy a trap. By his confident insinuation that they, knowing at first hand the power of love will understand, and understanding will pity, and pitying will forgive, the narrator manipulates his readers into sharing the guilt and the awareness of guilt that characterizes Pyrocles, Musidorus, and Sidney himself.[32]

This narrator is artful to a fault, not at all the clumsy, immature storyteller of Zandvoort's analysis. At the beginning of Book Four the narrator still appears to be in full sympathy with the lovers. Even when Pyrocles and Philoclea are surprised by Philanax in Philoclea's chamber, they are still portrayed as virtuous and worthy. Philanax is referred to as 'the hard-hearted Philanax' (p. 263), while Pyrocles becomes 'poor Pyrocles' (p. 262), and his qualities of virtue, selflessness and courage are stressed. We are guided by the narrator to feel compassion for the lovers as Pyrocles is taken away, and Philoclea left to grieve for her father's apparent death. Philanax leaves her in 'revengeful choler' (p. 265), while she remains a 'desolate lady; to whom now fortune seemed to threaten unripe death and undeserved shame among her least evils' (p. 265). The woman reader is convinced, once again, that her sympathies were rightfully with the lovers, despite the premature consummation of their passion.

However, this seemingly safe and reassuring state is radically threatened in the very next paragraph (p. 265) when we read, in a subordinate clause veiled in euphemism, that Musidorus has been restrained from raping Pamela only by a timely interruption. The disjuncture, both in timing and in grammar, is violently disruptive.[33] The clause, describing Pamela, begins unremarkably enough, but gradually as the subordinate clauses pile up on each other, so too does their significance:

> . . . who, having delivered over the burden of her fearful cares to the natural ease of a well refreshing sleep, reposing both body and mind upon the trusted support of her princely shepherd, was with the braying cries of a rascal company robbed of her quiet, at what time she was in a shrewd likelihood to have had great part of her trust in Musidorus deceived and found herself robbed of that she had laid in store as her dearest jewel − so did her own beauties enforce a force against herself.

> (p. 265)

It is one of Sidney's most grammatically tortuous passages, and one of his most sophisticated; the passive mode effectively appears to remove responsibility and blame from Musidorus, and the metaphorical terms in which it is couched at first gloss over his offence, until it is made more explicit in the following sentence which describes his 'tyrannical fire of lust' (p. 265). This has the effect of making the woman reader feel 'caught out': it is easy to read the first part of the passage without fully understanding its meaning, and it is with a shock that the reference to Musidorus' lust alerts us to the full implication of what we have just read, and to the realization that we have nearly allowed Musidorus' intent to rape pass without judgement. It is a discomforting experience: the nature of the sympathy for the enamoured princes which Sidney has asked of us comes dangerously close here to involving a complete abandonment of all responsibility. Immediately after this, however, the narrator deftly moves on to a swift battle scene, in which Musidorus single-handedly takes on the 'scummy remnant of those Phagonian rebels' (p. 265), and thus immediately becomes once again 'the worthy Musidorus' (p. 266) and 'the valorous Musidorus' (p. 267); and by a few pages later Musidorus has, with Pamela, achieved such a quality of 'excellent virtue' that it 'wrought a kind of reverence' in their guards (p. 272).

Sidney has pushed his thesis to its logical conclusion – that passion unrestrained by reason inevitably leads to violence – and finally withdraws from its literal enactment. C.S. Lewis, coming to this passage from a reading of the *New Arcadia* (which omits it), simply refuses to believe in it:

> We cannot suspend our disbelief in a Musidorus who commits indecent assaults: it is as if, in some re-discovered first draft of *Emma*, we were asked to accept a Mr Woodhouse who fought a duel with Frank Churchill.[34]

But in order fully to express the dilemma with which he is struggling, Sidney is obliged to push the woman reader's sympathy with the lovers perilously close to a state of moral irresponsibility; that our sympathy with them remains, shaken but intact, is a measure of Sidney's confident narrative technique in effectively moulding and directing our responses.

By the time we reach the trial scene, then, our greatest need is for those responses to be validated, and for the traditional happy ending to come about. But the trial is Sidney's opportunity to introduce the strongest ethical condemnation of the princes' actions. It is profoundly unsettling, for Euarchus, the judge, has been presented as the epitome of justice and wisdom. Thus, at precisely the time when we most need our sympathy for the princes to be proved appropriate, our responses are radically undermined by Euarchus' judgement.

As the trial scene proceeds, the text ensures that the two sets of reader responses – the sympathy for the lovers' passion, and simultaneous condemnation of their actions – become increasingly at odds. After almost two full pages of the narrator's celebration of Euarchus' greatness of mind, his virtue, his constancy, integrity and justice (pp. 309–310), the narrator turns back to the accused and, perversely it would seem, tries to encourage our admiration and pity for them: 'But first it shall be well to know how the poor and princely prisoners passed this tedious night' (p. 316). And as he turns from one to other of them, he pictures them at their most virtuous and sincere; even the wretched Gynecia stirs our compassion as we witness her 'crucify her own soul' with strange visions and cries of hellish ghosts, with guilt, shame and self-loathing (p. 316). Then we pass to the two sisters, 'excellent creatures' (p. 319), and watch their grief and patience, and recognize the purity of the 'tender Philoclea', and the 'virtuous mildness' of Pamela (p. 319). And, finally, to the princes, who in their supreme patience, courage, piety and selfless devotion to one another, and to their loved ones, achieve a kind of heavenly perfection. As Pyrocles speculates on the nature of the next world, Musidorus looks upon him 'with a heavenly joy' (p. 323), and sings about the need to accept death, while the narrator approvingly concludes:

> Thus did they, like quiet swans, sing their own obsequies, and virtuously enable their minds against all extremities which they did think would fall upon them.
>
> (p. 323)

And so, as the trial itself unfolds, and the princes come forward, their exquisite dress described in loving and reverent detail to enhance their stature and beauty, the woman reader is left in confusion. Euarchus pronounces sentence against them – they are to be killed – and by the laws of reason, Euarchus' logic is flawless, and by the laws of Arcadia, just; and in his rejection of their extenuating plea that love directed all their actions, he looks forward to that sort of love which will be explored by Sidney in his revised text, the *New Arcadia*:

> . . . love may have no such privilege. That sweet and heavenly uniting of the minds, which properly is called love, hath no other knot but virtue; and therefore if it be a right love, it can never slide into any action that is not virtuous.
>
> (p. 352)

Euarchus here forces us to acknowledge that the princes' love has not been truly virtuous, and that we have allowed our responses to be manipulated; the role which Sidney has held out to us, and the attitudes which we have been encouraged to adopt, are undermined. It is only by a miraculous resurrection that the lovers can be reunited, and the woman reader's sympathies be gratified.

This *deus ex machina* type ending is still disturbing, however. Richard McCoy articulates the uneasy awareness that, somehow, the princes do not deserve to be let off:

> The heroes should not be so easily forgiven for ravishing the girls and threatening the social order, but they still must be rescued from death at the hands of Euarchus. Basilius is restored, and Pyrocles and Musidorus receive the conventional rewards of pastoral romance as their paternal opponents are reduced to benign confusion. Yet these rewards cannot be administered within a clear or coherent ethical scheme . . . . The happy ending could not come

as the result of the heroes' own exertions; instead, it must derive from the indulgent and confused goodwill of others.[35]

But that is precisely the point, and the confusion is, I would argue, deliberate. Sidney has purposely brought into collision the two parts of the implied reader's dual role, and forcefully demonstrated – in a way which our frustrated reading experience forces us to *feel* intensely – that the claims of reason and passion cannot be reconciled without recourse to a 'higher' sort of love. As the 'skirmish betwixt Reason and Passion' in the Second Eclogue concludes:

> Then let us both to heav'nly rules give place,
> Which Passions kill, and Reason do deface.

> (p. 120)

It is a dilemma which Sidney continues to explore, most vividly in his sonnet sequence, *Astrophil and Stella*, where the tension and dynamism of the sonnets derive from the uneasy binding of authority and love, honour and desire. The famous concluding couplet of 71 contains the essence of this dilemma, the rhyme yoking together even more firmly the inseparableness of the two ideas:

> As fast thy Vertue bends that love to good:
> 'But ah', Desire still cries, 'give me some food!'[36]

Basilius' resurrection allows a temporary solution, although McCoy complains that Sidney is not playing fair:

> ... he gets away with several things: filial claims are satisfied without being fully vindicated, and paternal authority is thwarted without being denied. It is a kind of compromise solution, however precarious.[37]

All this is true, but intentionally so; and Sidney's manipulation of the role of the implied woman reader has demonstrated that until the levels of divinely virtuous love are reached (as they are in the *New Arcadia*) the reconciliation of reason and passion can always only be a compromise.

The first and foremost reader envisaged by the *Arcadia* is, as we have said, Sidney's sister Mary, Countess of Pembroke. In many ways it is a remarkably strange text for an aristocratic gentleman to write for his sister, and her response to it sadly remains unknown. It might be significant, however, that in the version which she published in 1593, the attempted rape of Pamela and the consummation of the passion between Pyrocles and Philoclea are written out.[38]

But if we do not know Mary Sidney's response to the *Arcadia*, we do at least know that she was the reader for whom it was first intended. Clark Hulse has stimulated critical debate about Sidney's later work, *Astrophil and Stella*, by provocatively suggesting that its primary reader was meant to be the woman he believes to have been Stella, Penelope Devereux Rich.[39] Most critical analysis has assumed that Stella is simply a blind, through whom Sidney addresses his more intelligent, subtle and presumably male critical audience. Hulse reverses the argument, and claims that the historical audience, the ideal reader, and the principal reader described within the poems, are all one person, Lady Rich. From this premise, Hulse constructs a critical reading of the poems which makes her an equally powerful co-producer of the meaning of the text:

> ... the love-game enacted in the sonnets is a struggle between her and Sidney for control not only over their relationship but over the poems as well ... and ... this struggle follows a pattern that characterizes the political milieu of the Elizabethan court.[40]

For Hulse, the narrative of *Astrophil and Stella* unfolds as a contest between the wits of Sidney and Penelope Rich, played out under the veil of synechdoche. Such poetry, Hulse maintains, is ultimately a struggle for power between the reader and writer, and in Penelope Rich, Sidney addresse a reader of unusual skill.

This struggle for power between woman reader and male writer replays the process we have seen in Sidney's *Arcadia*. It would appear, then, that the woman reader is crucial to the structure of Sidney's texts, and it is precisely in the dynamic interaction between woman reader and male discourse, with the conflicts and contradictions which it generates, that we can most fully experience Sidney's subject and design.

Afterword

Elizabethan romances are complex and contradictory, at once appearing to offer women so much and at the same time limiting it, qualifying it, and, on occasion, withdrawing it altogether. This book has been an attempt to re-open a conversation with these romances, to change our relationship to them from one of passive receptivity to one of active dialogue. I have aimed to interrogate them, to challenge them, to resist the male appropriation of the woman reader's response, and ultimately to give the woman reader a voice with which to name her own reality and to inscribe her own position within the literary discourse. The space opened up by the discrepancy between the role offered to us by these texts, and the role which we, as women readers and feminist critics, might wish to adopt can be a fertile one: for it is here that we can name the sexual/textual strategies which are being used against us, and resist them, rereading the romances instead as the strongly woman-centred texts which they can be.

The dialogue is not only between the woman reader and the text, however, but also with literary history itself. Gary Waller describes this as '. . . the perpetual struggle to write ourselves into our own history, and to do so in the company of as many of those who have struggled before us'.[1] This study is offered, then, as part of that struggle, and as part of the feminist commitment to reclaiming our own cultural history.

What would the Elizabethan women readers themselves have made of all this? Sadly, Mary Sidney left no journal recording her response to her brother's romance, nor did any of the other women readers leave any evidence of how they read the romances which were written for them.

They would probably never have thought of themselves as resisting readers nor of what they were reading as fantasies of female power, but the popularity of the romances suggests that sixteenth-century women might have individually and perhaps unconsciously adopted similar strategies; that they might, for example, have found Pettie's accounts of history, in which women are firmly centre-stage, more relevant to their lives than the originals in Tacitus or Livy. Catherine Morland, in Jane Austen's *Northanger Abbey*, explains her preference for fiction over history on precisely these grounds: '. . . history, real solemn history, I cannot be interested in . . . the men are all so good for nothing, and hardly any women at all'.[2]

Until recently, history has been an account of the actions of men written by men and for men. The romances record a different sort of history: a history about women, for women, and, increasingly after the end of the sixteenth century, written by women.[3]

The Elizabethan romances, written for women by men, are more ambiguous and ambivalent than most. What we can conclude from this about real attitudes to women during this period might only be that they were paradoxical. Although there are dangers of assuming any too simplistic correlation between literature and life, there is perhaps even greater danger in the opposite extreme of assuming no relation between the two or, worse, of assuming that what is intended as literature can have no effect on human attitudes and perceptions. Chaucer's Wife of Bath was made to observe long ago that women in literature influence the opinions and behaviour of readers, and her own response to the misogyny of her husband's anti-marriage manual was, as we have seen, to destroy it by ripping out the offending pages.

Reading as women readers, we do not have to destroy the text; we can instead read against the grain and, by naming and exposing the designs these texts have on us, reclaim and reappropriate them for our own use, recognizing that in romantic fiction women can find a power and independence which are not necessarily limited to the pages of a book.

Notes

Introduction

1 Judith Fetterley, *The Resisting Reader: A Feminist Approach to American Fiction* (Bloomington and London, 1978), p. xxii.

2 Jacob Burckhardt, *The Civilization of the Renaissance in Italy*, 2 vols, trans. S.G.C. Middlemore (1860; reprinted New York and London, 1958), vol. 2, p. 389.

3 Joan Kelly-Gadol, 'Did women have a Renaissance?', in Renate Bridenthal and Claudia Koonz (eds), *Becoming Visible: Women in European History* (Boston, Mass., 1977), pp. 137–64.

4 Peter Laslett, 'The wrong way through the telescope: A note on literary evidence in sociology and in historical sociology', *British Journal of Sociology*, **27** (1976), 319–42.

5 Ralph Houlbrooke, *The English Family 1450–1700* (1984; reprinted London and New York, 1985), p. 88.

6 Alan Macfarlane, *Marriage and Love in England 1300–1840* (Oxford, 1986), pp. 206–7.

7 See, in particular: Margaret Jensen, *Love's Sweet Return: The Harlequin Story* (Toronto, 1984); Tania Modleski, *Loving With a Vengeance: Mass-produced Fantasies for Women* (1982; reprinted New York and London, 1984); and Janice Radway, *Reading the Romance: Women, Patriarchy and Popular Literature* (Chapel Hill, N.C. 1984).

8 Linda Woodbridge, *Women and the English Renaissance: Literature and the Nature of Womankind 1540–1620* (Brighton, 1984), pp. 323–4.

9 Gary Waller, 'Struggling into discourse: The emergence of Renaissance women's writing', in Margaret Hannay, ed., *Silent but for the Word: Tudor*

Women as Patrons, Translators, and Writers of Religious Works (Ohio, 1985), p. 247.

10 Ann Rosalind Jones, 'Mills and Boon meets feminism', in Jean Radford, ed., *The Progress of Romance: The Politics of Popular Fiction* (London and New York, 1986), p. 198.

11 Radford, op. cit.

12 See, for example, J.J. O'Connor, *Amadis de Gaule and its Influence on Elizabethan Literature* (New Brunswick, 1970); M. Patchell, *The Palmerin Romances in Elizabethan Prose Fiction* (New York, 1947); and H. Thomas, *Spanish and Portuguese Romances of Chivalry* (Cambridge, 1920).

13 Juliet Mitchell, *Women: The Longest Revolution* (1966; reprinted London, 1984), p. 108.

14 Clara Reeve, *The Progress of Romance* (London, 1785), p. 111.

15 Jane Spencer, *The Rise of the Woman Novelist: From Aphra Behn to Jane Austen* (Oxford, 1986), p. 183.

16 Ibid.

17 Ibid, p. 184.

18 Rachel Brownstein, *Becoming a Heroine: Reading about Women in Novels* (1982; reprinted Harmondsworth, 1984), p. xv.

19 Charlotte Lennox, *The Female Quixote; Or, The Adventures of Arabella*, 2 vols (1752; reprinted London, 1970).

1. The background

1 Juan Luis Vives, *The Instruction of a Christian Woman* (trans. Richard Hyrde *c.* 1540); reprinted Foster Watson, ed., *Vives and the Renascence Education of Women* (London, 1912), p. 58.

2 Instruction books containing guidelines for women's reading include: Vives, op. cit.; Edward Hake, *A Touchestone for this time present . . . Whereunto is annexed a perfect rule to be observed of all Parents and Scholemaisters, in the trayning up of their Schollers and Children in learning* (1574); Thomas Salter, *A Mirrhor mete for all Mothers, Matrones, and Maidens, intituled the Mirrhor of Modestie* (1574); Richard Mulcaster, *Positions wherein those primitive circumstances be examined which are necessarie for the training up of children* (1581); reprinted in R.H. Quick, ed., *Positions of Richard Mulcaster* (London, 1888).

3 Suzanne Hull, *Chaste, Silent and Obedient: English Books for Women, 1475–1640* (San Marino, Calif., 1982). Hull has undertaken some excellent research into the bibliographical details of books written for women. The parameters of her study, however, preclude her from making any literary analysis.

4 Ibid., p. 1.

5 There is some debate over why the 1570s and 1580s should see such a sudden increase in books for women. Hull (op. cit., p. 1) suggests that it 'appears to be related to certain social and educational changes in fifteenth and sixteenth-century England and to the changing economics of the book trade'. Among these changes she includes the continuing growth of a middle class with some leisure for its women, increased opportunities for education, the continuing controversy about women, the rise of a professional class of

writers dependent upon book buyers as well as patrons, and the booksellers' need for new markets. Retha Warnicke questions the extent to which the Protestant reformation, with its emphasis on scripture reading, really did boost literacy levels among women (*Women of the English Renaissance and Reformation*, London, 1983), while Joan Kelly-Gadol challenges the whole notion of any kind of renaissance for women during this period ('Did women have a Renaissance?', in R. Bridenthal and C. Koonz (eds), *Becoming Visible: Women in European History* (Boston, Mass., 1977), pp. 137–64).

6 Sterg O'Dell, *A Chronological List of Prose Fiction in English Printed in England and Other Countries* (Cambridge, Mass., 1954), pp. 36–40. Cited by Hull, op. cit., p. 7.

7 Hull, op. cit., p. 7.

8 Ibid.

9 Thomas Tusser, *His Good Pointes of Husbandrie*, ed. Dorothy Hartley (London, 1931).

10 John Lyly, *Complete Works*, ed. R. Warwick Bond, 3 vols (Oxford, 1902), vol. 1.

11 Ibid., vol. 2, pp. 8–9.

12 Ibid.

13 Hull, op. cit., p. 6.

14 Ibid.

15 *A Booke of Curious and strange Inventions, called the first part of Needleworkes* (1596). Cited by Louis B. Wright, *Middle-Class Culture in Elizabethan England* (1935; reprinted New York, 1980), p. 110.

16 Lady Anne Clifford, *Diary* (1922; reprinted London, 1924); Dorothy M. Meads, ed., *Diary of Lady Margaret Hoby 1599–1605* (London, 1930); Rachel Weigall, 'An Elizabethan Gentlewoman: The Journal of Lady Mildmay, circa 1570–1617', *Quarterly Review* 215 (1911), 119–38.

17 See George C. Williamson, *Lady Anne Clifford, Countess of Dorset, Pembroke & Montgomery, 1590–1676* (London, 1922), p. 139; and Lady Anne Clifford, *Diary* (London, 1924), pp. 90–91.

18 Hull, op. cit., p. 125. On the subject of the controversy, see F.L. Utley, *The Crooked Rib* (Columbus, Ohio, 1944) for a comprehensive, annotated bibliography of Controversy titles before 1568. See also Linda Woodbridge, *Women and the English Renaissance: Literature and the Nature of Womankind 1540–1620* (Brighton, 1984). Woodbridge firmly maintains that the spirit of the formal controversy was that of a game, and it did not represent the genuine attitudes towards women at the time. Early in the seventeenth century at least three women appear to have joined in the literary debate: Rachel Speght, Esther Sowernam and Constantia Munda (Woodbridge, op. cit., pp. 87–104).

19 Hull, op. cit., p. 71.

20 George Pettie, *A Petite Pallace of Pettie his Pleasure* (London, 1576), ed. Herbert Hartman (London, 1938). A dedication to 'ladies' or 'gentlewomen' need not be taken as a proof of a work's aristocratic appeal; it was often simply meant to be flattering to a predominantly middle-class readership.

21 John Grange, *The Golden Aphroditis* (London, 1577), ed. Hyder Rollins (New York, 1939).

22 Selections of women's writing of the period include Betty Travitsky, ed., *The Paradise of Women: Writings by Englishwomen of the Renaissance* (London, 1981); Mary R. Mahl and Helene Koon, eds, *The Female Spectator* (New York, 1977). Valerie Wayne addresses the question of why Renaissance women wrote comparatively little, and points to the overwhelming social, political, cultural and psychological constraints in 'Some sad sentence: Vives' *Instruction of a Christian Woman*', in Margaret Hannay, ed., *Silent But For the Word: Tudor Women as Patrons, Translators, and Writers of Religious Works* (Ohio, 1985), pp. 15–29.

23 Margaret Tyler, trans., *The First Part of the Mirrour of Princely Deedes and Knighthood* (London, 1578), sigs. A$_3$^{v}–A$_4$^{v}.

24 Ibid., sig. A$_4$^{v}.

25 Hull, op. cit., p. 18. See also Hannay, op. cit.

26 Franklin Williams, *Index of Dedications and Commendatory Verses in English Books Before 1641* (London, 1962).

27 Hull, op. cit., p. 21.

28 J.W. Adamson, 'The extent of literacy in England in the fifteenth and sixteenth centuries: Notes and conjectures', *The Library*, 4th Ser., 10 (1929–30), 163–93.

29 Ibid., pp. 172–3.

30 R.S. Schofield, 'The measurement of literacy in pre-industrial England', in Jack Goody, ed., *Literacy in Traditional Societies* (Cambridge, 1968), pp. 311–25. David Cressy, *Literacy and the Social Order: Reading and Writing in Tudor and Stuart England* (Cambridge, 1980).

31 Cressy, op. cit., chs 6 and 8.

32 Keith Thomas, 'The meaning of literacy in early modern England', in Gerd Baumann, ed., *The Written Word: Literacy in Transition* (Oxford, 1986), pp. 97–131.

33 Ibid., p. 130.

34 Schofield, op. cit., pp. 312–13.

35 Cressy, op. cit., p. 51.

36 Cressy, *Education in Tudor and Stuart England* (London, 1975), p. 106.

37 Margaret Spufford, 'First steps in literacy: The reading and writing exprinces of the humblest seventeenth-century spiritual autobiographers', *Social History* 4 (1979), 407–35.

38 Ibid., p. 412.

39 Ibid., p. 414.

40 Adamson, op. cit., p. 188.

41 Sears Jayne, *Library Catalogues of the English Renaissance* (Berkeley and Los Angeles, 1956).

42 The three women he cites are Alice Edwards (1546), Lucy, Countess of Bedford (1628), and Judith Ishlam (*c.* 1636). Jayne points out that the collections of the first two women clearly belonged to their deceased husbands. In any case, these catalogues are of little use for a study of popular literature, since they rarely include the ephemeral works of the period. Such materials were excluded almost as a matter of principle from most large libraries: Spenser and Elyot were admissible; Shakespeare and Greene were not (p. 54).

43 Peter Clark, 'The ownership of books in England, 1560–1640: The example of some Kentish townsfolk', in Lawrence Stone, ed., *Schooling and Society: Studies in the History of Education* (London, 1976).

44 Ibid., p. 97.

45 Ibid., p. 98.

46 Ibid., p. 99.

47 Ibid.

48 Works relating to the book-trade include Phoebe Sheavyn, *The Literary Profession in the Elizabethan Age* (1909; 2nd ed. revised by J.W. Saunders, Manchester, 1967); E.H. Miller, *The Professional Writer in Elizabethan England* (Cambridge, Mass., 1959); H.S. Bennett, *English Books and Readers 1558–1603* (Cambridge, 1965); Francis Johnson, 'Notes on English retail book-prices, 1550–1640', *The Library*, 5th Ser., (1950), 83–112.

49 Clark, op. cit., p. 97.

50 Ibid.

51 Cited by Rachel Weigall, op. cit., especially pp. 120–1 and p. 134.

52 Meads, op. cit., pp. 93, 94 and 175.

53 Clifford, op. cit.; especially pp. 52, 66 and 104.

54 Ibid., p. 76.

55 Woodbridge, op. cit., p. 3.

56 William Browne, 'Fido, an Epistle to Fidelia', in *Whole Works*, ed. W. Carew Hazlitt, vol. 2 (London, 1869), pp. 300–1.

57 Philip Massinger, *The Guardian*, in *The Plays and Poems of Philip Massinger*, eds Edwards and Gibson (Oxford, 1976), Act 1, sc. ii.

58 Wye Saltonstall, *Picturae Loquentes. Or Pictures Drawne forth in Characters. With a Poeme of a Maid* (London, 1631), sig. B_1^v. Reprinted from the 1631 and 1635 editions for the Luttrell Society by Basil Blackwell (London, 1946) , 1, p. 47.

59 Edward Hake, op. cit., sig. C_4.

60 Thomas Salter, op. cit., sig. B_{ii}^v.

61 Ibid.

62 Ibid., sigs B_{ii}^v–B_{iii}.

63 Ibid.

64 See Chapter 4.

65 Richard Mulcaster, op. cit., pp. 176–7.

66 See Foster Watson, op. cit.

67 Ibid., p. 61.

68 Ibid., pp. 59–60.

69 Ibid., p. 60.

70 Ibid., p. 62.

71 Virginia Woolf, *A Room of One's Own* (1929; reprinted London, 1984), p. 70.

72 Louis B. Wright, *Middle-class Culture in Elizabethan England* (1935; reprinted New York, 1980), p. 382.

73 Quoted in Margaret Jensen, *Love's Sweet Return: The Harlequin Story* (Toronto, 1984), p. 15.

74 Nick Cohen, 'Feminist formula and fine romance', *The Independent*, 23 January 1988, p. 3.

75 Sandra Barwick, 'Working girls search for a novel kind of hero', *The*

Independent, 31 March 1988, p. 1. John Ezard, 'Writers labour for love', *The Guardian*, 31 March 1988, p. 1.

76 Angela Levin, 'At home with Barbara Cartland', *You: The Mail on Sunday Magazine*, 30 June 1985, pp. 17–21.

77 Daisy Maryles and Robert Dahlin, 'Romance fiction', *Publishers Weekly*, **220** (13 November 1981), p. 25. Quoted in Jensen, op. cit., p. 15.

78 Jensen, op. cit., pp. 15–16.

79 Sally Ann Lasson, 'Confessions of the blue stocking romantics', *Sunday Express Magazine*, 24 February 1985, pp. 36–8.

80 Peter H. Mann, *The Romantic Novel: A Survey of Reading Habits* (London, 1969); Peter H. Mann, *A New Survey: The Facts about Romantic Fiction* (London, 1974).

81 Ibid., p. 6.

82 Ibid., pp. 8–10.

83 Wright, op. cit., p. 376.

84 Jane Spencer, *The Rise of the Woman Novelist* (Oxford, 1986), has indicated the resistance of seventeenth- and eighteenth-century writers and moralists to romances, and to romance elements within the novel, on the grounds, that they posed a threat to female chastity and subordination. See pp. 186–7.

85 Foster Watson, ed., *Vives and the Renascence Education of Women* (London, 1912), pp. 58–9.

86 Germaine Greer, *The Female Eunuch* (1970; reprinted London, 1981), pp. 201–22.

87 Ibid., pp. 211–12.

88 Shulamith Firestone, *The Dialectic of Sex* (1970; reprinted London, 1972), p. 139.

89 John Cawelti, *Adventure, Mystery, and Romance* (Chicago, 1976), p. 8.

90 *The Writer's 1978 Yearbook*, p. 103. Quoted in Tania Modleski, *Loving With a Vengeance: Mass Produced Fantasies for Women* (1982; reprinted New York and London, 1984), pp. 35–6.

91 Modleski, op. cit., p. 36.

92 Polly Toynbee, *The Guardian*, 22 July 1985, p. 10.

93 Janet Batsleer, 'Pulp in the pink', *Spare Rib*, **109** (1981), pp. 52–5.

94 Ibid., p. 53.

95 Ibid., p. 54.

96 Ibid., p. 55.

97 Valerie Hey, 'The necessity of romance', *Women's Studies Occasional Papers* (University of Kent, 1983), No. 3.

98 Ibid., p. 15.

99 Modleski, op. cit., p. 26.

100 Ibid., p. 57.

101 Ibid., p. 58.

102 Jensen, op. cit., p. 24.

103 Ibid., p. 25.

104 Sara Barratt and John Illmann, 'Beware of romance', *Daily Mail*, 29 August 1985, p. 3.

105 Ibid.

106 *The Overburian Characters* (1614), ed. W.J. Paylor, The Percy Reprints 13 (Oxford, 1936), p. 43.

107 Chapman, Jonson and Marston, *Eastward Ho*, ed. C.G. Petter (London, 1973), Act 5, sc. i.

108 Janice Radway, *Reading the Romance: Women, Patriarchy, and Popular Literature* (Chapel Hill, N.C., 1984).

109 Ibid., p. 17.

110 Ibid., p. 211.

111 Ibid., p. 217.

112 Ibid., p. 17. It is, of course, possible to argue that women read romances because they are attracted to a world where the rules are clear, and where they can enjoy a 'vacation' from ideologically correct alertness, finding pleasure in recognizing (although not accepting) the codes used. This would, however, be equally true for any kind of formula fiction, and fails to account adequately for the *specific* appeal of romances to women.

113 Adrienne Rich, 'When we dead awaken: Writing as re-vision', *On Lies, Secrets & Silence* (1979; reprinted London, 1980), p. 35.

114 Annette Kolodny embraces the 'playful plurality' of feminist critical theory, a pluralism which she believes to be 'the only critical stance consistent with the current status of the larger women's movement' ('Dancing through the minefield: some observations on the theory, practice, and politics of a feminist literary criticism', *Feminist Studies* 6 (Spring 1980), 19–20). On the same subject, see Showalter, 'Literary criticism', *Signs* 1 (Winter 1975), 435–60, and a warning against an anti-theoretical approach by Toril Moi, *Sexual/Textual Politics* (London, 1985), pp. 74–5.

115 Toril Moi, op. cit., p. 84.

116 See Showalter's two key articles on feminist critical theory: 'Feminist criticism in the wilderness', in Elizabeth Abel, ed., *Writing and Sexual Difference* (Brighton, 1982), pp. 9–35; and 'Towards a feminist poetics', in Mary Jacobus, ed., *Women Writing and Writing about Women* (London, 1979), pp. 22–41.

117 Showalter, 'Towards a feminist poetics', p. 25.

118 Ibid., p. 28.

119 Gayle Greene and Coppelia Kahn, eds, *Making a Difference* (London, 1985), p. 24.

120 Carolyn J. Allen, 'Feminist(s) reading: A response to Elaine Showalter', in Elizabeth Abel, op. cit., pp. 298 and 301.

121 Toril Moi, op. cit., pp. 78–9.

122 Showalter, 'Towards a feminist poetics', p. 27.

123 Toril Moi, op. cit., p. 76.

124 Greene and Kahn, op. cit., p. 25.

125 Toril Moi, op. cit., p. 63.

126 Catherine Belsey, *Critical Practice* (London and New York, 1980), pp. 134 and 136; cited in Greene and Kahn, op. cit., p. 25.

127 Elizabeth A. Flynn and Patrocinio Schweickart, eds, *Gender and Reading: Essays on Readers, Texts, and Contexts* (Baltimore and London, 1986), p. ix.

128 Sir Philip Sidney, *A Defence of Poetry*, ed. J.A. Van Dorsten (1966; reprinted Oxford, 1978).

129 Ibid., p. 25.

130 Ibid., p. 27.

131 Ibid., pp. 40–1.

132 Foster Watson, ed., *Vives and the Renascence Education of Women* (London, 1912), p. 58.

133 Gary Waller, *English Poetry of the Sixteenth Century* (London and New York, 1986), p. 57.

134 Key works on reader–response criticism include: Wolfgang Iser, *The Implied Reader: Patterns of Communication in Prose Fiction from Bunyan to Beckett* (Baltimore, 1974); Wolfgang Iser, *The Act of Reading: A Theory of Aesthetic Response* (1976; reprinted London, 1978); Wayne C. Booth, *The Rhetoric of Fiction* (Chicago, 1961). Both Booth and Iser privilege the text in their theories of the production of meaning. Umberto Eco, *The Role of the Reader* (Bloomington, 1979); Geoffrey Hartman, *The Fate of Reading* (Chicago and London, 1975); Stanley Fish, *Is There A Text In This Class?: The Authority of Interpretive Communities* (Cambridge, Mass., 1980), p. 23; Susan B. Suleiman and Inge Crosman, eds, *The Reader in the Text: Essays on Audience and Interpretation* (Princeton, 1980); and Jane P. Tompkins, ed., *Reader Response Criticism: From Formalism to Post-Structuralism* (Baltimore, 1980).

135 Stanley Fish, op. cit., p. 17. All further references to Fish in the text are from his introduction to this work.

136 Susan Schibanoff, 'The art of reading as a woman', in Flynn and Schweickart, eds, op. cit., pp. 83–106.

137 Joseph L. Baird and John R. Kane, trans., 'La Querelle de la Rose', *Letters and Documents*, N. Carolina Studies in Romance Languages and Literatures, no. 199 (Chapel Hill, N.C., 1978), cited by Schibanoff.

138 Cited by Schibanoff, op. cit., p. 93.

139 Ibid., p. 94.

140 Ibid., p. 95.

141 Ibid.

142 Ibid. The Wife of Bath opens her Prologue with just such a premise, pitting her own experience of marriage against the male 'authorities' who have written about it:

　　Experience, though noon auctoritee

　　Were in this world, is right ynough for me

　　To speke of wo that is in mariage (11.1–3)

'The Wife of Bath's Prologue', in F.N. Robinson, ed., *The Works of Geoffrey Chaucer* (1933; reprinted London, 1957), p. 76.

143 Schweickart, 'Reading ourselves: Toward a feminist theory of reading', in Flynn and Schweickart, op. cit., p. 36.

144 Judith Fetterley, *The Resisting Reader* (Bloomington and London, 1978), p. xx.

145 Ibid.

146 Jonathan Culler, *On Deconstruction* (1982; reprinted London, Melbourne and Henley, 1983), p. 49.

147 Ibid.

148 Ibid.

149 Maggie Humm, *Feminist Criticism* (Brighton, 1986), p. 13.

150 Ibid.
151 Christine de Pisan, *The Book of the City of Ladies*, trans. Earl Jeffrey Richards, Foreword by Marina Warner (1982; reprinted London, 1983). See Schibanoff, op. cit., p. 86.
152 De Pisan, op. cit., pp. 4–5.
153 Ibid., p. 7.
154 Schibanoff, op. cit., p. 98. Reason's instructions serve 'Christine' well, and the rest of the *City* contains her re-readings of women's history as presented by male writers.
155 Chaucer, 'The Wife of Bath's Prologue', 11.788–791; 816; in Chaucer, *Works*, op. cit., pp. 83–4.
156 Kate Millett, *Sexual Politics* (1969; reprinted London, 1983).
157 Fetterley, op. cit., pp. xxii–xxiii.
158 Wayne C. Booth, op. cit., pp. 137–8.
159 The word 'enjoy' is important here: one does not need to share the author's beliefs in order to understand the work, to analyse it or, indeed, to appreciate it.
160 Wolfgang Iser, op. cit., p. 33.
161 Gibson, 'Authors, speakers, readers, and mock readers', *College English* **XI** (February 1950), 265–9; cited by Booth, op. cit., p. 138.
162 Fetterley, op. cit., p. xi.

2. Out of the literary doghouse: Elizabethan courtly romance

1 John Carey, 'Sixteenth and seventeenth century prose', in *English Poetry and Prose, 1540–1674*, ed. Christopher Ricks (1970; reprinted London, 1986), p. 348.
2 J.J. Jusserand, *The English Novel in the Age of Shakespeare* (1890; translated by Elizabeth Lee, reprinted London, 1901).
3 Margaret Schlauch, *Antecedents of the English Novel* (1963; reprinted London 1965).
4 Ernest Baker, *History of the English Novel* (London, 1929), p. 32.
5 Ibid., p. 44.
6 A.C. Hamilton, 'Elizabethan prose fiction and some trends in recent criticism', *Renaissance Quarterly* 37 (1984), p. 23.
7 Hamilton, 'Elizabethan romance: the example of prose fiction', *ELH* **49** (1982), pp. 297–8.
8 Hamilton, 'Elizabethan prose fiction', p. 32.
9 William Painter, *The Palace of Pleasure* (1566), 3 vols, ed. Joseph Jacobs (London, 1890).
10 For influence of Bandello on the fiction of the period, see René Pruvost, *Matteo Bandello and Elizabethan Fiction* (Paris, 1937).
11 H.S. Canby, *The Short Story in English* (New York, 1909), pp. 117–18.
12 Painter, op. cit., vol. 1, p. 5.
13 Painter, op. cit., vol. 2, p. 152.
14 Ibid., p. 165.

15 Linda Woodbridge, *Women and the English Renaissance: Literature and the Nature of Womankind, 1540–1620* (Brighton, 1984), p. 117.
16 Painter, op. cit., vol. 3, pp. 54–5.
17 Painter, op. cit., vol. 2, p. 261.
18 Geoffrey Fenton, *Certaine Tragicall Discourses* (1567), ed. R.L. Douglas (London, 1898).
19 Ibid., pp. 157–8.
20 Ibid., p. 160.
21 Ibid., p. 161.
22 Ibid.
23 George Pettie, *A Petite Pallace of Pettie his Pleasure* (1576), ed. Herbert Hartman (London, 1938).
24 Paul Salzman, *English Prose Fiction 1558–1700: A Critical History* (1985; reprinted Oxford, 1986), pp. 18–19.
25 Ibid., p. 20.
26 Barnaby Rich, *Farewell to Militarie Profession* (1581), ed. T.M. Cranfill (Austin, Texas, 1959).
27 Canby, op. cit., p. 128.
28 George Gascoigne, *The Adventures of Master F.J.* (1573; revised version 1575). First version in C.T. Prouty, ed., *A Hundreth Sundry Flowers* (Columbia, Miss., 1942); second version in J.W. Cunliffe, ed., *Poesies, Complete Works*, vol. 1 (Cambridge, 1907–10).
29 George Whetstone, *The Rocke of Regard* (1576), sig. ii^v.
30 John Grange, *The Golden Aphroditis* (1577), ed. Hyder Rollins (New York, 1939).
31 Rollins, 'John Grange's "The Golden Aphroditis" ', *Harvard Studies and Notes in Philology and Literature* 16 (1934), p. 177.
32 Ibid., p. 178.
33 Grange, op. cit., sig. B$_{ii}$.
34 Ibid., sig. C$_i$.
35 Ibid., sig. C$_{iii}$.
36 Ibid.
37 John Lyly, *Euphues: The Anatomy of Wit* (1578) and *Euphues and his England* (1580), in R.W. Bond, ed., *The Complete Works of John Lyly*, 3 vols (Oxford, 1902).
38 Preface to reader in *Six Court Comedies* (1632), ed. Edward Blount. Critical studies of *Euphues* and euphuism include Jonas A. Barish, 'The prose style of John Lyly', *ELH* 23 (1956), 14–35; Morris Croll, 'The sources of the euphuistic rhetoric', in *Style, Rhetoric and Rhythm*, ed. J. Max Patrick and Robert O. Evans (Princeton, N.J., 1966), pp. 241–95; Albert Feuillerat, *John Lyly* (Cambridge, 1910); Madelon Gohlke, 'Reading "Euphues" ', *Criticism* 19 (1977), 103–17; G.K. Hunter, *John Lyly: The Humanist as Courtier* (London, 1962); William Ringler, 'The immediate source of euphism', *PMLA* 53 (1938), 678–86.
39 Baker, op. cit., p. 59.
40 Ibid.
41 Lyly, *Works*, vol. 1, p. 184.
42 Feuillerat, op. cit., p. 412.

43 George Saintsbury, *The English Novel* (1913; reprinted London, 1919), pp. 34–5.

44 Ibid., p. 34.

45 Lyly, op. cit., vol. 1, p. 205.

46 Ibid., vol. 2, pp. 8–9.

47 See Samuel L. Wolff's study of the influence of the Greek romances on Elizabethan prose romance, *The Greek Romances in Elizabethan Prose Fiction* (Columbia, N.Y., 1912).

48 A.B. Grosart, ed., *Life and Complete Works of Robert Greene*, 15 vols (1881–6; reprinted New York, 1964).

49 Philip Sidney, *The New Arcadia* (1590), in *Works*, ed. Albert Feuillerat (Cambridge, 1912–26).

50 Rowland Edmund Ernle, *The Light Reading of our Ancestors* (New York, 1927), p. 122.

51 Wolff, op. cit., p. 150.

52 Ibid., pp. 131–2.

53 Thomas Hägg, *The Novel in Antiquity* (1980; reprinted Oxford, 1983), pp. 95–6.

54 Thomas Lodge, *Rosalynde* (1590), in Edmund Gosse, ed., *Complete Works of Thomas Lodge* (Glasgow, 1883).

55 Anthony Munday's translations include *Palmerin d'Oliva*, Part 1, and *Palladine of England* in 1588, and the *Historie of Palmendos* in the following year. In 1590 came *Amadis de Gaule*, Part 1; then *Primaleon of Greece* (1595) on which Munday was only a minor collaborator, and *Palmerin of England*, Part 1 (1596). Sequels, revisions and re-editions continued well into the seventeenth century. See Henry Thomas, *The Palmerin Romances* (London, 1916) and Mary Patchell, *The Palmerin Romances in Elizabethan Prose Fiction* (Columbia, N.Y., 1947).

56 Richard Johnson, *The Most Famous History of the Seaven Champions of Christendome* (1596/7), ed. R. Kennedy (Portland, Oreg., 1967).

57 Patchell, op. cit., p. xii.

58 Ibid., p. 72.

59 Julia Kristeva, 'Women's time', in Toril Moi, ed., *The Kristeva Reader* (Oxford, 1986), pp. 187–213. Marilyn French, *Shakespeare's Division of Experience* (1981; reprinted London, 1983). See also Nancy K. Miller, 'Emphasis added: Plots and plausibilities in women's fiction', in Elaine Showalter, ed., *The New Feminist Criticism* (1985; reprinted London, 1986), pp. 339–60.

60 French, op. cit., p. 32.

61 Ibid., p. 33.

62 Ibid.

63 John Marston, *The Dutch Courtezan,* ed. M.L. Wine (Lincoln, Nebr., 1965), Act 4, sc. i.

64 Spufford, op. cit., p. 234.

65 Samuel Richardson, *Clarissa* (1747–8; Harmondsworth, 1985), p. 723, L.225.

3. George Pettie and the premature closure of the text

1 Little is known about the author. He was born in Oxfordshire around 1548, and took a degree at Christ Church before spending some time travelling. He is known to have translated from the French into English Guazzo's *The Civil Conversation*, books 1–3. He died 'a captain and a man of note' in Devon in 1589. Pettie's great–nephew, Anthony à Wood, to whom we are indebted for these scanty details of Pettie's life, had little respect for his work. The *Petite Pallace* he dismisses in a few lines: '. . . 'tis so far now from being excellent or fine, that it is more fit to be read by a Schoolboy, or rustical amoratto, than by a Gent. of mode or language'. Cited in the introduction to *A Petite Pallace of Pettie His Pleasure*, ed. Herbert Hartman (London, 1938), p. ix. It was a popular work, however, and went through at least six editions by 1613. My suggestions for the most likely sources of these stories are based on those of Douglas Bush, 'The Petite Pallace of Pleasure', *Journal of English and Germanic Philology* **27** (1928), pp. 162–9. Bush also notes influences from Painter's *Palace of Pleasure*, Guevara (in Sir Thomas North's translation, *The Diall of Princes*), and the Italian novelle. For details of the different editions, see Hartman, op. cit., pp. xviii–xx. All further references in the text to Pettie's *Pallace* are from the Hartman edition.

2 William Painter, *The Palace of Pleasure*, 2 vols, 1566–7, ed. Joseph Jacobs, 3 vols, 1890.

3 Janet Batsleer, 'Pulp in the pink', *Spare Rib* **109** (1981), p. 54.

4 Douglas Bush, op. cit., p. 164.

5 William Hazlitt started the tradition of regarding 'R.B.' as the reversed initials of Barnaby Rich. See Hartman, op. cit., p. xvii.

6 Bush, op. cit., p. 164.

7 Linda Woodbridge, *Women and the English Renaissance: Literature and the Nature of Womankind 1540–1620* (Brighton, 1984), pp. 114–15.

8 I. Gollancz, ed., *A Petite Pallace of Pettie his Pleasure* (London, 1908), 2 vols, vol. 1, p. x.

9 Adrienne Rich, *On Lies, Secrets & Silence* (1979; reprinted London, 1980), p. 204.

10 Restrictions of space have prohibited my discussion of all twelve tales. The two which I omit, *Minos and Pasiphae* and *Cephalus and Procris*, contain varieties of the narrative strategies which I explore in Pettie's other works, without producing any new ones.

11 Ovid, *Metamorphoses*, trans. Golding (London, 1961), vi, 424ff.; Chaucer, *Legend of Good Women*, in Chaucer, *Complete Works*, ed. Robinson (London, 1957), VII, 2228–393.

12 Chaucer, ibid., 2251–4.

13 Ovid, op.cit., vi, 550–6.

14 Chaucer, op. cit., 2267–9.

15 I would argue that verbal puns and alliteration suggest the author's detachment from the rape which he describes. In Shakespeare's violent and bloody *Titus Andronicus*, the elaborate rhetorical descriptions of the raped and mutilated Lavinia actually work counter to the awful visual spectacle of the

girl on the stage, and a tension is generated between the horror of the reality, and the inadequacy of words to describe it in a meaningful way (Act 2, sc. iv).

16 Ovid, op. cit., vi, 743–4.

17 The deliberate punning at this highly emotionally charged point in the story is again similar to *Titus*.

18 Ovid, op. cit., vi, 787–800. Chaucer ends with the two women grieving together, omitting the story of Itys altogether. Condemnation of Tereus is clear.

19 It has been suggested that one of the main ideas in Ovid's account is to juxtapose 'barbarous' Thrace and 'civilized' Athens, and to indicate that in certain circumstances Athens can be as barbarous as Thrace. Akiko Kiso suggests that Ovid's story is based on a lost play by Sophocles which demonstrated that 'brutality in human nature, regardless of nationality, is veiled until it is disclosed in its sheer nakedness at a certain point in the action'. Kiso, *The Lost Sophocles* (New York, 1984), p. 77. In his elaboration of this theory, Kiso implies that the relative guilts of Progne and Tereus would be equal.

20 The Epistle, 11.134–40, in Ovid, op. cit.

21 Ovid, op. cit., vi, 842.

22 George Sandys, *Commentary*, Book Six, in Ovid, *Metamorphoses*, ed. Sandys (Lincoln, Nebr. 1970), p. 300.

23 Ovid states that Tereus was transformed into a lapwing 'through sorrow and desire of vengeance' (vi, 849). It is suggested that the lapwing is an appropriately aggressive bird, with a tuft of feathers like a helmet and his bill shooting out in the fashion of a long sword: 'all armed seemes his face' (vi, 853).

24 *The History of Titus Livius*, 3 vols (London, 1814), vol. 1, Bk. III, pp. 205–7. William Painter, *The Palace of Pleasure*, 2 vols, 1566–7, ed. Joseph Jacobs, 3 vols (London, 1890), I, p. 38.

25 The three most readily accessible versions of the story were in: Plutarch, *Moralia*, ed. Bernardakis (Leipsic, 1889), II, 234; Castiglione, *The Courtier*, trans. Hoby (London, 1956), Bk. iii, p. 208; Thomas North, trans., *The Diall of Princes*, selections ed. K.N. Colvile (London, 1919), pp. 33ff.

26 Donne's *Holy Sonnet*, xiv, 'Batter my heart, three person'd God' is perhaps a culmination of this association of sexual and military metaphors:

> . . . I, like an usurpt towne to'another due,
> Labour to admit you, but Oh, to no ende . . .
> Yet dearly I love you, and would be lov'd faine,
> But am bethroth'd unto your enemie,
> Divorce mee, untie, or breake that knot againe
> Take mee to you, imprison me, for I
> Except you enthrall mee, never shall be free
> Nor ever chaste, except you ravish me.

27 The Lady in Milton's *Comus* lacks precisely this momentary vacillation; arguably, this renders her a less appealing character, at least to modern readers.

28 Compare Castiglione's version, in which the only qualification to the story is not over her virtue (about which all, including the opponents of women, are convinced) but about the dearth of such women today, *The Courtier*, ed. Hoby, Book III, p. 209.

29 One might speculate on how the presence of Queen Elizabeth I on the throne might have affected the experience of reading about powerful, independent women at this time (especially when they are single women of means, like Eriphile in Pettie's story *Of Amphiarus and Eriphile*). Stevie Davies, in *The Idea of Woman in Renaissance Literature* (Brighton, 1986), suggests that the Queen's 46-year reign, mythologized in her own time, informed the idea of Woman in literature not only in contemporary writing but also for many years afterwards: 'Nearly fifty years of myth-making do not terminate with the merely human being who is their pretext', she remarks (p. 28). Linda Woodbridge warns against drawing any simple correlation between the power of the woman on the throne, and the power of the majority of ordinary women, and indicates that it is only a more extreme example of a system which allowed a very tiny minority of aristocratic women a power and independence unheard of among their middle- and lower-class sisters:

> In England, the upper-class girls shared her brothers' Latin and Greek tutor, while the middle-class girls were barred from grammar school; the artistocratic lady fought off the Roundheads and held the manor together in her husband's absence, while the middle-class wife was debarred from the weavers' guild. The aristocracy gave England a queen who reigned as one of the nation's greatest monarchs; the middle-class could boast no lady mayor of London.
>
> (*Women and the English Renaissance*, Brighton, 1984, pp. 54–5)

30 Livy, op. cit., vol. 1, Bk. 1, p. 46 or Painter, op. cit., vol. 1, Bk. 1. Pettie's version extends the role of Horatia, and invents details of the courtship between Horatia and Curiatius, during which Horatia remains in control. She is an independent, witty woman with no illusions about the realities of marriage:

> Way againe that the happy life of the wife only consisteth in the loyall love of her husband, and that shee reposeth her selfe only in the pleasure shee hath in him. She for the most part sitteth still at home, shee hawketh not, shee hunteth not, shee diseth not, shee in a manner receiveth no other contentation but in his company ... hee is the field shee delighteth to walke in, hee is the forrest shee forceth to hunt in (p. 176).

A married woman could usually enjoy the activities of public life only vicariously, and she was dependent on her husband for entertainment outside the home. There is a significant shift from 'delighteth' to 'forceth' at the end of the passage, which suggests that while a woman may enjoy the company of her husband, she is aware at the same time that she has no other option. The claim that Horatia was guilty of Curiatius' death is Pettie's own.

31 Tacitus, *Annals*, trans. George Gilbert Ramsay (London, 1904), i, 33, 69; ii, 43, 73ff.; iii, 1–6, etc.

32 Bush, op. cit., p. 163.

33 Tacitus, op. cit., p. 83.

34 Bush, op. cit., p. 163.

35 Possible sources: Ovid, *Metamorphoses*, Bk. VIII, 1ff.; Apollodorus, *The Library*, III, xv, 8.

36 Possible sources: Hyginus, *Fabulae*, 50–1; Apollodorus, *The Library*, I, ix, 15–16; Euripides, *Alcestis*.

37 Pettie is clearly uneasy with supernatural incidents. His euhemeristic approach suggests that he is not completely at home in the romantic genre.

38 Lawrence Stone, *The Family, Sex and Marriage in England 1500–1800* (1977; abridged edition Harmondsworth, 1979), p. 136.

39 Most likely sources: Hyginus, *Fabulae*, 69–73; Apollodorus, *The Library*, III, vi, 1–2.

40 Joyce Youings, *Sixteenth Century England* (Harmondsworth, 1984), p. 368. It is interesting to note that the words 'wilful' and 'calculating' seem to reflect her own opinion as much as those of Elizabethan men, suggesting perhaps her own absorption of the patriarchal fear of independent women.

41 Stone, op. cit., p. 136.

42 According to Apollodorus, Amphiarus was a soothsayer who had foreseen that if he went to war, he would not return alive. Although he concealed himself, hoping to avoid Adrastus' search, Eriphile betrayed him, and he went with the Seven to Thebes; he fought courageously and was escaping from an enemy when Zeus cleft the earth by throwing a thunderbolt, and Amphiarus vanished with his chariot. Zeus made him immortal. *The Library*, III, vi, 8.

43 Barbara Todd, 'The remarrying widow: A stereotype reconsidered', in Mary Prior, ed., *Women in English Society 1500–1800* (London, 1985), p. 55.

44 In Apollodorus it is done in accordance with an oracle from Apollo; in Hyginus, in remembrance of his father's instructions.

45 Linda Woodbridge, op. cit., p. 115.

46 Ovid, op. cit., Bk. X, 243ff.

47 The story of *Alexius* has its source in *The Golden Legend*, trans. William Caxton (London, 1900), 7 vols, 6, pp. 205–12: 'Saint Alexis' is a much beloved son who, initially, makes no objection to marriage. On the evening of his espousal, he gives his wife a ring and the gold buckle of his girdle, and enjoins her to keep her virginity. Then he goes away, and becomes a God-loving beggar. Meanwhile his parents and wife are desperate with worry about him, having no idea where he is. At last he returns home, and, his identity still concealed, lives as a beggar and is treated as such in his father's house. After 17 years his identity is revealed through a letter he has left; it is too late for reconciliation, however, for he has died the same day. In this version Alexis is still a strangely unsympathetic character. His desertion of his wife, and his 'trick' (for that is how it appears) at his father's house do not seem evidence of a 'saintly' nature.

4. Robert Greene: the heroine as mirror

1 Jusserand maintains that there 'seems no doubt' that Thomas Nashe's reference to 'The Homer of Women' (*Anatomie of Absurditie*, p. 12) alludes to

Robert Greene. J.J. Jusserand, *The English Novel in the Time of Shakespeare* (London, 1901), p. 169.

2 They have been variously categorized. While René Pruvost divided his work into eleven periods, Walter Davis, following Jusserand's earlier classification, reduces it to a more manageable four: experiments in the euphuistic mode (1580–4); collections of short tales or novelle (1585–8); pastoral romances strongly influenced by Greek romance (1588–9); and pamphlets of repentance and roguery, in the main non-fictional (1590–2). Walter Davis, *Idea and Act in Elizabethan Fiction* (Princeton, 1969), p. 139. See also René Pruvost, *Robert Greene et ses Romans* (Paris, 1938), chs 3–13 and J.J. Jusserand, op. cit., p. 167.

3 *The Repentance of Robert Greene* in *The Complete Works of Robert Greene*, ed. A.B. Grosart, 15 vols (1881–6; reprinted New York, 1964), vol. 12. All references to Greene's work are from this edition.

4 *The Overburian Characters* (1614), ed. W.J. Paylor, The Percy Reprints XIII (Oxford, 1936), p. 43.

5 Thomas Nashe, *Anatomie of Absurditie*, in *Works*, ed. R.B. McKerrow, 5 vols (Oxford, 1904–10), vol. 1, p. 11.

6 Ben Jonson, *Every Man Out of His Humour* (Act 3, sc. i).

7 R.B.'s *Greenes Funeralls* (1594), cited in L.B. Wright, *Middle Class Culture in Elizabethan England* (1935; reprinted New York, 1980), p. 115.

8 Storojenko, *Life of Robert Greene*, in *Works of Robert Greene*, ed. Grosart, vol. 1.

9 Pruvost, op. cit., p. 320.

10 Ibid., p. 574.

11 J.C. Jordan, *Robert Greene* (New York, 1915), p. 16. In the drama also, Greene's female characters are strong, lively women, particularly Margaret in *Frier Bacon and Frier Bungay* and Dorothea in *The Scottish Historie of James the Fourth*, in *Works*, ed. Grosart, vol. 13.

12 Storojenko, op. cit., pp. 159–60.

13 Samuel Lee Wolff, *The Greek Romances in Elizabethan Prose Fiction* (New York, 1912), p. 411.

14 Ibid., p. 400. Pruvost echoes him: 'La plupart des personages féminins de Greene souffrent et sont fidèles' (Pruvost, op. cit., p. 121), but neither develops the idea.

15 Storojenko, op. cit., p. 18.

16 Jordan, op. cit., p. 205.

17 Ibid., p. 203.

18 Nashe, *Anatomie of Absurditie*, in *Works*, ed. McKerrow, vol. 1, p. 287.

19 Wolff, op. cit.

20 Jordan, op. cit., p. 32.

21 Greene, *Penelope's Web*, in *Works*, vol. 5.

22 Herbert Grabes, *The Mutable Glass* (Cambridge, 1982), p. 32. Grabes notes that the number of mirror-titles in the second half of the sixteenth century increased quite rapidly. After 1580, almost as many can be listed from the two closing decades (29) as appeared during the whole of the preceding 80 years (32).

23 Ibid., p. 33.

24 Patricia Crawford has drawn attention to the association of women and

mirrors in another context. She quotes Pliny on the dangers of women menstruating: apparently 'A looking-glass will discolour at her glance' if a menstruating woman looks into one. Crawford, 'Attitudes to menstruation in seventeenth century England', *Past and Present* **91** (1981), 59.

25 John Berger, *Ways of Seeing* (1972; reprinted Harmondsworth, 1984), pp. 46–7.

26 Greene, *Perimedes The Blacke-Smith*, in *Works*, vol. 7, p. 79.

27 *Euphues: The Anatomy of Wyt*, in *Complete Works*, ed. R.W. Bond, 3 vols (Oxford, 1902), vol. 1.

28 Jordan, op. cit., p. 15.

29 I am indebted to J.C. Jordan for this comparison, op. cit., p. 15. *Mamillia* was entered in the Stationers Register in 1580, although it was not published until 1583. It was written, then, just two years after *Euphues* appeared.

30 Pruvost, op. cit., p. 105.

31 *Merchant of Venice*, Act 4, sc. i.

32 I use 'feminist' in its broadest sense here to indicate a recognition of, and resistance to, women's enforced subordination to men, and a concern for women's rights.

33 Chaucer, *Wife of Bath's Prologue*, in *Complete Works*, ed. Robinson (London, 1957), p. 82, 11.693–6.

34 Storojenko, op. cit., p. 71.

35 Ibid.

36 Berger, op. cit., p. 50.

37 Ibid., p. 51.

38 Ovid, *Metamorphoses,* Book 6, in *Shakespeare's Ovid*, ed. Arthur Golding (London, 1961), 11.542–853. Tereus, King of Thrace, marries the Athenian Progne. After five years, Progne wants to see her sister Philomela, and asks her husband to fetch her from Athens. In doing so, Tereus finds his lust enflamed by her and, on arrival back in Thrace, he rapes her, and cuts out her tongue to prevent her revealing it. She is kept in a grange, where she weaves a tapestry illustrating the crime against her. She has it delivered to Progne, who had thought that she was dead. In revenge on her husband, Progne kills their son Itys and feeds the body to the unknowing Tereus. When he realizes, he rushes after the two sisters with his sword. The women are turned into birds (a swallow and a nightingale) and Tereus into a lapwing.

This story seems to have had particular appeal towards the end of the sixteenth century, for Pettie also uses it. Its sensational plot, with its vivid description of cruelty to women, and by women, appears to be more than usually open to multiple interpretations.

39 Davis, op. cit., p. 147.

40 Simon Shepherd, *Amazons and Warrior Women* (Brighton, 1981), p. 177.

41 In *Comus*, the Elder Brother's conviction that if his sister is chaste she cannot be raped, has similar implications:

'Tis Chastity, my brother, Chastity:
She that has that, is clad in complete steel . . .
. . . No savage fierce, bandit, or mountaineer
Will dare to soil her virgin purity

(11.420–21, 425–6)

If a woman *is* raped, then, she could never have been chaste. Milton, *Comus*, in *Complete Shorter Poems*, ed. John Carey (London, 1978), 11.420–21, 425–6.

42 Homer tells the story of Penelope, wife of Odysseus (Ulysses). She tricked her suitors by asking them to cease their suits to her until she had finished weaving a winding-sheet for Lord Laertes, but every night she undid the work that she wove during the day. Homer, *The Odyssey*, Book II, trans. E.V. Rieu (Harmondsworth, 1980), pp. 39–40.

43 Christopher Thaiss, 'Robert Greene The Popular Writer', Diss. North-Western University, 1976, p. 144.

44 Men typically underestimate the value of women's talk, and refer to it in a condescending and dismissive way as 'prattle' or 'gossip'. Deborah Jones reclaims the word and defines it as 'A way of talking between women in their role as women, intimate in style, personal and domestic in topic and setting, a female cultural event which springs from and perpetuates the restrictions of the female role, but also gives the comfort of validation.' Cited in *A Feminist Dictionary*, ed. Kramarae and Treichler (London, 1985), p. 179.

45 Margaret Schlauch, *Antecedents of the English Novel 1400–1600* (London, 1963), p. 194.

46 The division of the kingdom according to the virtues of the three sons' wives suggests a possible influence on Shakespeare's *King Lear*, where Lear plans to divide his kingdom between his three daughters in proportion to the amount of love they profess to him, Act 1, sci. i.

47 Shepherd, op. cit., p. 33.

5. Barnaby Rich, reluctant romancer

1 Preface 'To the noble Souldiours bothe of England and Irelande', in T.M. Cranfill, ed., *Rich's Farewell to Military Profession* (Austin, Texas, 1959), p. 9.

2 Cranfill, ed., *Rich's Farewell*, p. 1. All further references to the *Farewell* are from this edition.

3 Edward M. Hinton, 'Rych's *Anothomy of Ireland*, with an account of the author', *PMLA* 55 (1940), 73–101.

4 Quoted in Cranfill and Bruce, *Barnaby Rich: A Short Biography* (Austin, Texas, 1953), p. 126; from a 'Warrant to pay to Barnaby Rich, the eldest Captain of the kingdom, 100 l. as a free gift', *CSPD*, 1611–18, 378.

5 John Lievsay quarrels with this figure (Rich's own), arguing that material was often duplicated under different titles, and much of it stolen from others; see Lievsay, 'A word about Barnaby Rich', *JEGP* 55 (1956), p. 384.

6 Henry Webb, 'Barnabe Riche – sixteenth century military critic', *JEGP* 42 (1943) 240–52. Webb lists the five works as follows: *A right excelent and pleasaunt Dialogue, betweene Mercury and an English Souldier*, 1574; *Allarme to England*, 1578; *A Path-way to Military practise*, 1587; *A Martiall Conference*, 1598; *The Fruites of Long Experience*, 1604; also published as *A Soldier's Wish to Britons Welfare*, 1604.

7 Webb, op. cit., p. 252.

8 Cranfill, ed., *Rich's Farewell*, p. xvi.

9 Ibid., p. liii.

10 E.J. O'Brien, ed., *Elizabethan Tales* (London, 1937), p. 23.

11 H.S. Canby, *The Short Story in English* (New York, 1932), p. 128.

12 Lievsay, op. cit., p. 392.

13 Lievsay, *Stefano Guazzo and the English Renaissance 1575–1675* (Chapel Hill, N.C., 1961), p. 145.

14 Cranfill, op. cit., p. xxi. Some of the most thorough examinations of Rich's texts other than those listed above are: Cranfill, 'Barnaby Rich: An Elizabethan reviser at work', *Studies in Philology* 46 (1949), 411–18; Cranfill, 'Barnaby Rich and King James', *ELH* 16 (1949), 65–75; Robin Hood, 'Studies in Some Collections of Romantic Novelle', Diss. Oxford, 1973; Edwin Miller, 'Repetition in Barnaby Rich', *Notes and Queries* (1953), 511–12; Mary Patchell, *The Palmerin Romances in Elizabethan Prose Fiction* (New York, 1947), pp. 111–13; René Pruvost, *Matteo Bandello and Elizabethan Fiction* (Paris, 1937); D.T. Starnes, 'Barnabe Riche's "Sappho Duke of Mantona": A study in Elizabethan story-making', *Studies in Philology* 30 (1933), 455–72.

15 In Castiglione's *The Courtier*, Count Lodovico, praising the military prowess of the ideal courtier, makes an important distinction between behaviour appropriate to the battlefield, and that suitable in social circles. A certain man, being asked to dance by a worthy lady, refuses on the grounds that his business is fighting:

> 'Well then', the lady retorted, 'I should think that since you aren't at war at the moment and you are not engaged in fighting, it would be a good thing if you were to have yourself well greased and stowed away in a cupboard with all your fighting equipment, so that you avoid getting rustier than you are already.'

Lodovico's audience laughs at the way the lady shows her contempt for the man's foolish presumption, and Lodovico concludes: 'Therefore . . . the man we are seeking should be fierce, rough and always to the fore, in the presence of the enemy; but anywhere else he should be kind, modest, reticent and anxious above all to avoid ostentation.' Castiglione, *The Book of the Courtier*, trans. George Bull (1967; reprinted Harmondsworth, 1980), pp. 58–9.

16 Cranfill notes that the editions of 1583, 1594 and 1606 print 'a tale' not 'at all'; Cranfill, ed., *Rich's Farewell*, p. 232.

17 Cranfill charts the repetition of this phrase, for which Rich became famous. See Cranfill, op. cit., p. lviii. Rich's bawdy innuendo, wishing women 'what your selves doe beste like of' (i.e. the penis) is repeated in Webster's *The Duchess of Malfi* where, according to Ferdinand, 'women like that part, which, like the lamprey, /Hath nev'r a bone in't'. Elizabeth M. Brenan, ed. (London, 1983), Act 1, sc. ii.

18 Rich returns to the theme of men wearing female dress in *My Ladies Looking Glasse* (1616).

19 Robin Hood, 'Studies in Some Collections of Romantic Novelle', Diss. Oxford 1973, p. 114.

20 Cranfill, op. cit., p. lv.

21 A similar ambivalence is revealed in a later work, the Second Part of *Don Simonides*, published in 1584. When Simonides discovers that his mistress has

married someone else in his absence, he rails at length against the whole female sex; to this Rich appends 'The Authors conclusion to the Ladies and Gentlewomen' (V_i^v), assuring the woman reader of his own anger at Simonides' 'unseemly upbraidings' and 'prejudicial exclamations'. Simonides responds that he did not mean to include English women in his condemnation, and offers a fulsome praise of the 'faire damoselles of England', which is reiterated by Rich himself.

22 Hood, op. cit., p. 117.

23 The word 'forged' seems to be deliberately ambiguous. According to the *OED* it means both to falsify as one's own, to imitate fraudulently, to counterfeit (which would seem to be an admission of the degree to which his stories are derived from other sources), and to make, fashion, frame or construct.

24 Master L.B. is probably Lodowick Bryskett. See Cranfill, pp. xxii–xxxvi. These three stories – *Of Nicander and Lucilla*, *Of Fineo and Fiamma* and *Of Gonsales and his vertuous wife Agatha* – are derived from Cinthio's *Gli Hecatommithi* (1565). It is unclear how much these works owe to Bryskett and how much to Rich. Cranfill points out that, 'there are turns of expression, even whole passages, so characteristic of Rich that they could have been written by no one else' (p. xxvi). Hood assumes Rich means that L.B. was the translator (op. cit., p. 143).

25 They are: *Sappho, Duke of Mantona*, *Of Apolonius and Silla*, *Of Two Brethren and their Wives*, and *Of Phylotus and Emelia*. *Of Aramanthus* is also a story of Rich's 'forging', but it contains no addresses to the woman reader.

26 For sources of *Sappho*, see D.T. Starnes, 'Barnabe Riche's "Sappho Duke of Mantona": A study in Elizabethan story-making', *Studies in Philology* 30 (1933), 455–72. The reasoning behind Rich's naming of Sappho remains unclear; Cranfill suggests Rich saw the name in Painter's 'Faustina the Empress' (*Palace*, II, 264) and considered it appropriate for a man since it ends in -o. See Cranfill, op. cit., p. 246. See also Cranfill's Appendix: 'Sources and Analogues', pp. 339–50 for sources of the five tales of Rich's own forging.

27 *OED* 'pretend': (8) To intend, purpose, design, plan (obs.); (15) To make pretence, to make believe, to counterfeit, feign.

28 See Cranfill, op. cit., pp. 257–9 for sources; especially Pettie and Painter.

29 To give Rich his credit, he refrains from characterizing Julina as the stereotypic lustful widow. See Barbara J. Todd, 'The remarrying widow: A stereotype reconsidered', in Mary Prior, ed., *Women in English Society 1500–1800* (London, 1985), pp. 54–92. When Rich does mock her later on, it is not on these grounds.

30 For all three translations, see Cranfill, pp. xxii–xxxvi. *Nicander* comes from Cinthio's Decade VI, Novel 3. See Cranfill, op. cit., pp. 276–82 for close comparison with original.

31 From Cinthio's Decade II, Novel 6. See Cranfill, op. cit., pp. 282–9 for comparison with original.

32 From Cinthio's Decade III, Novel 5. See Cranfill, op. cit., pp. 306–16 for comparison with original.

33 See especially Mamillia and Philomela.

34 See Cranfill, op. cit., pp. xx and 346–9 for sources. The single name in the title

suggests that the story is not strictly a romance. All Rich's other tales bear or suggest two names, with the exception of *Sappho* which, after *Aramanthus*, contains the most about military affairs.

35 See Cranfill, op. cit., pp. 342–6 for sources.
36 Ibid., p. xx.
37 In particular, in the preface to the soldiers. Cranfill comments that Rich apologizes for his own bluntness and plainness, the traditional 'failings' of the soldier, in a dedication to Queen Elizabeth in *A Pathway to Military Practise* (1587): 'Pardon me (most gracious Princesse) in discharging my duetie though simplie yet truely, Souldiours are but blunte, but sure they loove plainnes', Cranfill, op. cit., p. 295.
38 Cranfill, op. cit., pp. 298–300.
39 Michel Foucault, *Madness and Civilization*, trans. Alan Sheridan (New York, 1965).
40 See Cranfill, op. cit., pp. xxi, 321–6, and 349 for sources. For *Phylotus* as a source, see G.L. Moore-Smith, 'Riche's story "Of Phylotus and Emilia" ', *MLR* 5 (1910), 342–4.
41 Hood, op. cit., p. 173.
42 Compare the list of conditions within marriage on which Millamant insists when Mirabell courts her (Congreve, *The Way of the World*, Act 4, sc. v).
43 Hood, op. cit., p. 112.
44 The conclusion is addressed simply to the 'gentle reader', the non-gender-specific reader perhaps of the third preface.
45 For an explanation of why, in a later edition, Scotland and King James are changed to Constantinople and the Turk, see Cranfill, pp. lxxiv–v; also Cranfill, 'Barnaby Rich and King James', *ELH* 16 (1949), 65–75.
46 Cranfill, op. cit., p. 334.
47 Cranfill summarizes this: ibid., pp. 334–5.
48 Edmund Spenser, *The Faerie Queene*, ed. A.C. Hamilton (1977; reprinted London, 1980), Bk 5, canto vii, verse 37.
49 Ibid., verse 40.

6. Sir Philip Sidney: woman reader as structural necessity

1 John Buxton, *Elizabethan Taste* (London, 1963), p. 246.
2 Sidney, *The Old Arcadia*, ed. Katherine Duncan-Jones (Oxford, 1985), p. 3. All further references to the *Old Arcadia* are from this edition.
3 Richard Lovelace, 'Clitophon and Leucippe translated', in *The Poems of Richard Lovelace*, ed. C.H. Wilkinson (Oxford, 1930), p. 68.
4 Charles Cotton, 'The surprise', in *The Works of the English Poets, from Chaucer to Cowper*, 21 vols, ed. Alexander Chalmers (London, 1810), vol. 6, p. 750.
5 Wye Saltonstall, *Picturae Loquentes (or Pictures Drawne forth in Characters With a Poeme of a Maid)*, 1631, sig. B₁ᵛ. Reprinted from the 1631 and 1635 editions for the Luttrell Society by Basil Blackwell (Oxford, 1946), vol. I, p. 47.
6 Thomas Powell, *Tom of All Trades, or The Plaine Pathway to Preferment* (1631), in New Shakespeare Society Series, vol. VI, 2, ed. F.J. Furnivall (London, 1876), p. 173.

7 Horace Walpole, *A Catalogue of the Royal and Noble Authors of England* (London, 1758), p. 164.

8 William Hazlitt, *Lectures on the Age of Elizabeth* (1820; reprinted London, 1901) p. 211.

9 See Albert Feuillerat, ed., *The Complete Works of Sir Philip Sidney*, 4 vols (Cambridge, 1912–26), which contains the different versions of the *Arcadia*.

10 C.S. Lewis, *English Literature in the Sixteenth Century* (1944; reprinted Oxford, 1973), p. 333.

11 Sidney, *Works*, vol. 3, p. 132.

12 The letter is used as a preface to both the *Old* and *New*, although it clearly cannot refer to the latter, since it suggests that the work is finished; and the discrepancy between the letter's statement that the work's chief safety 'shall be the not walking abroad' and its position as a preface to a frequently published book, is an unsettling one.

13 R.W. Zandvoort, *Sidney's Arcadia: A Comparison Between the Two Versions* (1929; reprinted New York, 1968), p. 47.

14 Richard Lanham, *The Old Arcadia*, in Walter Davis and Richard Lanham, *Sidney's Arcadia* (New Haven and London, 1965), p. 197.

15 Gabriel Harvey, *Pierces Supererogation* (1593), in G. Gregory Smith, ed., *Elizabethan Critical Essays* (Oxford, 1904), vol. 2, p. 282.

16 Fulke Greville, *Life of Sidney*, ed. Nowell-Smith (Oxford, 1907), pp. 14–15.

17 Ibid., p. 15.

18 Kenneth Thorpe Rowe, 'Romantic love and parental authority in Sidney's *Arcadia*', *University of Michigan Contributions in Modern Philology* 4 (1947), 36.

19 Ibid., p. 35.

20 Franco Marenco, 'Double plot in Sidney's *Old Arcadia*', *MLR* 64 (1969), 248–83. See especially pp. 250–3.

21 Shakespeare, *Hamlet*, ed. George Rylands (1947; reprinted Oxford, 1974), Act 2, sc. ii. For further debate, see especially: Walter Davis, 'A map of Arcadia: Sidney's romance in its tradition', in Walter Davis and Richard Lanham, op. cit.; Walter Davis, *Idea and Act in Elizabethan Fiction* (Princeton, 1969), chs 2 and 3; Richard Lanham, op. cit.; Jon Lawry, *Sidney's Two Arcadias: Pattern and Proceeding* (Ithaca and London, 1972); Richard McCoy, *Sir Philip Sidney: Rebellion in Arcadia* (Brighton, 1979); Mario Praz, 'Sidney's original Arcadia', *The London Mercury*, March 1927, vol. 15, no. 89, pp. 507–14; Mark Rose, *Heroic Love* (Cambridge, Mass., 1968); R.W. Zandvoort, op. cit.

   For Myrick, it is simply a 'pastoral romance' (*Sidney as Literary Craftsman*, p. 194), and for Ringler, the *Old Arcadia* is 'a tragi-comedy in five acts, with a serious double plot . . . combined with a comic underplot' (*The Poems of Sir Philip Sidney*, Oxford, 1962, p. xxxvii). In 1913 Edwin Greenlaw proposed a reading of the *Arcadia* as a sustained account 'under hidden forms' of Elizabethan politics ('Sidney's *Arcadia* as an example of Elizabethan allegory', in *Kittredge Anniversary Papers* (1913; reprinted New York, 1967), pp. 327–37), and Richard McCoy (op. cit.) combines a socio-political reading with a psychological one. S.L. Wolff's *The Greek Romances in Elizabethan Prose Fiction* (New York, 1912) demonstrates that Sidney adopted methods and materials from the romances of Heliodorus and Achilles Tatius, and while Wolff admires Sidney's ingenuity in 're-weaving the *Old Arcadia* upon the loom of

Heliodorus', he condemns the result as a work of literary art. Indeed most critics – with the notable exceptions of Feuillerat and Zandvoort – see the revision as a failure.

22 Annabel M. Patterson, *Censorship and Interpretation: The Conditions of Writing and Reading in Early Modern England* (Wisconsin, 1984), p. 33.

23 Lanham, op. cit., p. 325.

24 Ibid., p. 324.

25 Gary Waller, *English Poetry of the Sixteenth Century* (London, 1986), p. 57.

26 Ibid., p. 54.

27 Catherine Barnes, 'The hidden persuader: The complex speaking voice of Sidney's *Defence of Poetry*', *PMLA* 86 (1971), 422–7, demonstrates the complexity of the *Defence*'s structure, with the sophistication of its different voices, and the ways in which it fashions its own audience. Any reading of the *Arcadia* which does not assume it is an equally sophisticated work will fail to do justice to Sidney's text.

28 Susan D. Gubar, 'Tudor Romance and Eighteenth Century Fiction', Diss. University of Iowa, 1972, p. 80.

29 When Hercules was taken captive by Omphale, Queen of Lydia, he was dressed as a woman and made to spin, while she took his club and lion skin.

30 Book Three, pp. 151, 152, 199, 211 (twice).

31 Gubar, op. cit., p. 65.

32 Quoted in McCoy, op. cit., p. 64.

33 Somewhat as we hear of Mrs Ramsay's death in Virginia Woolf's *To the Lighthouse* (1927; reprinted London, 1979), p. 120: '(Mr Ramsay stumbling along a passage stretched his arms out one dark morning, but, Mrs Ramsay having died rather suddenly the night before, he stretched his arms out. They remained empty).'

34 Lewis, op. cit., p. 332.

35 McCoy, op. cit., p. 136.

36 Sidney, *Astrophil and Stella*, in Maurice Evans, ed., *Elizabethan Sonnets* (London, 1977). See especially Nos 4, 5, 10, 52, 71 and 72.

37 McCoy, op. cit., p. 136.

38 It is not clear whether or not Mary Sidney was following her brother's instructions when she omitted certain passages from the *Old Arcadia* in her composite version.

39 Clark Hulse, 'Stella's wit: Penelope Rich as reader of Sidney's sonnets', in Margaret Ferguson, Maureen Quilligan and Nancy Vickers, eds, *Rewriting the Renaissance* (Chicago, 1986), pp. 272–86.

40 Ibid., p. 273.

Afterword

1 Gary Waller, *English Poetry of the Sixteenth Century* (London, 1986), p. 269.

2 Jane Austen, *Northanger Abbey* (London, 1963), p. 105.

3 Lady Mary Wroth, niece to the Sidneys, was probably the first woman to publish a romance in this country; her *Urania* came out in 1620.

Bibliography

Primary sources

Austen, Jane. *Northanger Abbey*. London, 1963.

Apollodorus. *The Library*. Trans. James Frazer. London, 1921.

Browne, William. 'Fido, an epistle to Fidelia'. In *Whole Works*. Ed. W. Carew Hazlitt. Vol. 2. London, 1869.

Castiglione, Baldassare, *The Courtier*. Trans. George Bull. 1967; reprinted Harmondsworth, 1980.

Castiglione, Baldassare. *The Courtier*. Trans. Thomas Hoby. London, 1956.

Caxton, William, trans. *The Golden Legend*. 7 vols. London, 1900.

Chapman, George, Ben Jonson, John Marston. *Eastward Ho*. Ed. C.G. Petter. London, 1973.

Chaucer, Geoffrey. *The Complete Works of Geoffrey Chaucer*. Ed. F.N. Robinson. 2nd ed. London, 1957.

Clifford, Lady Anne. *Diary*. With introductory note by V. Sackville-West. London, 1924.

Cotton, Charles. 'The surprise'. In *The Works of the English Poets, from Chaucer to Cowper*. Ed. Alexander Chalmers. Vol. 6. London, 1810.

Donne, John. *The Complete English Poems*. Ed. A.J. Smith. 1971; reprinted Harmondsworth, 1978.

Euripides. *Alcestis*. Trans. into English with introduction and notes by D.W. Lucas. London, 1951.

Fenton, Geoffrey. *Certaine Tragicall Discourses*. Ed. R.L. Douglas. 2 vols. London, 1898.

Gascoigne, George. *The Adventures of Master F.J.* 1573 ed. in *A Hundreth Sundry Flowers*. Ed. C.T. Prouty. Columbia, Miss. 1942; 1575 ed. in *Complete Works*. Ed. J.W. Cunliffe. Vol. 1. Cambridge, 1907–10.

Grange, John. *The Golden Aphroditis*. Ed. Hyder Rollins. New York, 1939.

Greene, Robert. *The Complete Works of Robert Greene*. Ed. A.B. Grosart. 15 vols. 1881–6; reprinted New York, 1964.

Hake, Edward. *A Touchestone for this time present . . . Whereunto is annexed a perfect rule to be observed of all Parents and Scholemaisters, in the trayning up of their Schollers and Children in learning*. 1574.

Harvey, Gabriel. *Pierces Supererogation*. In *Elizabethan Critical Essays*. Ed. G. Gregory Smith. Oxford, 1904.

Hazlitt, William. *Lectures on the Age of Elizabeth*. 1820; reprinted London, 1901.

Hoby, Lady Margaret. *The Diary of Lady Margaret Hoby 1599–1605*. Ed. Dorothy M. Meads. London, 1930.

Hoccleve, Thomas. *Hoccleve's Works*. Ed. F.J. Furnivall. 3 vols. London, 1892.

Homer. *The Odyssey*. Trans. E.V. Rieu. Harmondsworth, 1980.

Hyginus. *Fabulae*. In *Auctores Mythographi Latini*. Louvain and Amsterdam, 1742.

Johnson, Richard. *The Most Famous History of the Seaven Champions of Christendome*. Ed. R. Kennedy. Portland, Oreg., 1967.

Lennox, Charlotte. *The Female Quixote; or The Adventures of Arabella*. 2 vols. London, 1970.

Livy. *The History of Titus Livius*. With supplement of J. Freinsteim. Trans. by several hands. 3 vols. London, 1814.

Lodge, Thomas. *Rosalynde*. In *Complete Works of Thomas Lodge*. Ed. Edmund Gosse. 4 vols. Glasgow, 1883.

Lovelace, Richard. 'Clitophon and Lucippa translated'. In *The Poems of Richard Lovelace*. Ed. C.H. Wilkinson. Oxford, 1930.

Lyly, John. *Euphues: The Anatomy of Wit*, and *Euphues and his England*. In *The Complete Works of John Lyly*. Ed. R.W. Bond. 3 vols. 1902; reprinted Oxford, 1973.

Lyly, John. *Six Court Comedies*. Ed. Edward Blount. 1632.

Marston, John. *The Dutch Courtezan*. Ed. M.L. Wine. Lincoln, Nebr., 1965.

Massinger, Philip. *The Guardian*. In *The Plays of Philip Massinger*. Eds. Philip Edwards and Colin Gibson. Oxford, 1976.

Mulcaster, Richard. *Positions wherein those primitive circumstances be examined which are necessarie for the training up of children*. In *Positions of Richard Mulcaster*. Ed. R.H. Quick. London, 1888.

Nashe, Thomas. *The Anatomie of Absurditie*. In *Works*. Ed. R.B. McKerrow. 5 vols. Oxford, 1904–10.

North, Thomas, trans. *The Diall of Princes*. Ed. K.N. Colvile. London, 1919.

O'Brien, E.J., ed. *Elizabethan Tales*. London, 1937.

Overbury, Thomas. *The Overburian Characters*. Ed. W.J. Paylor. The Percy Reprints. Vol. 13. Oxford, 1936.

Ovid. *Metamorphoses*. Trans. Arthur Golding. London, 1961.

Ovid. *Metamorphoses*. Trans. George Sandys. Lincoln, Nebr., 1970.

Painter, William. *The Palace of Pleasure*. Ed. Joseph Jacobs. 3 vols. London, 1890.

Pettie, George. *The Petite Pallace of Pettie his Pleasure*. Ed. I. Gollancz. 2 vols. London, 1908.

Pettie, George. *The Petite Pallace of Pettie his Pleasure*. Ed. Herbert Hartman. Oxford, 1938.

Pisan, Christine de. *The Book of the City of Ladies*. Trans. Earl Jeffrey Richards. 1982; reprinted London, 1983.

Pisan, Christine de. *Epistle to the God of Love*. Trans. Thomas Hoccleve. In *Hoccleve's Works*. Ed. F.J. Furnivall. Vol. 1. London, 1892.

Plutarch. *Moralia*. Ed. Bernadakis. Leipsic, 1889.

Powell, Thomas. *Tom of All Trades, or The Plaine Pathway to Preferment*. Ed. F.J. Furnivall. London, 1876.

Rich, Barnaby. *A Farewell to Militarie Profession*. Ed. T.M. Cranfill. Austin, Texas, 1959.

Rich, Barnaby. *Don Simonides*. Part I. 1581.

Rich, Barnaby. *Don Simonides*. Part II. 1584.

Richardson, Samuel. *Clarissa*. Harmondsworth, 1985.

Salter, Thomas. *A Mirrhor mete for all Mothers, Matrones, and Maidens, intituled the Mirrhor of Modestie*. 1574.

Saltonstall, Wye. *Picturae Loquentes (or Pictures Drawne forth in Characters. With a Poeme of a Maid)*. Luttrell Reprints No. 1. Reprinted from 1631 and 1635 editions. Introduction by C.H. Wilkinson. Oxford, 1946.

Shakespeare, William. *Hamlet*. Ed. George Rylands. 1947; reprinted Oxford, 1974.

Sidney, Philip. *Astrophil and Stella*. In *Elizabethan Sonnets*. Ed. Maurice Evans. London, 1977.

Sidney, Philip. *A Defence of Poetry*. Ed. J.A. Van Dorsten. 1966; reprinted Oxford, 1978.

Sidney, Philip. *The Old Arcadia*. Ed. Katherine Duncan-Jones. Oxford, 1985.

Sidney, Philip. *Works*. Ed. Albert Feuillerat. 4 vols. Cambridge, 1912–26.

Spenser, Edmund. *The Faerie Queene*. Ed. A.C. Hamilton. 1977; reprinted London, 1980.

Tacitus. *Annals*. Trans. George Gilbert Ramsay. London, 1904.

Tusser, Thomas. *His Good Points of Husbandrie*. Ed. Dorothy Hartley. London, 1931.

Tyler, Margaret, trans. *The First Part of the Mirrour of Princely Deedes and Knighthood*. 1578.

Vives, Juan Luis. *The Instruction of a Christian Woman*. In *Vives and the Renascence Education of Women*. Ed. Foster Watson. London, 1912.

Walpole, Horace. *A Catalogue of the Royal and Noble Authors of England*. London, 1758.

Webster, John. *The Duchess of Malfi*. Ed. Elizabeth M. Brenan. London, 1983.

Whetstone, George. *An Heptameron of Civil Discourses*. 1582.

Whetstone, George. *The Rocke of Regarde*. 1576.

Woolf, Virginia. *A Room of One's Own*. London, 1984.

Woolf, Virginia. *To the Lighthouse*. London, 1979.

Secondary sources

Abel, Elizabeth, ed. *Writing and Sexual Difference*. Brighton, 1982.

Adamson, J.W. 'The extent of literacy in England in the fifteenth and sixteenth centuries: Notes and conjectures'. In *The Library*, 4th Ser. 10 (1929–30), 163–93.

Allen, Carolyn J. 'Feminist(s) reading: A response to Elaine Showalter'. In *Writing and Sexual Difference*. Ed. Elizabeth Abel. Brighton, 1982.

Baker, E.A. *History of the English Novel*. London, 1912.

Ballard, George. *Memoirs of Several Ladies of Great Britain, who have been celebrated for their writings or skill in the learned languages, arts and sciences*. Oxford, 1752.

Barish, Jonas A. 'The prose style of John Lyly'. *ELH* 23 (1956), 14–35.

Barnes, Catherine. 'The hidden persuader: The complex speaking voice of Sidney's *Defence of Poetry*'. *PMLA* 86 (1971), 422–7.

Barratt, Sara, and John Illmann. 'Beware of romance'. *Daily Mail*, 29 August 1985, p. 3.

Barwick, Sandra. 'Working girls search for a novel kind of hero'. *The Independent*, 31 March 1988, p. 1.

Batsleer, Janet. 'Pulp in the pink'. *Spare Rib*, August 1981, pp. 52–5.

Baumann, Gerd, ed. *The Written Word: Literacy in Transition*. Oxford, 1986.

Beer, Gillian. *The Romance*. 1970; reprinted London, 1982.

Bennett, H.S. *English Books and Readers 1558–1603*. Cambridge, 1965.

Berger, John. *Ways of Seeing*. 1972; reprinted Harmondsworth, 1984.

Booth, Wayne C. *The Rhetoric of Fiction*. Chicago, Ill., 1961.

Bridenthal, R. and C. Koonz, eds. *Becoming Visible: Women in European History*. Boston, Mass., 1977.

Brownstein, Rachel. *Becoming a Heroine: Reading About Women in Novels*. 1982; reprinted Harmondsworth, 1984.

Burke, P. *Popular Culture in Early Modern Europe*. London, 1978.

Burckhardt, Jacob. *The Civilization of the Renaissance in Italy*. 1860; reprinted and trans. S.G.C. Middlemore. 2 vols. London, 1958.

Bush, Douglas. 'The Petite Pallace of Pettie his Pleasure'. *JEGP* 27 (1928), 162–9.

Buxton, John, *Elizabethan Taste*. London, 1963.

Buxton, John. *Sir Philip Sidney and the English Renaissance*. London, 1954.

Canby, H.S. *The Short Story in English*. 1909; reprinted New York, 1932.

Carey, John. 'Sixteenth and seventeenth century prose'. In *English Poetry and Prose, 1540–1647*. Ed. Christopher Ricks. 1970; reprinted London, 1986.

Cawelti, John. *Adventure, Mystery, and Romance*. Chicago, 1976.

Clark, Peter. 'The ownership of books in England, 1560–1640: The example of some Kentish townsfolk'. In *Schooling and Society: Studies in the History of Education*. Ed. Lawrence Stone. London, 1976.

Cohen, Nick. 'Feminist formula on a fine romance'. *The Independent*, 23 January 1988, p. 3.

Coward, Rosalind. *Female Desire: Women's Sexuality Today*. 1984; reprinted London, 1985.

Cranfill, Thomas, and Dorothy Hart Bruce. *Barnaby Rich: A Short Biography*. Austin, Texas, 1953.

Cranfill, Thomas, 'Barnaby Rich and King James'. *ELH* 16 (1949), 65–75.

Cranfill, Thomas. 'Barnaby Rich: An Elizabethan reviser at work'. *SP* 46 (1949), 411–18.

Crawford, Patricia. 'Attitudes to menstruation in seventeenth century England'. *PP* 91 (1981). 47–73.

Cressy, David. *Education in Tudor and Stuart England*. London, 1975.

Cressy, David. *Literacy and the Social Order: Reading and Writing in Tudor and Stuart England*. Cambridge, 1980.

Croll, Morris. 'The sources of the euphuistic rhetoric'. In *Style, Rhetoric and Rhythm*. Eds. J. Max Patrick and Robert O. Evans. Princeton, N.J., 1966.

Crosman, Inge, and Susan B. Suleiman, eds. *The Reader in the Text: Essays on Audience and Interpretation*. Princeton, N.J., 1980.

Culler, Jonathan. *On Deconstruction: Theory and Criticism After Structuralism*. 1982; reprinted London, 1983.

Davies, Stevie. *The Idea of Woman in Renaissance Literature: The Feminine Reclaimed*. Brighton, 1986.

Davis, Walter R. *Idea and Act in Elizabethan Fiction*. Princeton, N.J., 1969.

Davis, Walter R. 'A map of Arcadia: Sidney's romance in its tradition'. In *Sidney's Arcadia*. Eds. Walter Davis and Richard Lanham. New Haven, Conn., 1965.

Dipple, Elizabeth. ' "Unjust justice" in the *Old Arcadia*'. *Studies in English Literature 1500–1900* 10 (1970), 83–101.

Dobell, Bertram. 'New light on Sidney's *Arcadia*'. *Quarterly Review* 420 (1909), 74–100.

Eagleton, Terry. *The Function of Criticism: From the Spectator to Post-Structuralism*. London, 1984.

Eagleton, Terry. *Literary Theory: An Introduction*. 1983; reprinted Oxford, 1985.

Eagleton, Terry. *Marxism and Literary Criticism*. 1976; reprinted London, 1983.

Eco, Umberto. *The Role of the Reader: Explorations in the Semiotics of Texts*. Bloomington, Ill., 1979.

Ellmann, Mary. *Thinking About Women*. 1968; reprinted London, 1979.

Ernle, R.E. *The Light Reading of our Ancestors*. New York, 1927.

Esdaile, Arundell. *A List of English Tales and Prose Romances Before 1740*. London, 1912.

Ezard, John. 'Writers labour for love'. *The Guardian*, 31 March 1988, p. 1.

Ferguson, Margaret, Maureen Quilligan, and Nancy Vickers, eds. *Rewriting the Renaissance*. Chicago, Ill., 1986.

Fetterley, Judith. *The Resisting Reader. A Feminist Approach to American Fiction*. Bloomington, Ill., 1978.

Feuillerat, Albert. *John Lyly: Contribution à l'histoire de la Renaissance en Angleterre*. Cambridge, 1910.

Firestone, Shulamith. *The Dialectic of Sex: The Case for Feminist Revolution*. 1970; reprinted London, 1972.

Fish, Stanley. *Is There A Text In This Class? The Authority of Interpretive Communities*. Cambridge, Mass., 1980.

Flynn, Elizabeth, and Patrocinio Schweickart, eds. *Gender and Reading: Essays on Readers, Texts, and Contexts*. Baltimore, Md., 1986.

Foucault, Michel. *Madness and Civilization*. Trans. Alan Sheridan. New York, 1965.

French, Marilyn. *Shakespeare's Division of Experience*. 1981; reprinted London, 1983.

Gohlke, Madelon. 'Reading "Euphues" '. *Criticism* 19 (1977), 103–17.

Goody, J., ed. *Literacy in Traditional Societies*. Cambridge, 1968.

Grabes, Herbert. *The Mutable Glass*. Cambridge, 1982.

Greene, Gayle, and Coppelia Kahn, eds. *Making a Difference: Feminist Literary Criticism.* London, 1985.

Greenlaw, Edwin. 'Sidney's *Arcadia* as an example of Elizabethan allegory'. In *Kittredge Anniversary Papers.* Boston, Mass., 1913, pp. 327–37.

Greer, Germaine. *The Female Eunuch.* 1970; reprinted London, 1981.

Greville, Fulke. *Life of Sir Philip Sidney.* Ed. Nowell-Smith. Oxford, 1907.

Gubar, Susan. 'Tudor Romance and Eighteenth Century Fiction'. Diss. University of Iowa, 1972.

Hägg, Thomas. *The Novel in Antiquity.* 1980; reprinted Oxford, 1983.

Hamilton, A.C. 'Elizabethan prose fiction and some trends in recent criticism'. *Renaissance Quarterly* **37** (1984), 21–33.

Hamilton, A.C. 'Elizabethan romance: The example of prose fiction'. *ELH* **49**, No. 2 (1982), 287–99.

Hannay, Margaret, ed. *Silent But for the Word: Tudor Women as Patrons, Translators, and Writers of Religious Works.* Ohio, 1985.

Harrison, G.B. 'Books and readers, 1599–1603'. *The Library* **13** (1933–4), 1–33.

Hartman, Geoffrey. *The Fate of Reading.* Chicago, Ill., 1975.

Hey, Valerie. 'The necessity of romance'. *Women's Studies Occasional Papers*, No. 3. University of Kent at Canterbury, 1983.

Hinton, Edward M. 'Rych's anothomy of Ireland, with an account of the author'. *PMLA* **55** (1940), 73–101.

Hood, Robin. 'Studies in Some Collections of Romantic Novelle, 1566–81'. Diss. University of Oxford, 1973.

Houlbrooke, Ralph. *The English Family 1450–1700.* 1984; reprinted London, 1985.

Hull, Suzanne. *Chaste, Silent and Obedient: English Books for Women, 1475–1640.* San Marino, Calif., 1982.

Hulse, Clark. 'Stella's wit: Penelope Rich as reader of Sidney's sonnets'. In *Rewriting the Renaissance.* Eds. Ferguson, Quilligan, and Vicks. Chicago, Ill., 1986.

Humm, Maggie. *Feminist Criticism: Women as Contemporary Critics.* Brighton, 1986.

Hunter, G.K. *The Humanist as Courtier.* London, 1962.

Iser, Wolfgang. *The Act of Reading: A Theory of Aesthetic Response.* 1976; reprinted London, 1978.

Iser, Wolfgang. *The Implied Reader: Patterns of Communications in Prose Fiction from Bunyan to Beckett.* Baltimore, Md., 1974.

Jackson, Rosemary. *Fantasy: The Literature of Subversion.* 1981; reprinted London, 1984.

Jacobus, Mary. *Reading Woman: Essays in Feminist Criticism.* London, 1986.

Jacobus, Mary, ed. *Women Writing, and Writing About Women.* London, 1979.

Jayne, Sears. *Library Catalogues of the English Renaissance.* Berkeley, Calif., 1956.

Jensen, Margaret Ann. *Love's Sweet Return: The Harlequin Story.* Toronto, 1984.

Johnson, Francis. 'Notes on English retail book-prices, 1550–1640'. *The Library*, 5th Ser. (1950), 83–112.

Jones, Ann Rosalind. 'Mills and Boon meets feminism'. In *The Progress of Romance: The Politics of Popular Fiction.* Ed. Jean Radford. London, 1986.

Jordan, J.C. *Robert Greene.* New York, 1915.

Jusserand, J.J. *The English Novel in the Time of Shakespeare.* 1890; 4th ed. trans. Elizabeth Lee, and revised by author. London, 1901.

Kelly-Gadol, Joan. 'Did women have a Renaissance?' in *Becoming Visible*. Ed. Bridenthal and Koonz. Boston, Mass., 1977.

Kelso, Ruth. *Doctrine for the Lady of the Renaissance*. Urbana, Ill., 1956.

Kiso, Akiko. *The Lost Sophocles*. New York, 1984.

Kolodny, Annette. 'Dancing through the minefield: Some observations on the theory, practice and politics of a feminist literary criticism'. *Feminist Studies* **6** (1980), 1–25.

Kramarae, Cheris, and Paula A. Treichler, eds. *A Feminist Dictionary*. London, 1985.

Lanham, Richard. 'The Old Arcadia'. In *Sidney's Arcadia*. Eds. Walter Davis and Richard Lanham. New Haven, Conn., 1965.

Laslett, P. *The World We Have Lost*. London, 1965.

Laslett, P. 'The wrong way through the telescope: A note on literary evidence in sociology and in historical sociology'. *British Journal of Sociology* **27** (1976), 319–42.

Lasson, Sally Ann, 'Confessions of the blue stocking romantics'. *Sunday Express Magazine*, 24 February 1985, pp. 36–8.

Lawry, Jon S. *Sidney's Two Arcadias: Pattern and Proceeding*. Ithaca, N.Y., 1972.

Levin, Angela. 'At home with Barbara Cartland'. *You: The Mail on Sunday Magazine*, 30 June 1985, pp. 17–21.

Lewis, C.S. *English Literature in the Sixteenth Century Excluding Drama*. 1954; reprinted Oxford, 1973.

Lievsay, John Leon. 'A word about Barnaby Rich'. *JEGP* **55** (1956), 381–92.

Lievsay, John Leon. *Stefano Guazzo and the English Renaissance 1575–1675*. Chapel Hill, N.C., 1961.

Lindheim, Nancy R. 'Sidney's *Arcadia*, Book II: Retrospective narrative'. *SP* **44** (1967), 159–86.

Macfarlane, Alan. *Marriage and Love in England 1300–1840*. Oxford, 1986.

Maclean, I. *The Renaissance Notion of Women*. Cambridge, 1980.

Mahl, Mary, and Helene Koon. *The Female Spectator: English Women Writers before 1800*. New York, 1977.

Mann, Peter. *A New Survey: The Facts About Romantic Fiction*. London, 1974.

Mann, Peter. *The Romantic Novel: A Survey of Reading Habits*. London, 1969.

Marenco, Franco. 'Double plot in Sidney's "Old Arcadia" '. *MLR* **64** (1969), 248–63.

Margolies, David. *Novel and Society in Elizabethan England*. London, 1985.

McCoy, Richard C. *Sir Philip Sidney: Rebellion in Arcadia*. Brighton, 1979.

Miller, Edwin, 'Repetition in Barnaby Rich'. *N & Q* **198** (1953), 511–12.

Miller, E.H. *The Professional Writer in Elizabethan England*. Cambridge, Mass., 1959.

Millett, Kate. *Sexual Politics*. 1970; reprinted London, 1983.

Mitchell, Juliet. *Women: The Longest Revolution. Essays in Feminism, Literature and Psychoanalysis*. 1966; reprinted London, 1984.

Modleski, Tania. *Living With a Vengeance: Mass-produced Fantasies for Women*. 1982; reprinted New York, 1984.

Moi, Toril. *Sexual/Textual Politics: Feminist Literary Theory*. London, 1985.

Monteith, Moira, ed. *Women's Writing: A Challenge to Theory*. Brighton, 1986.

Moore-Smith, G.L. 'Riche's story "Of Phylotus and Emilia" '. *MLR* **5** (1910), 342–4.

Myrick, Keneth O. *Sir Philip Sidney as a Literary Craftsman*. Cambridge, Mass., 1935.

O'Dell, Sterg. *A Chronological List of Prose Fiction in English Printed in England and Other Countries, 1475–1640*. Cambridge, Mass., 1954.

Patchell, M. *The Palmerin Romances in Elizabethan Prose Fiction*. New York, 1947.

Patterson, Annabel M. *Censorship and Interpretation: The Conditions of Writing and Reading in Early Modern England*. Wisconsin, 1984.

Praz, Mario. 'Sidney's original Arcadia'. *The London Mercury* 15, No. 89 (1927), pp. 507–14.

Prior, Mary, ed. *Women in English Society 1500–1800*. London, 1985.

Prouty, C.T. *George Gascoigne: Elizabethan Courtier, Scholar, Poet*. Columbia, 1942.

Pruvost, R. *Matteo Bandello and Elizabethan Fiction*. Paris, 1937.

Pruvost, R. *Robert Greene et ses Romans*. Paris, 1938.

Radford, Jean, ed. *The Progress of Romance: The Politics of Popular Fiction*. London, 1986.

Radway, Janice A. *Reading the Romance: Women, Patriarchy, and Popular Literature*. Chapel Hill, N.C., 1984.

Reeve, Clara. *The Progress of Romance*. London, 1785.

Rich, Adrienne. *On Lies, Secrets & Silence*. 1979; reprinted London, 1980.

Ringler, William. 'The immediate source of euphuism'. *PMLA* 53 (1938), 678–86.

Rogers, K.M. *The Troublesome Helpmate: A History of Misogyny in Literature*. Seattle, Wash., 1966.

Rollins, Hyder. 'John Grange's "The Golden Aphroditis" '. *Harvard Studies and Notes in Philology and Literature* 16 (1934), 177–98.

Rose, Mark. *Heroic Love: Studies in Sidney and Spenser*. Cambridge, Mass., 1968.

Rowe, George E. 'Interpretation: Sixteenth century readers and George Gascoigne's "The Adventures of Master F.J." '. *ELH* 48 (1981), 271–89.

Rowe, Kenneth Thorpe. 'Romantic love and parental authority in Sidney's "Arcadia" '. *University of Michigan Contributions in Modern Philology* 4 (1947), 14–58.

Ruthven, K.K. *Feminist Literary Studies: An Introduction*. Cambridge, 1984.

Saintsbury, George. *The English Novel*. 1913; reprinted London, 1919.

Salzman, Paul. *English Prose Fiction 1558–1700: A Critical History*. 1985; reprinted Oxford, 1986.

Savage, Howard J. 'The beginning of Italian influence in English prose fiction'. *PMLA* 32 (1917), 1–21.

Schlauch, Margaret. *Antecedents of the English Novel 1400–1600*. 1963; reprinted London, 1965.

Schibanoff, Susan. 'The art of reading as a woman'. In *Gender and Reading: Essays on Readers, Texts and Contexts*. Eds. Flynn and Schweickart. Baltimore, Md., 1986.

Schofield, R.S. 'The measurement of literacy in pre-industrial England'. In *Literacy in Traditional Societies*. Cambridge, 1968.

Sheavyn, Phoebe. *The Literary Profession in the Elizabethan Age*. 1909; 2nd ed. revised by J.W. Saunders. Manchester, 1967.

Shepherd, Simon. *Amazons and Warrior Women: Varieties of Feminism in Seventeenth-Century Drama*. Brighton, 1981.

Showalter, Elaine. 'Feminist criticism in the wilderness'. In *Writing and Sexual Difference*. Ed. Elizabeth Abel. Brighton, 1982.

Showalter, Elaine. 'Literary criticism'. *Signs* 1 (1975), 435–60.

Showalter, Elaine. 'Towards a feminist poetics'. In *Women Writing, and Writing About Women*. Ed. Mary Jacobus. London, 1979.

Simons, John. 'Medieval Chivalric Romance and Elizabethan Popular Literature: A Selective Study'. Diss. University of Exeter, 1982.

Spencer, Jane. *The Rise of the Woman Novelist: From Aphra Behn to Jane Austen.* Oxford, 1986.

Spufford, Margaret. *Small Books and Pleasant Histories: Popular Fiction and its Readership in Seventeenth-Century England.* London, 1981.

Starnes, D.T. 'Barnaby Rich's "Sappho Duke of Mantona": A study in Elizabethan story-making'. *SP* 30 (1933), 455–72.

Stone, Lawrence. *The Family, Sex and Marriage in England 1500–1800.* 1977; abridged edition, Harmondsworth, 1979.

Stone, Lawrence, ed. *Schooling and Society: Studies in the History of Education.* London, 1976.

Thaiss, Christopher. 'Robert Greene the Popular Writer'. Diss. North-Western University, 1976.

Todd, Barbara. 'The remarrying widow: A stereotype reconsidered'. In *Women in English Society 1500–1800.* Ed. Mary Prior. London, 1985.

Tompkins, Jane P., ed. *Reader-Response Criticism: From Formalism to Post-Structuralism.* Baltimore, Md., 1980.

Toynbee, Polly. 'Guardian women'. *The Guardian*, 22 July 1985, p. 10.

Travitsky, Betty, ed. *The Paradise of Women: Writings by Englishwomen of the Renaissance.* London, 1981.

Utley, F.L. *The Crooked Rib: An Analytical Index to the Argument about Women in English and Scots Literature to the End of the Year 1568.* Ohio, 1944.

Waller, Gary. *English Poetry of the Sixteenth Century.* London, 1986.

Waller, Gary. 'Struggling into discourse: The emergence of Renaissance women's writing'. In *Silent But For The Word.* Ed. Margaret Hannay. Ohio, 1985.

Warnicke, Retha M. *Women of the English Renaissance and Reformation.* Connecticut, 1983.

Wayne, Valerie. 'Some sad sentence: Vives' *Instruction of a Christian Woman*'. In *Silent But For the Word.* Ed. Margaret Hannay. Ohio, 1985.

Webb, Henry. 'Barnaby Rich – sixteenth-century military critic'. *JEGP* 42 (1943), 240–52.

Weigall, Rachel. 'An Elizabethan gentlewoman: The journal of Lady Mildmay, circa 1570–1617'. *Quarterly Review* 215 (1911), 119–38.

Wibberley, Mary. *To Writers With Love: On Writing Romantic Novels.* London, 1985.

Williams, Franklyn, ed. *Index of Dedications and Commendatory Verses in English Books Before 1641.* London, 1962.

Williamson, George. C. *Lady Anne Clifford, Countess of Dorset, Pembroke & Montgomery, 1590–1676.* London, 1922.

Wilson, John Dover. *John Lyly.* Cambridge, 1905.

Wolff, Samuel L. *The Greek Romances in Elizabethan Prose Fiction.* New York, 1912.

Woodbridge, Linda. *Women and the English Renaissance: Literature and the Nature of Womankind.* Brighton, 1984.

Wright, Louis B. *Middle-Class Culture in Elizabethan England.* 1935; reprinted New York, 1980.

Wright, Louis B. 'The reading of Renaissance English women'. *SP* 28 (1931), 671–88.

Youings, Joyce. *Sixteenth-Century England.* Harmondsworth, 1984.

Young, Robert, ed. *Untying the Text.* London, 1981.

Zandvoort, R.W. *Sidney's Arcadia: A Comparison Between the Two Versions.* 1929; reprinted New York, 1968.

Index